First Shots, Last Shots

First Shots, Last Shots

The Opening and Closing Campaigns of the First World War

ILLUSTRATED

Forty Days in 1914
and
The Last Four Months

Sir F. Maurice

First Shots, Last Shotst
The Opening and Closing Campaigns of the First World War
Forty Days in 1914
and
The Last Four Months
by Sir F. Maurice

FIRST EDITION IN THIS FORM

First published under the titles
Forty Days in 1914
and
The Last Four Months

Leonaur is an imprint of Oakpast Ltd
Copyright in this form © 2023 Oakpast Ltd

ISBN: 978-1-916535-52-7 (hardcover)
ISBN: 978-1-916535-53-4 (softcover)

http://www.leonaur.com

Publisher's Notes
The views expressed in this book are not necessarily those of the publisher.

Contents

Forty Days in 1914   7
The Last Four Months   139

Sir F. Maurice, the author

Forty Days in 1914

Contents

Preface	11
The German Plan	13
The French Plan	23
The German March Through Belgium	36
Namur, Dinant, and the Sambre	46
Mons	57
Pursuit and Retreat	69
Von Kluck Changes Direction	86
The Ourcq and the Marne	106
The Higher Command in War	126

Preface

This little book owes its origin to curiosity. I wanted to see if it was possible to discover what the Germans were planning and doing during the retreat from Mons. I found that by piecing together evidence obtainable from the accounts of the early parts of the war published in Germany, in neutral countries, in France, and by Belgian authorities, as well as from the reports of the very full investigations which have been conducted into the German atrocities, in Northern France and in Belgium, it was possible to work out the movements of the German Armies, and from these to deduce the German plans. The information obtained in this way threw what has been to me an entirely new light upon the campaign, and made clear what had previously been dark.

Much of what I have written about the Germans is necessarily conjectural, and therefore I make no claim to be writing history. But I believe that the positions I have ascribed to the German forces at various dates are in the main accurate, and I must leave my readers to judge of the deductions which I have drawn from those movements.

I have found that the accounts published in Allied and neutral countries, owing to lack of information, do but scant justice to the part played by our original Expeditionary Force. Even such an authority as M. Hanotaux, in his excellent little book, *L'Énigme de Charleroi*, makes the fighting at Mons begin only at 3 o'clock in the afternoon on August 23, and says that such fighting as, did take place was done by our First Corps, which was hardly engaged at all. I hope that what I have written here may at least have the effect of making clearer the influence which our operations had on the campaign as a whole.

For my account of the operations of the French Armies I am indebted chiefly to "*Quatre Mois de Guerre*," published in the official French *Bulletin des armées* for December 1914, to M. Hanotaux's *Histoire illustrée de la guerre*, and to his *L'Énigme de Charleroi*. My account of the operations of the Belgian Army is drawn from *L'Action de l'armée belge*, the official report of the Belgian General Staff, and from *The Invasion and the War* in Belgium, by Professor Leon van der Essen. To all of these I owe much valuable information as to the movements of the German Armies. I have also to express my indebtedness to my brother-in-law, Captain C. T. Atkinson, who has kindly read the proofs and made many valuable suggestions.

I have in my last chapter endeavoured to explain the strong and weak points in the German system of conducting war, and what we may learn from it to our advantage.

I must apologise for the fact that it has been necessary to limit the number of maps, and therefore I have to ask my readers in following the operations occasionally to refer both to the general map and to the maps of the battlefields.

F. Maurice.

CHAPTER 1

The German Plan

In the opening days of the war the opinion was general, both in Great Britain and in France, that Germany, having invaded Belgium and thereby compelled us, in defence of our honour, to take the field, had tilted against herself the balance of military power. The Dual Entente had never been considered to be conspicuously weaker in military power than the Triple Alliance, and when Italy refused to follow Germany and Austria into the field, and the clumsy diplomatists of Berlin had added the forces of Great Britain and Belgium to those of France and Russia, it was commonly held that Germany had overreached herself. When I landed at Havre on August 11, 1914, a French colonel who had come down to meet our party said to me, "Now that the British Army is coming the result is certain. This time the Germans have bitten off more than they can chew"; and this represented the common opinion of both armies at the time.

The news of the French invasion of Lorraine and of the stout resistance of Liège confirmed this view, and until the actual tidings of disaster arrived all seemed going well. It was then with amazement that the peoples of the Entente nations learned that the fortress of Namur had fallen in forty-eight hours and that the German Armies were sweeping through Belgium and Northern France, everywhere in overwhelming numbers. It was with consternation that Great Britain heard the news, for which she was completely unprepared, that her little army, all but surrounded, was as good as lost and that Paris lay at the mercy of the enemy. Then, still more amazing, came the later news that the Germans were in full retreat, that Paris was saved, and that our men were advancing victoriously, taking prisoners and guns.

How did our army escape? Why did not the Germans enter Paris? and why did they retreat? The answer has generally been—the miracle of the Marne. We owe much to Foch and the French soldiers of the

Marne, but the Marne does not account for all, and to get as complete a reply to these questions as in the present state of our knowledge it is possible to give, to find out why the Germans failed of complete victory, and why they achieved as much as they did, we must look at events, as far as may be, from the German side, see how their plans were laid and how they were carried through.

The basis of Germany's scheme of conquest, formed long before the war and put into execution in the autumn of 1914, was that she, holding a central position, would be opposed on the Western front by an enemy who could bring his forces quickly into the field and most quickly on the stretch of common frontier lying between Luxemburg and Switzerland, while on the Eastern front she would meet an enemy formidable in point of numbers, but slow and ponderous in his methods, and lacking means to develop rapidly his numerical strength.

From the days of Moltke onwards the German General Staff had studied deeply the problem of war on two fronts, and their studies had given them a very intimate knowledge of Russia's military strength, of which, as events proved, they had taken a more exact measure even than had Russia's own ally, France. Shortly after the South African War I paid a visit to Berlin, and there met the head of the Russian section of the German Great General Staff, an officer who, having been much in England, knew us well. He bemoaned the fact that he could never get his comrades on the General Staff either to understand or to take much interest in us. "There is no future in the English section, but I am very lucky where I am, because it is quite different as regards Russia. We have *got* to know Russia, for our existence depends on it, and you may be sure that we do."

The solution of the two-front problem, in the earliest stages, turned upon an accurate estimate of the amount of force required to hold Russia in check, with the aid of Austria, while the greatest possible strength was concentrated on the Western front in order to beat France quickly to her knees. Time was of the essence of the contract drawn by the German General Staff. To be sure of victory they needed a prompt and decisive success in the West, so that they could turn Eastwards before Russia was ready to strike with her whole power.

In deciding on the methods, they would employ to get these results they were greatly influenced by the events of the Russo-Japanese War, in which they found confirmation of their own pet theory of war. They assumed that the long-drawn-out battles in Manchuria made it clearer than ever that a direct attack against a front, no matter in what superiority of force it was made, must, owing to the delaying power of modern quick-firing weapons, and particularly of machine-guns, be a slow and costly business, and that decisive success could only be obtained quickly by envelopment.

Now the founder and trainer of the modern German General Staff, the elder Moltke, had taught and practised the theory that the surest road to victory was that which led round the enemy's flank, and the greatest victories of 1870 had been won by envelopment in one form or another. This theory of envelopment was studied and examined by von Schlieffen, the predecessor, as the *Kaiser's* chief military adviser, of the younger Moltke, who was responsible for perfecting and carrying out the plan I am now describing. Von Schlieffen's problem was how to apply envelopment to war between nations in arms, how to get round millions where before it had been a question of outflanking two or three, hundred thousand. Naturally he did not disclose his plan, but he developed in at least one treatise, which created a deep impression in military Germany, the theory that the only way to obtain decisive results quickly in modern war was to seek the enemy's flanks and roll them up, for quick results were Germany's special aim, a long-drawn-out war of exhaustion being abhorrent to her military philosophy.

Von Schlieffen, who was much interested at the time in the events of the South African War, sent for me while I was in Berlin, and after asking me a number of questions ended by saying: "Well, you have found in your Roberts a general who understands envelopment, and that is why you succeeded." Von Schlieffen was a very able man and a profound thinker, but his successor was little more than a well-trained German General Staff officer, with the advantages of a great name, a tactful manner, and the faculty of getting on with the emperor. I am convinced that the secret of much that happened in the early phases of the war lies in the fact that an inherited theory, which had been elevated into a gospel, was applied by an individual of but ordinary capacity.

Having received the endorsement of the emperor, the theory of envelopment was preached in the military text-books of Germany and practised sedulously at the German manoeuvres, yet it was obviously out of the question to get round the large and highly trained armies which France could place quickly on the 150 miles of common frontier. If the armies of Germany were confined to such narrow limits, they would find that frontier manned by the French from end to end before they could reach it in sufficient strength to develop their attack. Therefore, if the theory of war in which the German General Staff had believed for years, the theory which they held to be confirmed by the lessons of recent wars and by the developments of modern armaments, if this theory was to be translated into practice, it was absolutely necessary that a way round should be found by violating the neutrality of Belgium and Luxemburg.

No explanation of the invasion of Belgium which Germany has issued squares even superficially with the known facts, and on military grounds alone it is out of the question that what happened should have happened except as the result of deliberate, cold-blooded, and careful calculation. Honour and treaty obligations counted as nothing in the Prussian military mind where expediency appeared to point the way, and it does not appear to have taken the Prussian military mind long to convince the German political mind that its plan was the only safe one and that all questions of morality must go to the wall. No doubt Germany did not want to fight Belgium; fighting a secondary foe meant waste of time, men, and material, and delay in getting at the chief enemy; but she was quite determined to march through Belgium, and if Belgium refused to be terrorised into acquiescence, force would be necessary, so force was prepared.

The mobilisation of modern armies, even when their arrangements have been as perfected as were those of Germany, is a matter of time, and is a very intricate and complicated process, dependent upon the exact execution. of a detailed programme which is easily deranged. Therefore, in order to be able to prepare their armies for war in security all the great Continental nations had for long been accustomed to keep on their frontiers considerable forces of covering troops, so nearly mobilised as to be ready to take the field at a few hours' notice. There was not the least likelihood that Belgium would attempt to interfere with Germany's mobilisation, but if Belgium were to be foolish enough to resist it was before all things necessary that the advance of the mobilised armies should not be delayed by such resistance.

Therefore, one of the first items in Germany's programme was to arrange in peace time for a force of covering troops to be ready at very short notice to enter Belgium and clear the way for the armies that were to follow. The success of this plan depended on the rapid reduction of the Belgian fortresses on the Meuse, and in dealing with this problem the German General Staff showed that they were ahead of the rest of military Europe, in that they were the first to appreciate the possibilities of modern howitzer fire. Their early experiments in this direction did not aim at the rapid reduction of fortresses, but at the application of the howitzer and the high explosive shell to field warfare. For some time before the war, they began to neglect their field guns, which in August 1914 were very inferior both to our own and to the French, and to develop the light and the medium howitzer. While they were doing this the advent of the aeroplane opened up to them new possibilities. In the direction of artillery fire from the air they were again ahead of both the French and ourselves, and they were quick to grasp its effect, when applied to the use of heavy siege howitzers, upon the powers of resistance of modern fortresses. The Belgian fortresses consisted of a ring of detached forts, heavily armoured, and containing the fortress artillery. The Germans understood that these forts, the positions of which were accurately known and clearly marked on the maps, would be helpless against the fire of heavy howitzers from concealed positions unknown to the defenders. The one element that was wanted to make success certain was that the fire of these howitzers should be accurately observed, and this element was provided by the aeroplane.

I do not mean to imply that all this was as completely understood by the German General Staff before the war as it is today, for it is evident, from what happened at Liège, that they hoped to be able to reduce the place without waiting for the arrival of the siege artillery, but they did in fact have the right kind of weapon ready when the need arose, and appear to have formed a much truer estimate of the powers of resistance of the Belgian fortresses than did the soldiers of the Entente Powers.

Having found the means to overcome the resistance of Belgium in the time available, if she should dare to oppose their military power, the German General Staff were able to complete their plans for the destruction of the French Army. They proposed to leave in the East to hold off the Russian Armies with the help of Austria less than one-third of the total forces they would have available on mobilisation, while more than two-thirds were concentrated in the West. But force alone was not sufficient for the success of their plan. If they were to get a quick decision against the numerous and highly efficient armies of the French Republic, some element of surprise was necessary.

Now the size of the German active army, that is the army kept under training in peace time, and the position of each of its corps were perfectly well known to the military world. There was therefore no great difficulty in calculating the time required to mobilise these corps and move them into position on the frontiers. It was also well known that Germany had a large surplus of trained men above those needed to bring the active corps up to their war strength, and that she had made arrangements to create out of these men a number of reserve formations; but it was not known how many these would be or how quickly they could be placed in the field.

The German General Staff, in fact, knew that the French would be uncertain both as to the number of German troops that would be left to watch Russia in the East, and as to the number of reserve corps which could be placed in the field in the opening phases of the war, and they proposed to use these elements of uncertainty to obtain the surprise which they desired, first by completing immediately the formation of a large number of reserve corps, and secondly, having in this way very considerably increased their available force, by bringing to the West a very high proportion of the whole.

Actually, during the period with which my account deals; that is, during the first six weeks of the war, Germany placed on the Western front 21 active and 13 reserve corps, and followed these soon after with 4 more reserve corps. All these reserve corps were not ready at the same time, but the first 13 appeared in the field early enough to make it justifiable to include them in the original grouping of the German Armies. Now, in considering this grouping the German General Staff were no doubt influenced by the facts that the arrangements of the French railways, and the location of the French corps in peace time, lent themselves to a rapid concentration of the main French forces on the Franco-German frontier, and they doubtless anticipated from this and from their knowledge of the French character that the French would take the offensive into Alsace and Lorraine. It is also highly probable that they calculated that the French Government would be influenced by considerations of morality, and would not enter Belgium until invited to do so by the Government of that country.

In comparing the opposing forces, it is most convenient to take divisions as the basis, because at the beginning of the war the division was approximately of the same size in all armies. The 21 active and the 13 reserve corps, (a corps at this time normally consisted of 2 divisions, with other troops chiefly artillery), which the German General Staff proposed to deploy on the Western front, totalled 68 divisions—I am leaving cavalry divisions for the present out of account. They had to reckon that this force might be opposed by the little Belgian Army of 6 divisions, possibly by the English Expeditionary Force of 6 divisions, and the French Army of 45 active and 27 reserve divisions, or 84 divisions in all, while the French in addition were known to have a considerable number of Territorial troops.

This on paper looks a formidable array to attempt to overwhelm quickly with a force of 68 divisions; but there were many factors which simplified the problem when it was examined more closely. In the first place the little Belgian Army stood alone and could not be supported in time either by France or by England, while it was beyond the bounds of probability that the Belgian Government would permit their army to abandon the country to its fate, and march at once to join the French Armies. Therefore, there was every reason to expect that it would be possible either to overwhelm the Belgian Army completely and quickly, or, at the worst, to lock it up in its fortresses, where it could be held by reserve formations while the main German Armies were marching on France.

If Great Britain intervened in the war, which was by no means certain to the German mind, she would be late in the field, because her troops had to be shipped across the Channel, and the British military system did not lend itself to very rapid mobilisation, while the plan of a great enveloping movement through Belgium would tend, when prolonged into France, to cut the communications between the Channel ports and the South and prevent the despatch of British reinforcements. Of the French Army at least 3 active divisions had to come from North Africa, and would probably be late, many of the reserve divisions would be required for fortress garrisons, and the Territorial troops were known to be lacking in artillery, and to be incompletely trained.

Such then were probably the chief considerations which the German General Staff had before them when shaping their plan of campaign. They decided to draw up their armies on the Western front in two groups: (For the original grouping of the German Armies see Map 1). The first, which was to be the principal means of obtaining the quick decision they sought, along the Belgian frontier; the second, which was to meet and counter the probable French invasion of Lorraine and pin the main French forces in the south, was to be formed on the southern frontier of Luxemburg and in Lorraine. These two groups were to be connected by a comparatively weak link, and a fourth, and also weak, group was to take post in the extreme south and watch the Vosges and Alsace.

The first group, composed of the First, Second, and Third Armies under von Kluck, von Bülow, and von Hausen respectively, comprised no less than 16 corps (32 divisions) and a large force of cavalry, nearly one-half of the German forces in the West. The second group consisted of the Fifth and Sixth Armies, under the German Crown Prince and the Bavarian Crown Prince Rupprecht, and amounted to 12 corps (24 divisions). The connecting-link between the two groups was provided by the Fourth Army, under the Duke Albrecht of Würtemberg, who commanded 4 corps (8 divisions), and lastly, on the south, lay the Seventh Army under von Heeringen, with 2 corps (4 divisions) and some reserve formations, and troops from the garrisons of Metz and Strassburg.

There were two dangers to which this distribution exposed the German forces. The first was that a French offensive into Alsace and Lorraine might overwhelm the weak left flank under von Heeringen and lead to the envelopment of the armies of the two Crown Princes from the south, the second was that the weak link between the two main groups might be snapped by a French attack in force upon it, and the flanks of either or both of these groups be assailed. In appreciating these risks, they were most certainly guided by the principles I have already outlined.

They would argue that both the danger points lay in difficult and highly defensible country, the Vosges on the south and the Ardennes in the centre, that in such country their machine-guns, which they had developed highly both in numbers and efficiency, would have great delaying power, and the French 75's, the crack weapon of their chief enemy, little scope. In fact, they proposed to make skilful use of the nature of the country on the frontier so as to increase the weight of the blows they intended to deliver. The plan in the main hinged on the German belief that a frontal advance even against weak forces must be slow, and that therefore the armies of the two Crown Princes in the south must make their weight felt before a French advance into the Vosges had got very far, and that the great enveloping movement through Belgium, the strength of which they trusted would not be anticipated by the French, would become effective before an attack on their centre could make enough progress to be dangerous.

The German plan was in conception bold, simple, and based upon a careful abstract study of war. It was at the same time utterly ruthless and immoral in its cold-blooded contempt of national pledges and of the rights of the weak, and was fundamentally defective in its disregard of the psychology both of potential enemies and of possible allies. It was, in fact, a *chef d'oeuvre* of Prussian militarism naked and unashamed, and, like all plans which defy the laws of morality, it contained the germs of weakness which were to bring it to failure. For it made Great Britain a certain enemy, Italy a certain neutral, and turned against Germany the sentiment of the greater part of the civilised world.

Had it been carried through in the field with the skill with which it had been drawn up in the offices of the Great General Staff, it might have encompassed the destruction of our first five divisions, the fall of Paris, and the occupation of Northern France, but even so great a measure of success would not have brought victory over enemies who felt that life would not be worth living if such a plan and such methods were permitted to triumph. Luckily, we were not put to so terrible a test, for though the plan was good its execution was faulty, and, as will be seen, adherence to one idea caused opportunity after opportunity to be missed.

I do not wish to suggest that it was in any sense a rigid plan, or that the direction and objective of the great enveloping movement was fixed at the time when the march into Belgium began. The Germans are too good soldiers to commit a stupidity of that kind. War, so far as concerns the higher command, is a conflict between minds, and each Headquarters can only guess what is going on in the other. The German Headquarters could only conjecture what the Belgian Army would do; they could only guess whether, if Great Britain came into the war, her army would come at once to the help of Belgium, or prolong the French left, or lie back behind it; they could only surmise how far north the French left would extend.

Moltke had always taught that the preparation of a plan of campaign in detail should not be carried further than the first contact with the opposing troops, all beyond that depending upon the unforeseeable, the action of the enemy, who usually does what is least expected. In one of those flashes of humour which very occasionally light up his valuable but portentously dull pronouncements, he once said to his staff in criticism of a military exercise:

"Gentlemen, I have observed that there are always three courses open to the enemy, and that he usually takes the fourth."

In that teaching the German General Staff of the present day has been brought up; but fortunately for the world the successors of the elder Moltke were not in 1914 of his calibre, and though their plan was flexible and adaptable to the changes and chances of war, the idea of envelopment had become with them such a fetish that it was for a time at least regarded consciously or subconsciously as an end in itself rather than as a means to the one end of operations of war—the decisive defeat of the enemy.

CHAPTER 2

The French Plan

Though I propose to follow the course of events mainly from the German side my object is to make clearer the part played by our Expeditionary Force in the opening phase of the war, and for this it will be necessary from time to time to look at events both from our own and from the French point of view, and to examine the Allied scheme on the Western front as a whole. The French plan was, as might have been expected from the spirit and training of the French Army, offensive, the object being to carry the war into Germany as quickly as possible. Russian co-operation was assured, Italy had fallen out with the Triple Alliance, and, once it was known that English help was forthcoming, France had every reason to suppose that she would have sufficient force to carry through her plans, for there was no great disparity in strength between the active armies of France and Germany.

To obtain an approach to equality France, with her much smaller population, had had to keep with the colours in peace time a higher proportion of her manhood of military age than had her enemy, and the military superiority of Germany at the outbreak of war lay mainly in the mass of trained men who had passed through the ranks and were no longer in the active army.

The French Headquarters could not know how the enemy would solve the two problems which would decide the strength of the armies to be mobilised against them. Neither France nor any of her Allies suspected that Germany would dare to concentrate so great a proportion of her total strength on the Western front, nor was the perfection to which Germany had brought her arrangements for mobilising rapidly her reserve formations appreciated; and these two factors had, as will be seen, very great influence on the early course of the war in the West. But this difficulty in gauging accurately the enemy's strength in the West was not the only handicap from which French

Headquarters suffered.

Unlike the German, the French Government paid due respect to the rights of others, and therefore the French soldiers were limited in their plans of offence to direct attack across the German frontier between Metz and Switzerland, and a great envelopment, such as Germany carried through, was excluded on moral grounds. The French invasion of Alsace and Lorraine was not therefore, as has sometimes been said, a movement dictated by sentimental and political considerations. It was the one alternative either to waiting passively for the enemy's attack, and exposing French territory to the ravages of war, without an effort to prevent such a disaster, or to outvying the enemy in immorality by transferring the scene of battle to the country of a weak and neutral power.

These factors governed the arrangements for the first grouping of the French Army, which was designed to be as follows: (This grouping of the French Armies is shown on Map 1), an Alsace group of 5 divisions with 4 reserve divisions was to assemble about Belfort; along the Lorraine frontier south of Metz the main offensive group, consisting of the First Army of 4 corps (8 divisions) under General Dubail, and the Second Army of 5 corps (10 divisions) and 3 reserve divisions under General de Castelnau; the Third Army of 4 corps (8 divisions) and 3 reserve divisions under General Ruffey assembled round Verdun; the Fifth Army of 3 corps (6 divisions) and 3 reserve divisions under General de Lanrezac watched the exits of the Ardennes from Belgian Luxemburg as far north as the Belgian frontier near Rocroi; a Fourth Army of 4 corps (8 divisions) and 2 reserve divisions under General Langle de Gary was in reserve behind the centre.

Thus, Joffre had a total force for the field of 45 active and 15 reserve divisions. This grouping shows that the French commander-in-chief intended to employ, for an offensive across the Franco-German frontier, 30 out of his available 60 divisions, more than half his active troops being included in the 30, which could be readily reinforced from the Fourth Army in reserve. It also shows that he was prepared for the violation of the neutrality of Luxemburg, and of that part of Belgium south of the Meuse, but that he had not thought it probable that Germany would be strong enough to force the Meuse, brush aside the opposition of Belgium, and march through the plains of that country.

The possibility of such an eventuality does not, however, appear to have been overlooked, for the position of the Fourth Army in reserve was such that it could be pushed forward into the Ardennes, so as to strike at the flank and communications of any German force attempting a wide turning movement by the north, while the Fifth Army took ground to its left, so as to meet the enemy if he advanced north of the Meuse.

When the first groupings of the opposing armies are compared, we get at once the key to the mentality of the French and German leaders, and to the principles which guided them. As might be expected, these principles were the outcome of special study of the particular problems which confronted each nation, and in each case they show the influence of national thought and character. Strategy is not an abstract science, concerned with the grouping and movements of pieces on a level board, but has to occupy itself with the political questions of the day, with a most minute and careful study of the topography of the theatre of war, with examination of the time in which troops can be moved from one area to another, both by friend and by foe, and, above all, it is a clash of human minds, each with at best a very imperfect knowledge of the problem of the other, and each dealing with men of flesh and blood, who have limited powers of endurance, and require to be fed, clothed, equipped, and provided with the means to enable them to fight in the best possible conditions.

Consideration of all these factors by the French and German General Staffs during the years which preceded the outbreak of war had led each of them to inculcate certain methods of procedure, which were sometimes labelled, erroneously, the French and German doctrines of war. They were not doctrines applicable to war in general, but solutions of the special problems of a war between the Central Powers and the Entente in Western Europe.

The Germans, as we have seen, required quick results, and they relied upon obtaining them by concentrating from the very outset superior numbers on those parts of the front where they wished to obtain the decision, that is, particularly against the Allied left flank, and by the more rapid effect of attack by envelopment as compared with that of frontal attack. They had great confidence in the perfection of the training, organisation, and equipment of their armies, and in the capacity of their General Staff to deal promptly and accurately with the complicated problems of time and space which their plan of campaign involved.

The General Staff had gained the concurrence of the statesmen in the plan, and left them to devise a plausible story which should soothe such conscience as the German people possessed, and if possible hoodwink the neutral world; and, as the first article in the creed of the German Governments had, since the days of Bismarck, been that victory covers all sins, while from the *Kaiser* downwards all were absolutely persuaded that their arms were invincible, there had been no difficulty in the application of the old maxim that policy and strategy should go hand in hand. The principle of the German General Staff was then (to use a phrase dear to the German soldier) to impose their will upon the enemy from the outset, to compel him to conform to their plans, and, by employing at once the greatest possible force upon one general scheme, to leave him no time for counter-manoeuvre.

The defects of the plan, which sprang from the innate conceit of the Prussian mind, lay in the failure to grasp its effect upon certain or potential enemies and in its underestimate of the forces which it would bring into the field against Germany. The Prussian *Junker* in fact believed that Great Britain and Belgium would seize any excuse to avoid having to face the might of Germany. To these defects must be added a certain rigidity of thought, which long study of the problem of war against France upon one fixed principle had produced in the minds of the German leaders.

The French General Staff, limited by political conditions in their field of manoeuvre, could not by any possibility use, as the Germans proposed to do, the whole of their available offensive power upon one prearranged plan, because there was no room on the stretch of frontier, much of it mountainous, between Basle and Metz, for the employment of such masses of troops. They had therefore to trust that the rapidity of mobilisation would enable them to forestall the enemy, and upset his concentration before it was complete; while a considerable body of troops was held in reserve as a mass of manoeuvre, ready either to confirm and complete a success or to ward off any danger which might suddenly develop.

It was not because they did not believe in envelopment that they did not attempt it, for Joffre did in fact bring about the breakdown of the enemy's plans by enveloping one of the German flanks at the very first opportunity he had of carrying out such a manoeuvre; but because under the particular political and geographical conditions which confronted the French at the outbreak of the war envelopment was impossible. That this would be so had been long recognised by French students of war and particularly by Foch, who had taught the French Staff how to counter envelopment by a return to the Napoleonic principle of manoeuvre with a general reserve. The French had therefore by force of circumstances adopted an opportunist policy, which sought rather to create occasions for the action of a reserve held back for the purpose of delivering a decisive blow at the right time and place, than to put the whole of their armies into line at once, each having from the first assigned to it a mission in accordance with a plan prepared before the enemy had been encountered.

So, throughout the period of the war which I am about to describe we find Joffre, as soon as he has sent off his reserve upon some task, at once creating another, and continuously on the watch for opportunities, until at last the opportunity comes.

France declared war on the evening of August 8, and the next morning General Joffre announced this fact to his troops in the following order:—

> War is declared. Italy has issued a declaration of her complete neutrality. Germany will endeavour, by spreading false information, to cause us to violate the neutrality of Belgium. All our troops are expressly forbidden, until orders to the contrary are issued, to enter Belgium or Swiss territory even with patrols or single horsemen. No flying is to take place over these territories.

Not until the evening of August 5, that is, after Germany had violated the neutrality of Belgium, and Belgium had appealed to the Allies for help, was the following order issued:—

> (1) French airships and aeroplanes are authorised to fly over Belgian territory. As, however, the Belgian troops had orders up till yesterday to fire at all aircraft, and orders to the contrary may not yet be known to all concerned, pilots are to be directed to fly high.
> (2) Cavalry reconnaissances may also proceed into Belgian territory, but they are not yet to be supported by large detachments....
> (3) All parties entering Belgium are to be specially warned that they are entering the country of a friendly and Allied Power. They are not to carry out requisitions of any kind until the agreement with regard to these, which is in preparation, has been made known. They are only to make voluntary purchases against cash payments.

These orders do honour to the French Government, and display their anxiety to respect the rights and wishes of an Ally, and if anything were needed to do so, they should suffice to bring France the sympathy and support of the civilised world, for this scrupulous respect for the code of national honour gave the unprincipled enemy an advantage from which he profited to the full. Had it been possible to make preparations earlier for obtaining information as to what was happening on the German-Belgian frontier, the surprise which the Germans sprang upon the Allies at the time of the Battle of Mons would have been unmasked much sooner and the story of the war materially changed. As it was, the Germans had leisure to complete their arrangements for concealing their designs before the French Headquarters could get their means of investigation to work.

On August 7, (for these events see Map 1), the French covering troops about Belfort moved forward into Alsace, and occupied Mulhausen on the 8th, but were unable to hold the town in face of superior German forces, and fell back the next day. By August 14 the First and Second Armies and the Alsace group were ready for the general advance, and Alsace and Lorraine were invaded in force. Mulhausen was again occupied, the outskirts of Colmar were reached, and patrols pushed forward towards the Rhine, while the main chain of the Vosges as far east as the Donon was secured. In Lorraine the First and Second Armies fought their way forward against steadily increasing opposition, and on the 19th penetrated as far as Saarburg, cutting direct communication between Strassburg and Metz.

But before the French main offensive had reached its full development events in the north had forced Joffre to divert troops from the south, and it was a weakened force which on the 20th met the Sixth and Seventh German Armies advancing to the attack, the enemy's main blow falling on their northern flank between Saarburg and Metz. Generals Dubail and de Castelnau were forced slowly back to positions covering Nancy and Lunéville, where we may leave them for the present to return to the events on the extreme left of the French line.

Here to the north of Sedan, on the frontier of Belgian Luxemburg, was placed in the first concentration General Sordet's cavalry corps of three divisions. This corps crossed the Belgian frontier on August 6, and advancing south of the Meuse on the 8th got to within a few miles of Liège, but without discovering any large bodies of German troops. The French cavalry then fell back again towards the frontier, and after a short rest carried out further reconnaissances between the 11th and the 15th through the Ardennes towards Neufchâteau, and north of the Meuse towards Namur and Charleroi. All these enterprises brought only negative results.

Eastern Belgium had been explored and no considerable German forces had been discovered on the move against the French left flank. The French Headquarters to that extent found confirmation of their views that such a movement was improbable. Sordet's expedition was in fact too early to find the German columns on the march, and his troopers could not get through far enough to discover and interrupt the enemy's concentrations. The German cavalry when met gave way, but did not allow their screen to be pierced, and the French horsemen found great difficulty in obtaining information in face of the rifle and machine-gun fire coming from the cyclists and *Jägers* brought up in motor lorries in support of the German cavalry.

This first experiment in cavalry reconnaissance on a large scale in the present war illustrates very clearly how easily the old eyes of the army can, in these days, be blinded by an enemy who knows how to make skilful use of rifles and machine-guns. The textbook opening of a great war which had fired the imagination of the Continental cavalryman proved to be a fiction. The French cavalry encountered no great masses of opposing horsemen, to be ridden down in thrilling charges. Instead, they were met by rifle fire coming from they knew not where, fire to which with their light carbines they could make no effective reply. Nor were the new eyes much more successful in clearing up the fog of war.

The distances from their bases in France to the Meuse north of Huy, to which place, and to Liège still farther north, the German columns marched to cross the river, made it impossible for the French aircraft of those days to keep up regular and sustained reconnaissances of the roads along which the enemy was moving. The part of Belgium which lies east of the Meuse is densely wooded, and in particular the forests of the Ardennes formed an impenetrable screen to the eyes of the French airmen. Further, the enemy frequently took the precaution of marching his infantry by night.

It had been very generally supposed before the war that air reconnaissances would make surprise impossible, and that generals would find themselves in the happy position of no longer having to guess, like Wellington, at what was happening on the other side of the hill. In practice, however, human ingenuity usually arrives at some more

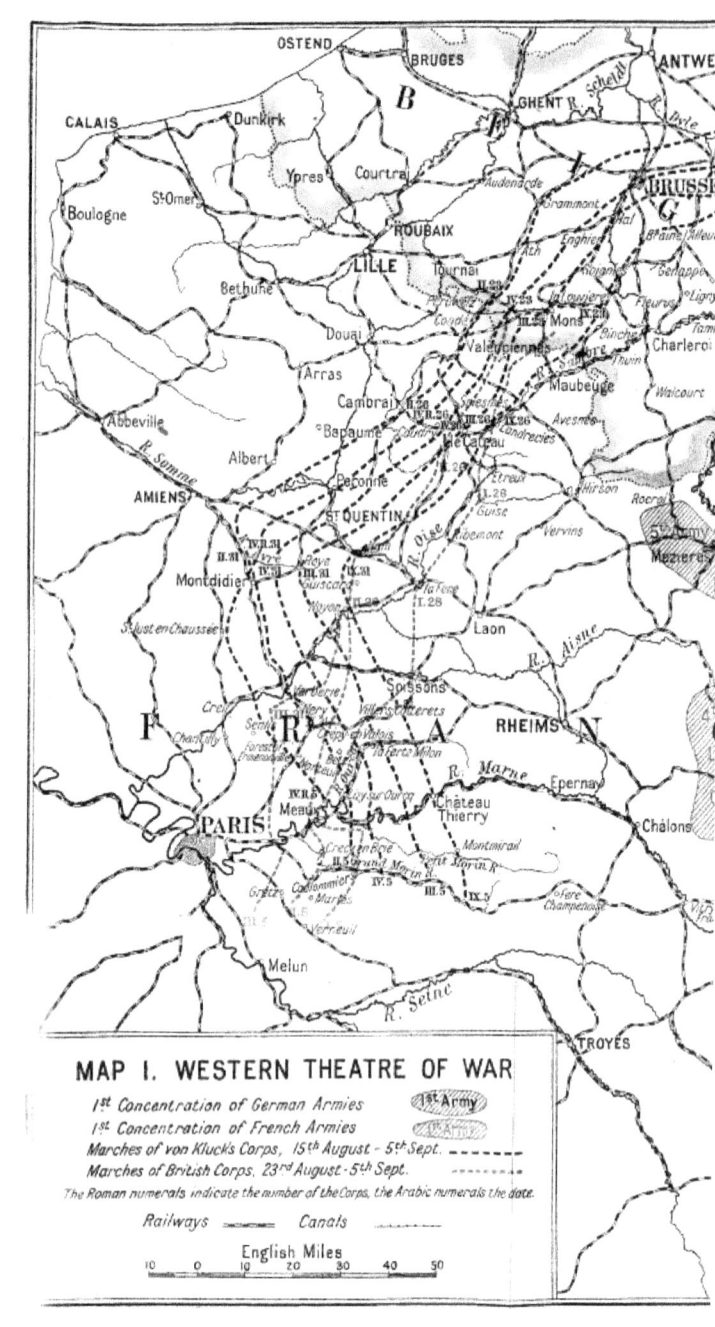

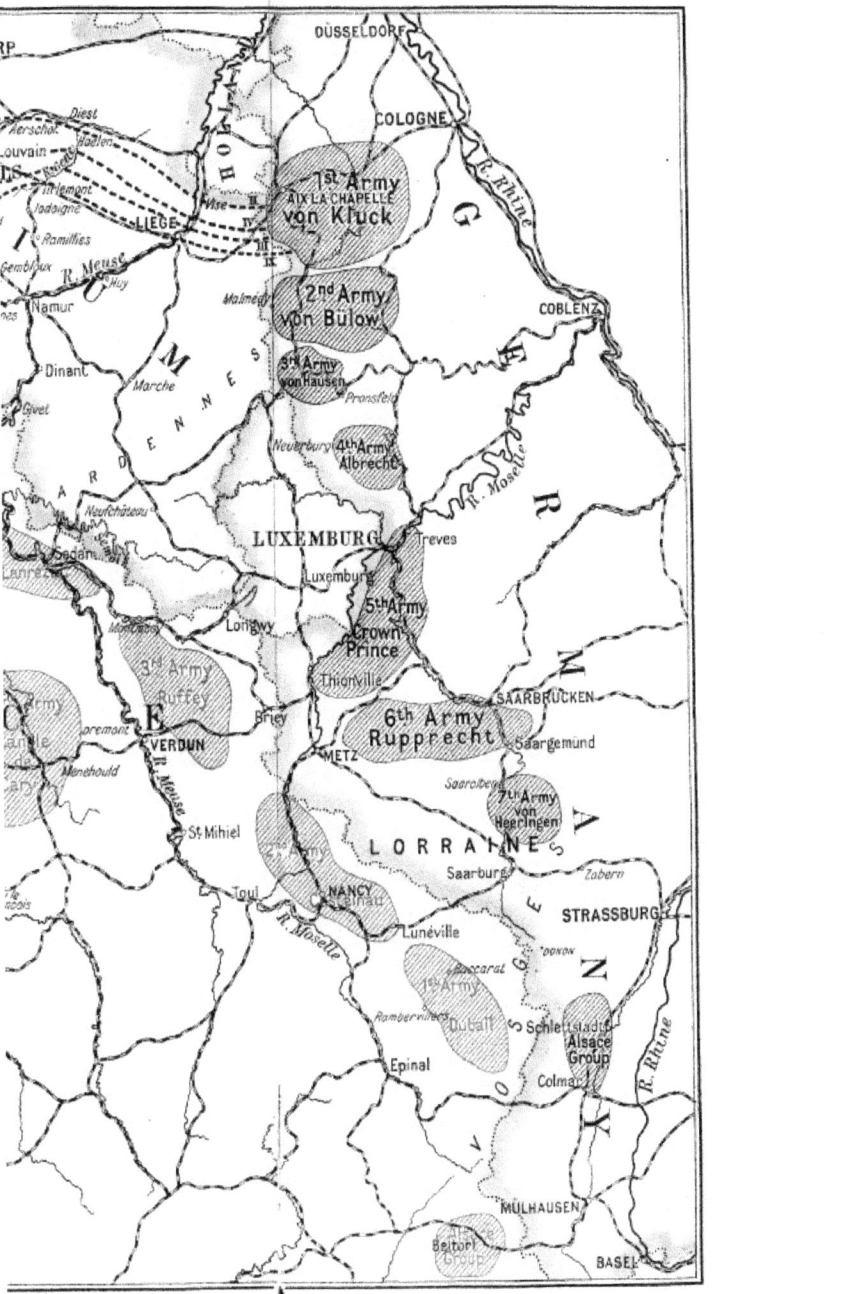

or less effective antidote to every new development of science which is applied to war. Revolutions in warfare, which are sometimes announced as the necessary and immediate consequence of a startling invention, are in fact slow to mature. In the story which I am now telling of the first six weeks of the war, will be found, successfully carried through, one by each side, two great surprises, each as dramatic and as far-reaching in its consequences as any to be found in military history.

There was nothing in this early exploration to shake the opinion of French Headquarters that the enemy was unlikely to advance in strength north of the valley of the Meuse, and it was not until August 15 that General Joffre received definite information that large German forces were moving westwards through Liège. He at once issued orders to strengthen his left, and to extend it northwards to meet the threatened enveloping movement of the enemy. The Fifth Army was ordered to move across the Belgian frontier into the angle formed by the Sambre and the Meuse between Charleroi, Namur, and Dinant, and it was reinforced by the Eighteenth Corps, which was withdrawn from the Second Army, then moving forward into Lorraine. The Second Army had also to give up the Ninth Corps, and the three divisions from North Africa, which were to have joined in the invasion of Alsace, were sent northwards.

Thus, the effect of the discovery that the enemy was in strength in the north was to reduce the main French striking force in the south by no fewer than seven divisions. The Fourth Army, which had been in reserve, was moved up to the frontier of Belgian Luxemburg to take the place vacated by the Fifth Army and to connect that army with the Third.

Lastly, as it was definitely known that a large force of German cavalry, estimated at three cavalry divisions at least, had crossed the Meuse and was moving westwards through Belgium, it was necessary to take precautions against raids into French Flanders, which the enemy might attempt, either in order to interfere with the concentration of the British Expeditionary Force then on its way, or even to interrupt communication between the Channel ports and the rest of France. General d'Amade was therefore sent to Arras to take command of a group of Territorial divisions consisting of the Eighty-Fourth at Douai, the Eighty-Second at Arras, and the Eighty-First about St. Omer. To this group was added in a few days' time the Eighty-Eighth Territorial Division, which assembled south of Lille, while two reserve divisions from the garrison of Paris were placed under orders to move north to join General d'Amade's command. We shall meet most of these troops again during the retreat of the British Army from Mons.

These movements were not completed until August 21, and at that time French Headquarters were still unaware of the full strength which the enemy was bringing against them, and more especially of the strength of the enemy's forces moving north of the Meuse through Belgium. General Joffre was far from renouncing all idea of attack. He had been forced to weaken his offensive in the south, but this was to be remedied by a blow in the north, and therefore his central reserve, the Fourth Army, was brought up towards the Ardennes, ready to strike if it were found that the enemy were moving in force north of the Meuse, while if the Germans were not in strength there the British would come in on the left of the Fifth Army and with it envelop the German right. The idea still prevailed that the Germans could not be strong enough to secure their centre in the Ardennes against attack and at the same time carry out a great attack upon the Allied left.

By August 20, (for these movements see Map 2), the British Expeditionary Force of a cavalry division and 2 corps, each of 2 divisions, in all about 70,000 combatants, had completed its concentration just south of Maubeuge, and on the 21st began its march northward, the British cavalry advancing towards the Canal de Condé, to the east of Mons, and gaining touch with General Sordet's cavalry on its right. On August 22 the First and Second British Corps reached positions about Mons, the First Corps, on the right, being in touch with the left corps of General de Lanrezac's Fifth Army near Thuin, south-west of Charleroi. This left corps was the Eighteenth, which had entrained at Toul on receiving orders to leave the Second French Army, had detrained at Avesnes to the south of Maubeuge at the same time that the British were assembling, and had marched thence across the Belgian frontier towards Marchienne.

Farther to the right about Charleroi lay the Third French Corps, while the Tenth Corps was disposed along the Sambre between Charleroi and Namur, and the First Corps on the line of the Meuse, between Namur and Dinant. The Tenth and Third Corps were by this time being reinforced each by one of the French divisions from North Africa. The First Corps expected a reserve division, the Fifty-first, which had not actually arrived, and two reserve divisions were on their way to join the Eighteenth Corps, these reinforcements bringing General de Lanrezac's Fifth Army up to a total of 280,000 men, but of these some 80,000 were not actually in place; so that about the time when the German blow first fell on the Franco-British left flank there were, exclusive of the garrison of Namur, 270,000 Franco-British troops in position between Dinant, Namur, and Mons, facing German Armies which, as we shall see, totalled over 400,000 men.

Even as late as August 22 the view held at French Headquarters appears to have been that it would be possible to envelop the Germans north of the Meuse by an advance of the British Army and of the French Fifth Army pivoting on Namur, and it was with this general idea of an advance to be continued northwards into Belgium that our army marched to Mons on August 22.

On the morning of August 23, the two reserve divisions attached to the French Eighteenth Corps, the Fifty-Third and the Sixty-Ninth, reached the line Montignies-Jeumont, just north-east of Maubeuge and directly behind the point of junction of the French left and the British right. But by then the German surprise had already been sprung, the French Fifth Army had been heavily attacked, and a few hours later both General Joffre and Sir John French were for the first time aware of the imminent peril which menaced the Allied left wing. In order to make the extent of this surprise clear I cannot do better than quote Sir John French's first despatch. He says, *(Naval and Military Dispatches relating to Operations in the War, September-October and November, 1914)*:—

> At 6 a.m., on August 23, I assembled the commanders of the First and Second Corps and Cavalry Division at a point close to the position and explained the general situation of the Allies, and what I understood to be General Joffre's plan. I discussed with them at some length the immediate situation in front of us.
>
> From information I received from French Headquarters I understood that little more than one, or at most two, of the enemy's army corps, with perhaps one cavalry division, were in front of my position; and I was aware of no outflanking movement by the enemy. I was confirmed in this opinion by the fact that my patrols encountered no undue opposition in their reconnoitring operations. The observations of my aeroplanes seemed also to bear out this estimate.
>
> About 3 p.m. on Sunday, the 23rd, reports began coming in to the effect that the enemy was commencing an attack on the

Mons line, apparently in some strength.

The right of the Third Division, under General Hamilton, was at Mons, which formed a somewhat dangerous salient; and I directed the Commander of the Second Corps to be careful not to keep the troops too long on this salient, but, if threatened seriously, to draw back the centre behind Mons. This was done before dark. In the meantime, about 5 p.m. I received a most unexpected message from General Joffre by telegraph, telling me that at least three German Corps, *viz*. a reserve corps, the Fourth Corps and the Ninth Corps, were moving on my position in front, and that the Second Corps was engaged in a turning movement from the direction of Tournay. He also informed me that the two reserve French Divisions and the Fifth French Army on my right were retiring, the Germans having on the previous day gained possession of the passages of the Sambre between Charleroi and Namur.

CHAPTER 3

The German March Through Belgium
(See Map 1)

The three German Armies destined for the attack on the Allied left flank were concentrated, the First, under von Kluck, about Aix-la-Chapelle, the Second, under von Bülow, about Malmedy and Stavelo, and the Third, under von Hausen, about Prün. They were to move into Belgium, the First Army by Liège, the Second mainly through Huy and thence along the north bank of the Meuse upon Namur, the Third through the Ardennes by Marche on Dinant. Each army required several roads, but these places give the general direction of the line of march. Von Kluck's army, which was to be on the outside of the wheel, and was therefore intended to carry out the final envelopment, had the most difficult task and was considerably the strongest.

It consisted of no less than seven corps (14 divisions), the Second, the Third, Third Reserve, Fourth, Fourth Reserve, Ninth, and Ninth Reserve, and three cavalry divisions, the Second, Fourth, and Ninth. Two of these corps, the Third Reserve and Ninth Reserve, were, as will be seen, left in Belgium for a time, but it is probable that at first at least they formed part of von Kluck's command. Two of the cavalry divisions, the Second and Fourth, formed a cavalry corps under the command of von Marwitz, and may possibly have been independent of von Kluck; but as they worked throughout in the closest touch with his army it is reasonable to consider them as under his orders.

As I explained in the first chapter, a very small proportion of the fighting strength of Germany was left on the Eastern frontier. Actually, only four out of a total of twenty-five active corps were, with a number of reserve formations, to hold back the Russians till France had been defeated. It is necessary to keep this in mind in order to understand the early phases of the campaign in the West, throughout which the German General Staff had one eye on the East, and were gauging to a nicety the time available for the completion of their programme in France. Von Kluck's line of march was barred by the important fortress of Liège, and he had the longest way to go.

Therefore, not only was it of the first importance that he should be able to get through Liège as soon as possible, but the whole German plan of envelopment depended upon getting early possession of the place, for within the circle of its forts lay the railway junction upon which centred the lines connecting Belgium and northern France with Northern Germany, and without those railways the mass of troops assembling for the march round the Allied left could not be fed or furnished with the thousand-and-one things which an army must have if it is to keep the field.

It must for these reasons have been a grievous disappointment to the German command when Belgium stoutly refused them permission to march their troops through her territory, but it is abundantly clear from the course of events that they had drawn up plans long beforehand to meet the possibility of Belgian resistance to their demands. It was von Kluck's army that was to march through Liège, but many of his corps came from the East, and not only would it cause delay to wait for these to come up in order to attack the fortress, but it was very important to conceal the presence on the Western front of troops whose natural task would be to oppose the Russians.

Therefore, the duty of clearing the road for von Kluck fell upon covering troops from von Bülow's Second Army, which were drawn mainly from his Seventh and Tenth Corps. As these corps came from Westphalia and Hanover respectively, their presence on the Western front would be expected by the enemy, and would not arouse any suspicions as to the real strength of the armies by which France was to be attacked.

War was declared by France on the evening of August 3, and early on the following day the German Second and Fourth Cavalry Divisions entered Belgium and crossed the Meuse at Visé to the north of Liège, overcoming the resistance of a Belgian detachment holding the bridge. They then proceeded to cover on the west the attack on Liège. Similarly, to the south, along the valley of the Meuse and in the Ardennes, the Ninth, Fifth, and Guard Cavalry Divisions established a screen covering the concentration of the Second and Third Armies, and this screen was, with the assistance of armoured cars, infantry cyclists, and *Jägers* brought up in lorries, effectively established before the French cavalry were free to cross the Belgian frontier. While the cavalry were moving into position the infantry of the Seventh and Tenth Corps marched on Liège, and after a last vain attempt to open a road by persuasion, attacked and drove in the Belgian outposts. The next day, August 5, von Emmich, the commander of the attacking troops, attempted to carry the place by assault, and failed with very heavy loss.

Simultaneously with the attack on Liège, the attack on the moral of the Belgian people was begun. It is not my purpose to describe in any detail the German campaign of frightfulness in Belgium—that has already been done authoritatively with the aid of many who were brought into direct contact with its horrors. The savagery with which it was conducted has been ascribed to such various causes as exasperation at the heavy losses suffered in the capture of Liège, the natural brutality of the German soldiery, and anger at the audacity of little Belgium in daring to resist the commands of the War Lord of Europe.

All these very probably, indeed one may say certainly, contributed to the rage of lust and cruelty which swept over such parts of Belgium as lay on the track of the German columns, but I am convinced that the vast amount of evidence which has been collected admits of no other conclusion than that the inspiration came from above, and was as much part of the calculated and cold-blooded German plan as was the concentration on the frontier. It was, in fact, an element in the scheme to save the time which was so precious to the German General Staff, and to secure by terrorism, deliberately and scientifically applied to military purposes, the uninterrupted march of the main forces to their goal.

The first attack on Liège on the morning of August 5 had been carried out mainly by troops of the Seventh Corps. The Belgian *commandant*, General Leman, had been reinforced by the Third Belgian Division shortly before the attack was delivered, and had entrenched and manned the intervals between the detached forts. Von Emmich in his haste had tried to carry these entrenchments in a rush after what is now recognised as a short and inadequate artillery bombardment. This rash experiment had proved very costly, but time was of more value than men's lives. Troops of the Tenth Corps arrived during the afternoon from the south-east, and about the same time the first of von Kluck's infantry, the men of the Ninth Corps, who had crossed the Meuse to the north of Liège in the neighbourhood of Visé, came down on the fortress from the north.

With these additions to his strength, and with an increased amount of artillery at his disposal, von Emmich organised a fresh assault on a larger scale. During the late afternoon a bombardment was opened which continued until dark, and this was followed by a series of Infantry attacks on the northern, eastern, and southern defences, which were pressed home throughout the night regardless of loss. By the morning of August 6, the German infantry had forced their way between two of the eastern forts, but the Belgians still held the villages between the circle of forts and the town, and the Germans were too exhausted to follow up their success immediately.

Thus, it was not until the morning of August 7 that the town was entered, and before then the Third Belgian Division had evacuated the place, for General Leman, finding the Germans gradually encircling the fortress, and his defences pierced, ordered it away to join the Belgian Army, which was assembling behind the Gette, 30 miles west of Liège, in order that this division might not be involved in the capitulation which he saw was inevitable. At the same time, he determined to hold the forts to the last, so as to prevent the Germans as long as possible from using the railways passing through Liège.

The first hasty infantry assaults had proved too costly to be repeated, and once the town was entered the task of reducing the forts was left to the howitzers. To open a road for the siege train, which did not arrive until the 11th, the concentrated fire of the heavy field howitzers was turned on the two easternmost forts immediately south of the Meuse, and these fell on the 9th and 10th. On the 12th the siege train began its work, and the steel and cement cupolas which protected the guns of the forts were in turn smashed by the German heavy high explosive shell. Fort Lencin, which barred the main line of railway connecting Liège with Brussels, held out until the 15th, and there the gallant Leman was captured after he had been rendered senseless by the final explosion which destroyed the work.

The brave resistance of the forts of Liège sent a thrill of admiration throughout the countries of the Entente Powers, but the actual military effect of this resistance was greatly exaggerated, because it was not possible to appreciate at the time the skill with which the Germans, in making their plans for the attack upon the place, had reduced the delay it would cause them. From first to last the siege lasted twelve days, and during the greater part of this time the mobilisation and concentration of von Kluck's army was proceeding. Several of his corps, as I have pointed out, had to come from great distances, and it is improbable that his main bodies could have been ready to march across the frontier before the 12th at the earliest.

It is not less than four marches from the neighbourhood of Aix la Chapelle to the River Gette, about halfway between Liège and Brussels, and von Kluck had actually reached this river in force on the evening of August 17. Had the road been open it is improbable that he could have been there more than two days earlier, for it is unlikely that he would have dared to approach the main Belgian force with partially mobilised troops, small as it was in comparison with his great army. Even if he had done so, it is certain that he would have had to wait until his army was completely equipped and concentrated before marching southward against the left wing of the main Allied forces; so that, apart from the serious losses that the Germans suffered, the military effect of the resistance of Liège may be estimated at a delay to von Kluck's Army of forty-eight hours in reaching the battlefield of Mons.

This delay may appear very short and as hardly worth the sacrifices made by the brave defenders of the Belgian fortress, but, in fact, it was of priceless value. Had von Kluck's Army appeared north of Maubeuge two days earlier than it did, it is very possible that it would have caught the British Army and the French Fifth Army, which were, as we know, very incompletely informed as to its strength, much less prepared for battle than they were, and that neither would have been able to escape from disaster. At best they could only have retired Immediately, without Inflicting on the enemy the loss and delay which were later to give Joffre his opportunity.

But this was not the only service which the defenders of Liège rendered to the cause of the Allies. The spectacle of a little army, partially trained and insufficiently equipped, standing up for King and country against the most powerful and perfect military machine of modern times was an inspiration to every soldier of the Entente Armies, and still more did the proud refusal of Belgium's king and people to admit that might is right, with the certainty before them of having to make such sacrifices for honour and faith as no nation in civilised times has been asked to endure, bring into the struggle against Germany moral forces which in her eagerness for immediate and material military results she despised and neglected.

Even today, (1919), Germany fails to grasp the effect on Great Britain of the violation of Belgian neutrality. The German people are deceived into believing that by the skill of their leaders and the valour of their troops a British attack on Germany through Belgium was just anticipated, and England's motive in entering the war is still held, not merely for purposes of propaganda, but in the mind of the German masses, to have been greed of gain and the annihilation of her chief commercial rival. The Hymn of Hate merely makes us smile, but it was a sincere expression of the popular conviction which yet prevails in Germany that England brought about the war for her own base ends—so easy is it for an autocratic government to make its people think as they are told to think when it has drilled and disciplined them for generations.

This failure to appreciate the psychology of her enemies is one of the weak spots in the German armour. It is responsible for the sinking of the *Lusitania*, the shooting of Miss Cavell, (*vide Nurse Edith Cavell* by William Thomson Hill: Leonaur 2011), the bombing of open towns, the bombarding of Paris, and other methods of "frightfulness," the only military effect of which has been to increase the number of Germany's enemies, and to steel their hearts to endure all in order to remove for all time this pest which threatens civilisation. Perfect in many respects as have been the planning and organisation of the German General Staff—and I am here making no attempt to conceal their good points—they have failed because they are incapable of grasping the fact that there are higher forces in war than the scientific application of physical power to the gaining of an immediate military advantage.

Before the last fort of Liège had fallen the Second and Fourth German Cavalry Divisions, which had been covering the siege on the west and south, set out to discover the strength and position of the Belgian Army, and attempted at the same time to secure the crossings over the Gette, (see Map 1), for von Kluck's main bodies, which had completed their concentration round Aix-la-Chapelle. The Belgian forces watched the crossings of the Gette from near Diest, as far south as Jodoigne, with detachments from their main army, which lay between the Gette and the Dyle, and consisted of five infantry divisions, including the greater part of the reduced and sorely tried Third Division escaped from Liège, and a cavalry division.

The remaining Belgian division, the Fourth, was posted at Namur and the crossings of the Meuse immediately below that fortress. On the 12th the German cavalry attacked the Belgians near Haelen, and after a sharp fight were repulsed, from which von Kluck must have gleaned that it would require infantry in force to drive back the little Belgian Army. He therefore made certain of being able to overcome any resistance he might meet with, and on the 17th approached the Gette with three corps, the Second, Fourth, and Ninth, flanked on the north by the Second and on the south by the Fourth Cavalry Division. The remaining active corps of his army, the Third, and his three reserve corps followed at no great distance.

The German advanced guards attacked the line of the Gette early on the 18th, and in the course of the morning succeeded in forcing their way across on the Belgian left at Haelen and Diest. Farther to the south they met with greater opposition, and it was not until the evening that the whole line of the river was in von Kluck's hands. By then it had become abundantly clear to the Belgian commander-in-chief that he was face to face with an enemy in greatly superior numbers, that the German cavalry were working steadily round his flanks, and that no French or British help could reach him in time to avert disaster if he held his ground.

Sordet's cavalry had, indeed, appeared on the 18th near Gembloux, but had again been stopped by the rifle and machine-gun fire with which they had been received by the *Jägers* of von Kluck's cavalry corps, and had had to fall back without being able to gather any definite indications of the strength of the German forces. Left to itself the Belgian Army could only retreat or be overwhelmed, and it therefore withdrew behind the Dyle on the night of the 18th-19th, and on the morning of the 20th was within the circle of the outer forts of Antwerp.

Von Kluck's road being thus opened, he pressed his advance with all possible vigour. (The marches of von Kluck's Corps are shown on Map 1.) The trail of blood and outrage left by the Germans in their progress through Belgium makes it a matter of no great difficulty to trace the march of many of their corps. On the 19th, the Second Corps, after a short skirmish with a Belgian detachment covering the withdrawal of their army, passed through Aerschot and preceded and flanked by the Second Cavalry Division marched on to get round Brussels by the north and east of the Belgian capital. The Fourth Corps moved direct through Louvain on to Brussels, which it entered on the 20th, the Third Corps, on its left, passing through the southern suburbs of the town to gain the main road to Hal and Mons.

The last of von Kluck's active corps, the Ninth, marched west from the Gette towards Braine l'Alleud. The three reserve corps of the First German Army were in second line, but the only indication of the routes they followed is that the Ninth Reserve Corps made itself for ever infamous by the sack of Louvain. It and the Third Reserve Corps were sent towards Antwerp to watch the Belgian Army, while von

Kluck consummated his great wheel to the south, which was now beginning. The Fourth Reserve Corps appears to have entered Brussels and to have, remained in and about the town probably until the other two reserve corps were established in their position round Antwerp, for it did not appear at Mons.

On the morning of August 21, the German plan of envelopment had taken definite shape, and all von Kluck's active corps were marching south-westwards from Brussels. The head of the Second was approaching Grammont, that of the Fourth was nearing Enghien, the Third Corps was passing through Hal, and the Ninth Braine l'Alleud. The march of the army was covered by the Fourth and Ninth Cavalry Divisions, which advanced towards the line of the canal which connects Charleroi, Mons, and Condé. The outer flank of the wheel was covered by the Second Cavalry Division, which moved towards Ghent and Audenarde.

Von Bülow's Second Army had, while von Kluck was moving through and round Brussels, got into position. On August 12 his advanced troops had seized the only railway bridge which spans the Meuse between Namur and Liège, that at Huy, and begun to pass to the left bank of the river. Both this army and the Third, to its south, had to cross the Ardennes, and the Second Army, of which the Seventh and Tenth Corps must have been delayed by the operations at Liège, could only cross the Meuse at a few points; but as both armies had to wait upon von Kluck, who had much longer marches to make, these difficulties did not affect the perfect timing of the German deployment.

The morning of the 21st found the Second Army, with four and a half corps north of the river, (it seems probable that at least half the Tenth Corps had been detained at Liège and had not come up), also moving in a generally south-westerly direction, on a rough arc extending from Genappe, where the right of the army was in touch with von Kluck's left, by Gembloux to within a few miles of Namur, which the Seventh Reserve Corps was approaching. At the same time the most northerly corps of the Third German Army, the Twelfth Saxon Corps, was marching' through the Ardennes on Dinant.

Thus, nine and a half German corps, covered by a large force of cavalry, were deployed on a front of seventy-five miles extending from Grammont on the right by Hal and Gembloux towards Dinant, ready to strike a concerted blow at the British Army and the French Fifth Army. On the morning of the 21st three of the corps of this French

Army were moving into their positions on the Sambre and the Meuse, in the expectation of being able to continue their forward march and with the help of the British Army to come down on the flank of such German forces as were believed to be marching through Belgium north of the Meuse; but the remaining corps of this army, the Eighteenth, was still on the march northwards from Avesnes, and was a long way off, as were several of the reserve divisions.

The British Army of two corps was leaving its billets to the south of Maubeuge, where it had assembled in glorious August weather, the men rejoicing in the friendly welcome of the French peasants and in the comparative comfort of the French billets, which contrasted very favourably with the damp bivouacs of our own autumn manoeuvres, and marched forward towards Mons in complete and cheery ignorance of what fate had in store.

Thus, almost before they had fired a shot the French and British Armies on the left flank were compromised. The enemy had already won the initiative, because he had carried through remorselessly and without material change a carefully-thought-out plan, and by combining great skill with complete lack of scruple had succeeded in shrouding in mystery both his strength and his intentions. The French Headquarters had been compelled by circumstances which they could not control to change their plan at the last moment, and were not until a later date able to recover the loss of time this change involved.

These first manoeuvres for position had brought into real and practical conflict the principles of the two opposing schools of military thought, which had, as I have described, for many years before the war been engaged in paper controversy. In accordance with their theory of war the Germans had developed from the outset, and in the shortest possible time, the maximum of force which was to go relentlessly forward until the decisive battle, the goal of the whole vast manoeuvre, had been fought and won. The numbers required to ensure that the decisive blow should have the necessary weight and strength had been obtained by a careful study of the characteristics of the enemy armies, and of the terrain upon which the opposing forces would first meet, by a bold acceptance of risk where no decision was sought, and above all by surprise, the supreme weapon of generalship.

The French theory of war aimed, as I have said, at keeping in hand a considerable reserve, or mass of manoeuvre, to be thrown into the conflict as occasion arose, either from the enemy's mistakes or from the success of other parts of the army. The enemy did make a mistake, and Joffre seized his opportunity, but not until the Germans had gained such a commanding position as could not wholly be wrested from them. The French commander-in-chief had to abandon his first project of offence, extend his left northwards, strengthen it by moving troops from his extreme right, throw his reserve immediately into the line, and set about creating a fresh mass of manoeuvre.

While all this was doing, the Germans were marching forward in agreement with their pre-arranged plan. The German General Staff had in effect out-manoeuvred the Allies in the first deployment by a combination of treachery and skill.

On the critical left flank, the Franco-British forces were coming into action piecemeal against an enemy not only in superior force but able to use his whole strength.

CHAPTER 4

Namur, Dinant, and the Sambre

The British Army and the French Fifth Army had assembled in the very area in which Napoleon had collected his forces for his last campaign: von Bülow's corps were marching to battle over the roads trodden, in 1815 by Blücher's men; Condé, Turenne, William of Orange, Marlborough, Villars, and Wellington are amongst the great commanders who led their troops to war on these fields.

The bridges over the Sambre, which the Fifth Army was guarding on the morning of August 21, 1914, had been forced by Napoleon's infantry, nearly one hundred years before, against the Prussians under Ziethen, and Wellington in Brussels hearing this news had sent out the orders which summoned the gallants of the British Army from the Duchess of Richmond's famous ball, and sent them marching to the field of Quatre Bras by the very routes taken by von Kluck's right columns. (Quatre Bras and Ligny, where Napoleon overthrew Blücher, lay in sight of de Lanrezac's outposts on the Sambre, and French troopers had passed over the field of Ramillies some miles to the north-east. Mons had been held by Wellington's men at the outset of the campaign of 1815, and now a British Army once more entering Belgium had crossed the field of Malplaquet on its march to Mons. Before battle was joined British cavalry patrols had penetrated northwards almost to within sight of Waterloo, and German horsemen flanking von Kluck's march had passed through Audenarde. The armies were closing on each other in the very centre of the cock-pit of Europe.

A great change had come over the face of the country since it had last seen British, French, and German troops locked in battle. (The country here described is shown on Map 2.) When Napoleon marched to the Sambre to open his last campaign he saw from the low hills which form the southern limit of the valley great stretches of open, rolling agricultural land, dotted with farming villages and woods, with here and there at the more important river-crossings a small town enclosed within the narrow limits of strong ramparts; a country of well-defined, broad-backed ridges and wide valleys watered by sluggish streams, a country in fact, abounding in the classic positions dear to the hearts of the writers of military text-books.

The ground on which, in the third week of August 1914, the German Armies were deploying for battle retained much of its old character, but a great part of the French and British forces found themselves taking up positions such as troops had never before been asked to hold in war, for the valley of the Sambre has been completely transformed by the industrial development of Southern Belgium. Around the little town of Charleroi now stretches north, east, and west a confusion of mines, blast-furnaces, and glassworks, connected by a network of cobbled streets and lanes, lined by close-packed, dull, uniform miners' cottages, between which rise tall chimneys, the headworks of mines, and great conical pyramids of smoking slack.

Industry has added a new feature to the countryside in the form of a canal, which runs eastward, its waters black with slime and reeking of chemical refuse, from the Scheldt at Condé past Mons to a point a few miles north of Charleroi, where it dips sharply southwards to join the Sambre. West of the Charleroi Black Country, which extends almost without a break for twenty-six miles along the Sambre and the canal, the country resumes its open and agricultural character for a short interval beyond La Louvière and Binche. This disappears again, when Mons is reached, in another medley of mine-works, factories, and mining villages, ending still farther west along the Condé Canal in an intricate area of small market gardens intersected by innumerable dykes, which drain the country and have converted the marshes of the Scheldt into rich productive land.

Altogether it was as unfavourable an area for defensive battle as could well be found, for the free movement of the defenders was much hampered by enclosures of all kinds natural to a great industrial district, and the scope of their artillery was limited by the masses of factories and buildings which on many parts of the battlefield obstructed the view to the front. Not the least of the difficulties of the Allies was that the teeming population of the district, ignorant of what was afoot or not knowing whether to fly, swarmed in the narrow streets, affording admirable cover for the enemy's spies, who were doubtless busy among them, while later these unfortunates were to be driven helpless before the German attacking columns to shield them from the bullets of our men.

Neither the British nor the French had marched to this curious battlefield intending to fight there defensively or, indeed, at all. Both armies had on arrival covered their front with outposts preparatory to a farther advance northwards, which would bring them clear of the mining districts. Battle was forced upon them by an enemy who had forestalled them in preparation and gained the initiative.

The gradual wheel of the German forces through Belgium had on August 21 brought von Bülow nearer to the Allied forces than was von Kluck, and the Second German Army was consequently the first to become engaged. It will therefore be convenient to follow its operations before turning to those of the First German Army.

The pivot of the Allied position was Namur, a fortress covering the junction of the Meuse and the Sambre, designed on the same system of cupola forts as had been adopted for the defence of Liège. The experience of the attack on Liège had confirmed the Germans in their views of the effect of heavy howitzer fire upon permanent works, and with this knowledge it was neither necessary nor desirable to repeat the infantry assaults which had cost them so heavily in their first attempts to rush the Belgian fortifications.

The siege artillery from Liège accompanied the infantry of von Bülow's Seventh Reserve Corps in its advance towards Namur, and was reinforced by still more formidable weapons. Austria had before the war gone ahead even of Germany in the development of heavy siege howitzers, and she had succeeded in perfecting one with a calibre of 42 centimetres (16 in.). A battery of these monsters, hastily borrowed by Germany from her Ally, reached Cologne on August 15, and came into action against the Namur forts on August 22.

Meantime the German infantry had driven in the Belgian outposts and, without attempting further attack, took up entrenched positions covering the artillery. The siege howitzers at once began to pound the forts, while the field howitzers and guns bombarded the infantry entrenchments, which, as at Liège, had been thrown up in the intervals between the permanent works.

The garrison of Namur consisted of the Belgian fortress troops and the greater part of the Fourth Belgian Division, reinforced before the attack developed by some detachments which had been driven in from Huy, and later by three battalions of French infantry, bringing the total strength to over 30,000 men. This time the Belgian infantry had no chance of using their rifles, and had to endure the nerve-racking and demoralising experience of a prolonged and heavy bombardment to which no effective reply was possible; for the Belgian fortress guns were unable to discover the position of the enemy's howitzers, and the telephonic communication between the forts was very early destroyed, which made any systematic control of their fire impossible. This one-sided struggle did not last long. The forts were crushed in quick succession, and on the morning of the 23rd the German infantry advanced to the attack, entered the town, and cut off a considerable part of the garrison.

This rapid reduction of the fortress of Namur was a great blow to the Allied plans. The resistance of Liège had encouraged the hope that Namur, with the immediate support of the French Army, would be able to resist at least long enough to allow of the completion of the Franco-British concentration on the Allied left flank, to be followed at once by an offensive movement against the advancing enemy. Details of the attack on Liège were, of course, not obtainable, and it was not appreciated how short the resistance of its forts had been when once the German siege howitzers had come into action. It was the fate of Namur which gave the quietus to the system of defending fortresses with immobile guns in heavily armoured works.

While the final attack on Namur was in progress a fresh danger was developing against the right of the French Fifth Army. On the evening of the 22nd the advanced guards of the Twelfth Corps of von Hausen's Third German Army reached the Meuse at, and on either side of, Dinant, fifteen miles to the south of Namur. The Germans began the attack on Dinant early on the 23rd, and after a sharp struggle got possession of the town and crossed the river. The French defenders here, the Fifty-First Reserve Division, had only arrived the evening before, and had relieved de Lanrezac's First Corps, which moved north to the battlefield of the Sambre, where it was badly needed.

With Namur already in the enemy's hands, de Lanrezac could not neglect the fresh blow which threatened to cut his communications with the remaining French Armies in the south, and he had no course but to order the First Corps back again to Dinant, where it arrived in time to carry out a brilliant counter-attack against the Twelfth Saxon Corps, the farther progress of which was thereby arrested for the time being. The Saxons had, however, as we shall see, played their part in forcing the withdrawal of a large French force at a critical moment from the battlefield in the north, and it is to this battlefield that we must now turn, leaving the Germans established on the Meuse by the evening of the 23rd at both Namur and Dinant.

While the Seventh Reserve Corps were preparing to attack Namur on the morning of the 21st, the remainder of von Bülow's Army was advancing to the Sambre from the north, its centre being directed on Charleroi. His corps came into action in succession from left to right, the wheel having brought the inner or left flank nearer to the river. Thus, the Guard Corps moving from Gembloux was the first to become engaged, and after driving in the French outposts which were north of the river, discovered that the crossings between Ham and Tamines were held in strength. An attack on the bridges was begun soon after mid-day, and by 2.30 p.m. the German Guards had got across the river and were in possession of Auvelais, and soon after of Tamines.

Here they were fiercely counter-attacked by the French, but, being constantly reinforced, not only held their own but were able to make farther progress towards dusk, and by 9.30 p.m. were in possession of the village of Arsimont, which lies two miles south of the river. Meanwhile on their right the Tenth Corps, passing through Ligny, worked its way through the raining villages to the north of Charleroi, and beginning late in the afternoon an attack on the bridges to the east of the town, had by dusk established itself to the south of the river.

★★★★★★★★★★

> Being uncertain as to how much of the Tenth Active Corps took part in these battles and how much of this fighting was done by the Tenth Reserve Corps, I refer to the German troops on this part of the battle-front as the Tenth Corps, but it appears probable that part at least of both corps were engaged. The Germans claim that von Bülow's Second Army was not complete at this period, as all his troops had not come up from Liège.

★★★★★★★★★★

Still farther to the west the Seventh Corps moving south from Genappe crossed the canal to the east of Courcelles, and its advanced guard came into contact with French cavalry (Sordet's corps), which in the evening it pushed back to the main Charleroi—Mons road. Thus, by dark on the 21st von Bülow had obtained possession of the crossings of the Sambre as far west as Charleroi, and was in a position to deploy for attack south of the river, against the French who were known to be in strength.

This day had been one of preliminaries, the German advanced

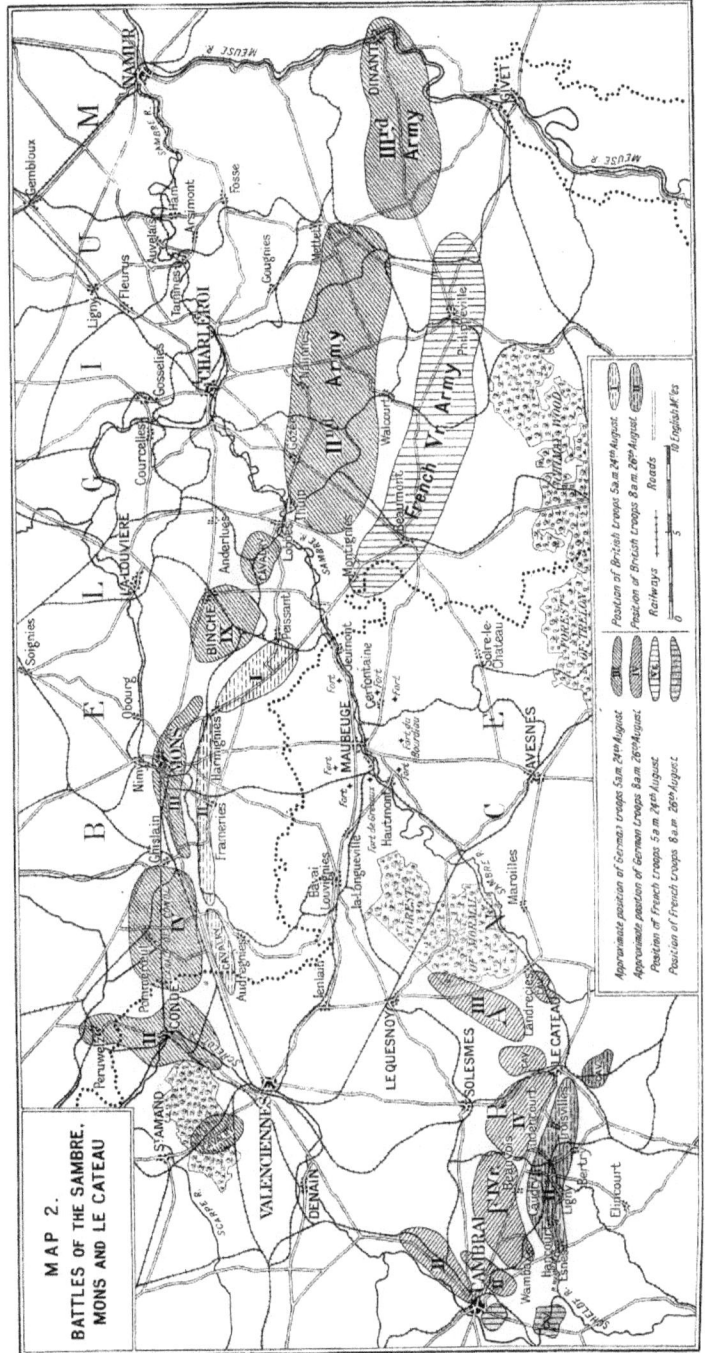

guards fighting their way forward against the French outposts, to gain room for the columns closing on the river from the north. Both sides had from time to time reinforced their covering troops in the struggle to gain or hold some important passage across the river, but neither von Bülow nor de Lanrezac had engaged their main bodies. Yet in these preliminaries the Germans had gained very real advantages, for though the French forces south of the Sambre were at least equal in numbers to those which von Bülow was bringing to the attack, the German troops were so placed as to give them superiority at the outset.

De Lanrezac was, in fact, compelled to accept battle at a time when he was preparing for an advance across the Sambre, to begin forty-eight hours later, and a considerable part of his army was still on the march to the battlefield. The Germans were already reaping the benefit of surprise, they had gained the initiative, thrown the French on the defensive, and had their troops so placed that the whole could be used together in one concerted plan of attack. It was in these conditions that battle was joined in earnest next day.

At dawn on the 22nd the troops of the Guard Corps south of the river were heavily attacked by the French, who regained possession of Arsimont, and fierce fighting ensued in this part of the valley of the Sambre, but as battery after battery of the Guard artillery came into action, and more infantry were pushed across the river, the Germans, despite very heavy losses, were able to force the French back by the close of the day to the main ridge overlooking the Sambre valley, between Fosse and Gougnies.

Simultaneously with this struggle of the Guard Corps, the Tenth Corps were heavily engaged to the south of Charleroi, and gaining ground in spite of repeated French counter-attacks, which made their advance slow and costly, they had, ere the light failed, established themselves four miles to the south of the river, and were in line with the Guards on the right. The Seventh Corps, advancing west of Charleroi after a stiff fight at Anderlues in the evening, discovered French infantry holding the Sambre in force on either side of Thuin. This was the French Eighteenth Corps which had come up the evening before, but its two reserve divisions, which were to fill the gap between its left and the British Army, were still a day's march to the south.

The 22nd had proved a hard but, on the whole, a successful day for the Germans. The battle was far from decided, but von Bülow had placed the whole of his corps on an east and west line, running about four miles south of Charleroi, had fought his way clear of the industrial districts, and now had beyond the river, room and positions which would allow him to make full use of his superiority in artillery.

General de Lanrezac's view of the situation on the evening of this day was:

> My opinion is that the enemy has not yet shown any numerical superiority, though he has perhaps considerable forces in the vicinity. The Fifth Army is shaken as the result of the battle, but is still intact. If it has suffered heavy losses, it has also inflicted heavy losses on the enemy. Having now been withdrawn into more open country, where the artillery of the army, which is still intact, can act effectively, the army should be able to bring the Germans to a stand. Our troops, by defending every yard of ground, can gain time to reorganise, and will shortly be in a position to counter-attack. (Hanotaux, vol. v.)

At the time when he wrote this General de Lanrezac's Eighteenth Corps had come up on his left, and had hardly fired a shot, its two reserve divisions were still on the march to the front, while his First Corps had just been relieved on the Meuse, and was now available to take part in the battle. The brunt of the fighting had been borne by two of his corps only, the Tenth and Third, and these in his own words though shaken were intact. The British Army had just reached its positions about Mons, and was quite fresh. The strength neither of von Kluck's army now coming down on the Mons canal from the north, nor of Von Hausen's army about to debouch from the Ardennes against Dinant, was yet suspected by General de Lanrezac. Therefore, although the German successes gained on the 22nd were disquieting, there was nothing in the information available as to the military situation to cause the Allies any real anxiety.

The early hours of the 23rd were spent by von Plattenberg, the commander of the German Guards, in reorganising his corps after the severe fighting of the day before, and preparing to attack the French, who were discovered to have fallen back during the night to a fresh position on either side of Mettet, five miles south of the Fosse ridge. His artillery had already started the preliminary bombardment when he was informed of the advance of a large French force on his left flank, and he had to break off his preparations for attack to meet this new enemy. This was the First French Corps, which, as we know, had handed over the defence of the Meuse about Dinant to the Fifty-First Reserve Division, and now made its first appearance on the Sambre battlefield. Unfortunately, at this time news arrived in quick succession at General de Lanrezac's headquarters of the fall of Namur and of the capture of Dinant by the Twelfth Saxon Corps. The First Corps had to turn about at once and march back to the Meuse to save the right flank and communications of the French Fifth Army from the danger which threatened them.

Had the French First Corps, which had not been engaged, been able to come down at this decisive moment on the flank of the German Guards, the result of the Battle of the Sambre might have been very different; and without in any way reflecting on General de Lanrezac, who, in the circumstances was compelled to provide for the safety of his right and rear, one cannot but recall that ninety-nine years before, on a field of battle a few miles to the north, there occurred a somewhat similar incident which vitally affected the fate of a campaign. Then the French were attacking the Prussians at Ligny, and d'Erlon's corps, marching and counter-marching between the fields of Ligny and Quatre Bras, was lost to Napoleon at a time when its aid might have allowed the emperor to inflict on Blücher such a defeat as would have made it impossible for the Prussians to appear at Waterloo.

Von Plattenberg, relieved of any further anxieties as to his left, renewed his preparations for attack on the French positions about Mettet, which he carried before dark. To the south of Charleroi, the Tenth Corps was engaged throughout the day in a fierce struggle with the French Third Corps about Malines, and had by dusk overcome its resistance and compelled it to retire on Walcourt, a village on the latitude of Maubeuge and eighteen miles to the east of the French fortress. Simultaneously the Seventh Corps attacked the French Eighteenth Corps on the front Gozée-Thuin-Lobbes, and after prolonged and fierce fighting carried all these places. The Eighteenth Corps, finding its right flank exposed by the retirement of the Third Corps, was in its turn compelled to fall back.

At nightfall on the 23rd General de Lanrezac was then in the position that his front everywhere had been driven in, his flank was threatened by the fall of Namur and by the appearance of the German Third Army at Dinant, and he had received information that the British Army was being attacked by three German corps, while a fourth was working round its left flank. This information was accompanied by an order to him to send off General Sordet's cavalry corps at once to the British left to prevent the threatened envelopment. In these circumstances General de Lanrezac ordered a general retirement, which took with it the two reserve divisions, the 53rd and 69th, coming up on the British right.

With this we may leave von Bülow's Second Army and the French Fifth Army opposed to it, and turn to von Kluck and the British Army, but it is important to remember, if the situation of the British Army at Mons is to be appreciated, that by the evening of the 21st, when the British were still on the march northwards, the Germans were already across the Sambre at and east of Charleroi; that by the morning of the 23rd, when the Battle of Mons opened, they were established some seven miles to the south of Charleroi, and were therefore even then to the south of the British right flank; and that at dawn on the 24th, before we had begun to withdraw from Mons, the French Fifth Army had been for some twelve hours in retreat.

GERMAN INFANTRY ADVANCING AT MONS

CHAPTER 5

Mons

(See Map 2)

We left von Kluck's army on the forenoon of the 21st marching south-west from Brussels by the roads running through Grammont-Enghein-Hal and Braine l'Alleud, covered in front and on his right flank by three cavalry divisions. The day's marches were completed without incident, but early on the 22nd the British and German cavalry came into conflict, particularly to the north-east and east of Mons, and between La Louviere and Binche. The German cavalry now experienced the same difficulties as had confronted Sordet's horsemen in obtaining information as to what was going on behind the mounted screen, for the British horsemen, though not supported as were the German cavalry by armoured cars and infantry transported in lorries, had since the South African War been armed with the infantry rifle, and were easily first of the cavalries of Europe in dismounted work.

The *Uhlans* got little beyond considerable losses from their morning's work, and it was not until late afternoon, when the British cavalry were withdrawn, that the Germans discovered that their enemy was in force at and to the west of Mons, and on a front running south-east from that town. The First and Second British Corps had by then arrived and taken up outpost positions, the line of the First Corps, under Sir Douglas Haig, extending from near Peissant, about five miles west of the left of the French Eighteenth Corps which was near Lobbes, to Harmignies, four miles south-east of Mons; that of the Second Corps, under Sir Horace Smith-Dorrien, running thence east of Mons to the canal at Obourg, and then westward along the canal to Pommeroeul. Here the line was extended next morning westwards to the Scheldt by the cavalry division, which had been moved during the evening from the right flank to the extreme left, where it arrived late at night.

Von Kluck's Army had continued its march forward, still in a

4TH BATTALION ROYAL FUSILIERS, 22ND AUGUST 1914, MONS

south-westerly direction, and on the evening of the 22nd appears to have been placed as follows: the Fourth and Ninth Cavalry Divisions were spread out along the British front, the Second Cavalry Division, which had sent patrols far to the west in the direction of Courtrai and Lille, had stronger bodies southwest and west of Ash about Peruwelz and Tournai: the left corps of the army, the Ninth, had halted on the road from Nivelles to La Louvière with its head near the canal: the Third Corps was along the main Brussels-Mons road, with its leading troops to the south of Soignies, while the Fourth Corps moving from Enghien, reached the Mons-Ath railway about halfway between those places. On the right the Second Corps was along the Lessines-Ath road, with its head just south of the latter place.

Von Kluck's troops had come far and fast, the Second Corps on the outer flank of the sweep having marched 150 miles in eleven days, which for a body of troops of such a size is a remarkable achievement in the early days of a campaign, when boots and equipment are new, and reservists, fresh from civil life, are in the ranks. The British reservists had found the marches to Mons in the sultry August weather and their first acquaintance with the cobbled roads of Belgium trying, and the Germans must have had similar experiences, though not to the same extent, for they had a much smaller number of reservists in the ranks of their battalions than we had, and their men had for the most part been a shorter time away from active training.

A Continental Army in time of peace in the month of August has just completed the training of the year's batch of recruits, and then requires comparatively few reservists to raise it to its war strength, which is one of the main reasons why the late summer has seen the outbreak of most Continental wars in recent history, and why this season has always been the danger period in times of European tension. The necessity for keeping up our foreign garrisons having long turned our army at home into a feeder for the army abroad, it was in consequence normally below strength, and contained a large number of young recruits, who, not being qualified either by age or training to take the field, had to be left at the depots on mobilisation.

For these reasons the British infantry at Mons contained a far higher proportion of men returned from civil life than did von Kluck's army, and the majority of them had completed their military training in the battalions abroad and did not know either their officers or non-commissioned officers. (In most of our battalions at Mons the reservists numbered 60 *per cent* of the total strength and in some cases 70 *per cent.*) On the other hand, they were mostly men who had served for seven years as against the German infantryman's two, and the British infantryman had received, since the Boer War, more and better training in the use of the rifle than the foot-soldier of any other Army, a training which was to bear good fruit in the coming battle.

When day broke on August 23 von Kluck had four active corps and three cavalry divisions of nine brigades, or about 160,000 men and 600 guns, within striking distance of the British force of two corps and five cavalry brigades, that is, about 70,000 men and 300 guns, and his neighbour von Bülow had for two days been engaged successfully with the French Fifth Army, which had been pushed back some way south of the Sambre, between Namur and Charleroi. Doubtless, if von Kluck had known the British strength at this time he would not have acted as he did, but if our mobilisation had been delayed (it did not in fact begin till four days after that of the French Army), once it was ordered the arrangements for the organisation, trans-shipment, and concentration in France of the British Expeditionary Force were carried out with remarkable secrecy and swiftness.

Von Kluck may therefore have been in some doubt as to the strength of the forces opposed to him, and he probably was in no less uncertainty as to the position the British were holding, and more particularly how far their left flank extended. This knowledge was of special importance to him, for his task being to envelop the Allied left, he had to find out where that left was in order to get round it. As the British cavalry had been engaged with his troops to the east of Mons throughout the day, and did not reach their position on the left of the British line till long after dark, it is almost certain that the Germans must have been in ignorance of this movement until after their plans for the 23rd had been formed.

Further, the German troops had been moving continuously since their fight on the Gette on August 18, and must therefore have been strung out in their marching columns for miles along the roads behind the places I have indicated as reached by the heads of the various corps. It would, in such circumstances, be a matter of time for von Kluck to close up his troops, deploy for battle, and deliver a concerted blow in overwhelming force against the enemy who apparently lay at his mercy. The Third Corps to the south of Soignies lay within five miles of the British outposts north of Mons, the Fourth Corps, on its right, was rather farther off, while the heads of the two flank corps, the Ninth on the left and the Second on the right, were between ten

The German attack on the Nimy Bridge, 23rd August, 1914

and twelve miles from the British positions.

Von Bülow had, it will be remembered, begun his attack on the French Fifth Army by bringing his corps into battle in succession from left to right; but they were so placed before he began to fight that he was sure of being able to keep up a steadily increasing pressure on his enemy. Von Kluck, on the other hand, had half his army at such a distance from the battlefield that it could hardly come into action before the evening of the 23rd, and yet without waiting to marshal his troops he flung those nearest his enemy into battle.

Possibly he underestimated the capabilities of the British force, for the German soldier had been wont to speak with contempt of our mercenaries, his favourite name for our Old Army, and our military reputation had not been enhanced by the story of the South African War, which was very imperfectly understood in the Fatherland: possibly he feared that we would run away from him at once, and was therefore anxious to come to grips at the earliest possible moment. Be that as it may, his only plan seems to have been to attack with his Third Corps, which was nearest to Mons, and to extend the battle front as soon as might be with the Fourth Corps, while the two flank corps continued to march forward in the general direction they had followed hitherto.

The early hours of the 23rd were spent in completing the defective reconnaissances of the day before, and the German cavalry were busy tapping at the British outposts along the whole front. The battle opened in earnest about 10.30 a.m. with a bombardment of some batteries of the Third Corps which came into action on a ridge to the north of Obourg, and from that time onwards the line of guns was gradually extended westwards as battery after battery, first of the Third Corps and then of the Fourth Corps, came into action, until by 1 p.m. the Germans had established a great superiority in artillery along the front of Sir Horace Smith-Dorrien's corps. (*Vide* also *Smith-Dorrien* by Horace Smith-Dorrien, Leonaur, 2009.) Under the cover of this bombardment the infantry of the Third Corps began soon after 11 a.m. an attack in mass on the loop of the canal to the north of Mons.

This was the first occasion in which the corps had met modern rifle-fire, for it had not been engaged either in the assault on Liège or with the Belgian Army on the Gette, and it came forward to within close range of our rifles in the column formations preceded by skirmishers, which had often been noted by British observers of the German manoeuvres, who, with memories of the South African War fresh in their minds, had speculated as to what would happen if such tactics were employed against us. Now the day had come, and as had been expected the dense columns of German infantry made an easy target for the rapid and accurate fire of the British riflemen, and our artillery, though impeded in finding positions on a great part of the front of our Second Corps by the mass of buildings and slagheaps south of Mons, and overweighted by the numbers and power of the German guns, nevertheless succeeded for the most part in supporting their infantry comrades effectually.

It was, therefore, not until the Germans had crossed the canal to the east of Obourg, where it was not defended, and began, in conjunction with their troops to the north of the canal, a converging attack on Mons from the north and east, that the British were gradually pushed back on to and south-east of the town. The one complaint of our men was that they could not shoot fast enough to keep down the grey masses which surged against them, and yet they shot so fast that they could not touch the breeches of their rifles, and some of the German reports say that we had lined the canal with masses of machineguns, a weapon with which we were peculiarly ill-provided.

This attack of the Third Corps had been made chiefly against the British Third Division, whose commander, General Hubert Hamilton, had prepared a main position to the south of Mons connecting with the left of Sir Douglas Haig's First Corps, near Harmignies, and it was to this position that the infantry defending the canal were withdrawn by order, fighting desperately hard to the east of Mons, where the German attack, unhampered by buildings and enclosures, was made in great strength, but not pressed to the immediate west of the town. The infantry of the Third Corps, taught by heavy losses to respect the British rifle fire, felt their way cautiously forward through the town of Mons, and the mining villages to the west of it, and did not come into touch with the main British position until dusk, when they contented themselves with putting out outposts and restoring order after the losses and confusion of the day's fighting.

Farther west along the canal the attacks of the extreme right of the Third Corps and of the Fourth Corps, which had rather farther to go to reach the battlefield, developed somewhat later than the attack on Mons itself, and were, if anything, less successful, despite the great superiority of the German artillery. Less than half of the infantry of Sir Charles Ferguson's Fifth Division met these attacks, and was able to hold the general line of the canal until dusk, when it, like the

Third Division, was withdrawn to an entrenched position in rear. Still farther to the west Allenby's cavalry, supported later in the day by the 19th Infantry Brigade, beat off all attempts to cross the canal without much difficulty. (The 19th Infantry Brigade was made up from battalions sent out for duty on the lines of communication.)

The Ninth German Corps, on von Kluck's left, seems to have made a leisurely march to the battlefield, and perhaps spent the day in closing up its columns preparatory to attacking the next day. In any event little more than its advanced guard became engaged partly with the right of the Third Division and partly with Sir Douglas Haig's First Corps, which had a comparatively quiet day as far as fighting was concerned.

This, then, is a bare outline of the events of the first day's fighting at Mons, and it is not easy to disentangle from it any clear-cut German plan of battle. It seems that von Kluck, being unaware how far the British left extended, thought that his Fourth Corps by continuing its march south-westwards would overlap his enemy's flank, and on that understanding allowed his Third Corps to press in at once. Then finding himself committed to a direct frontal attack, which was costing him very heavy losses, he appears later in the day to have ordered his Third and Fourth Corps to hold the British until he could bring his two outer corps down on their flanks and annihilate them. If this is the case his manoeuvre was slow and cumbrous, and he failed to take advantage of the chances open to him. Sir John French, as he says in his Mons despatch, had not expected to be attacked by more than one or, at the most, two corps, with perhaps one cavalry division, and it was not until 5 p.m. that he was aware of von Kluck's strength.

Two of his divisions, Smith-Dorrien's Third and Fifth, had, in fact, been attacked throughout the day by two corps and two cavalry divisions, which had only succeeded in driving back the British from their outpost positions, at a cost quite disproportionate to the losses of the defenders; while two more German corps and a third cavalry division had been within reach of the battlefield, but had not taken any real part in the struggle. The Ninth Corps had, as we have seen, got into touch with the Third Division and with Sir Douglas Haig's First Corps, but had done nothing more; the Second Corps appears to have continued its march from Ath on the Valenciennes road, its advanced guard coming into action in the evening on the canal near Condé.

Had von Kluck been able to press his attack on the evening of the 23rd the fate of the little British Army might have been very different. By then the right of our Third Division south-east of Mons was in a position of some difficulty owing to the fact that the enemy had penetrated through the town, and the withdrawal of this division to its main position having taken place earlier than that of the Fifth Division, a gap was for some time left in the centre of Sir Horace Smith-Dorrien's corps, which gap was actually penetrated by small parties of Germans. It was closed soon after dark, but till then there had certainly been critical moments.

Without more knowledge than we possess as yet of the state of von Kluck's corps on the evening of this first day of the Battle of Mons, criticism of his action at that time can only be guess-work, but there can be but little doubt that, if the Third Corps had continued to advance southeast of Mons and had simultaneously exploited the gap between our Third and Fifth Divisions, while the Fourth Corps pressed the Fifth Division and the Ninth and Second Corps began attacks on the British flanks, ordered retreat would have become impossible. It may be that the Third and Fourth Corps had had such a bellyful of British musketry that they were incapable of further effort, and that the Second and Ninth Corps were wearied with marching, and so strung out along the roads as to make it impossible to bring them into battle; but from what happened next day it appears certain that a considerable part of the infantry of the Fourth Corps, as well as the whole or almost the whole of the Ninth and Second Corps, were not employed on the 23rd.

It does not speak well for von Kluck's generalship if he approached us with his force so scattered that he could not make use of his strength and exhausted a part of his force before the remainder could become engaged, for both his cavalry and his aeroplanes must have given him timely notice of our presence. As to the effect of our rifle fire in the battle we have not only the evidence of our own men as to the heavy losses inflicted on the enemy, but a letter found on a German officer captured by the French, and printed by them, is very much to the point; it runs:

> We have already left Belgium several days, after having fought and beaten the Belgians at Tirlemont, and the British at Mons. The principal tactics of the English consist in entrenching themselves in villages and in opening murderous rifle and machine-gun fire. So, we only advance against them with artillery, and reduce these wasps' nests with the fire of our guns. We have

too heavy losses if we attack these positions with infantry, because our infantry marches like Blücher.

This letter was written about a week after the Battle of Mons, and the change in the German tactics to which it refers almost certainly took place in consequence of the experiences of the German infantry on August 23. It is probable, as I have said, that von Kluck, finding that his first plan was producing a frontal attack in which his infantry was making little progress at very heavy cost, changed his plan during the course of the battle, and checking his Third and Fourth Corps in the afternoon decided to wait for the attack upon the flanks of the British by his two remaining corps, which had not then been engaged. The German general's action in this battle may be judged by his conduct later when he was faced by somewhat similar circumstances, and from this it appears that he was a man of one idea. He saw in envelopment the one road to victory, and this was but the first of a number of opportunities which he let slip because he could think of battle in no other way.

Von Kluck had the extraordinary good fortune to bring to action an enemy very inferior in numbers and completely ignorant of the extent of this inferiority, and it was an occasion for a bold and comprehensive plan. But he seems to have made the mistakes, first of attacking before he was ready and thereby failing to employ sufficient force at the outset to make complete success certain, and next of relying on the slow process of envelopment by troops at a distance from the enemy, at a time when it was a question of seizing a chance which might disappear.

In the morning when he began the battle he struck with no considerable preponderance of strength; in the evening he had in immediate touch with Sir Horace Smith-Dorrien's two divisions more than sufficient force to overwhelm them, and it is to the undying glory of the infantry of the Old Army that by that time they had taken the sting out of such of the First Army as had attacked them, and had inspired the German commander with such respect that he was afraid to try for complete victory until the chance had slipped away. Up to 5 p.m. von Kluck had the advantage of surprise and was unable to make use of it. After 5 p.m. the surprise was gone and his hand was exposed, for by then Sir John French had received Joffre's message informing him of the strength of the German First Army, and of the retreat of the French Fifth Army. (*Vide* also *1914* by Sir John French:

Leonaur, 2009.)

In vain is the net spread in the sight of any bird, and the British commander-in-chief, once aware of the trap, took steps to escape from it before it was sprung, and during the night issued orders for a retreat on Bavai to the west of Maubeuge. These orders came as a shock to the British troops, who had on the whole every reason to be satisfied with their day's work. They were quite unaware of the danger which threatened them or of the fate of the French Fifth Army, but they knew that the enemy had suffered terrible losses, that their main positions were intact, and that in their first battle with the world's most famous soldiers they had more than held their own.

The First Corps had had some hard marching to reach the battlefield, followed by long spells of entrenching, but the bulk of its infantry had not fired a shot, and was dismayed at the idea of retreating without a fight. Of the Second Corps a part of the Third Division had been highly tried in the Mons salient, but the remainder had been nowhere hard pressed, while the cavalry, as the result of their first encounters with the enemy, were firmly convinced of their superiority, either on horseback or on foot. The army was, in fact, ready and eager to renew the battle where it stood.

A retreat is at any time a depressing experience, but it is doubly depressing to troops who, proudly conscious that they can beat the enemy on anything like fair terms, can see no reason for it in what has happened within their view, and are forced to surmise that something somewhere has gone wrong and that some vague danger is threatening from some unknown direction.

By the time when the orders for retreat reached the British divisions the French Fifth Army was already a day's march to the rear of the British right. On the British left General d'Amade's force of French Territorials had been assembling since August 20 between the Scheldt and the sea, and on the 23rd his Eighty-Fourth Division was at Valenciennes. This, the nearest force to us on this side, was therefore seven miles behind our left. Farther west the Eighty-Second Division, lying between the Scarpe and Lille, came in contact on the 23rd with part of the Second German Cavalry Division, and its advanced troops were turned out of Tournai.

The Eighty-First Division watched the frontier between Lille and Dunkirk, so as to prevent raiding parties of German cavalry and armoured cars from interrupting the British communications with the Channel ports, while d'Amade's last division, the Eighty-Eighth, had just arrived at Arras. These troops were therefore very scattered; they had been hastily organised and were lacking in equipment, so that while they were able to confine the activities of the German cavalry, they were not yet in a position to oppose the advance of von Kluck's main bodies. Thus, throughout the night of the 23rd-24th the British Army lay isolated in the presence of an enemy of more than twice its strength.

Von Kluck's plan for the 24th appears to have been to hold the British centre to the south of Mons while his flank corps enveloped the British right and left, but his troops, after the experiences of the previous day, set cautiously to work, and the German infantry was in no mind to approach the British trenches until they had been well pounded by artillery. Sir Douglas Haig on the British right had had information on the previous evening of the retreat of the Fifth French Army, and, before the receipt of Sir John French's orders, had made all preparations for the withdrawal, which he saw to be inevitable. On receipt of these orders, he was able to slip away early in the morning before von Kluck's Ninth Corps had completed its preparations.

On Sir Horace Smith-Dorrien's front, south and south-west of Mons, the German Third and Fourth Corps opened a heavy bombardment soon after dawn, and followed this some two or three hours later with infantry attacks in mass, which were again met and mowed down by the British rifle fire; while somewhat later the Second German Corps and the German cavalry, working forward from the neighbourhood of Condé against the British cavalry division and the 19th Brigade on the extreme left, began to make themselves felt. This German envelopment should, to have been effective, have taken place twelve hours earlier, for by the time it began the arrangements for the move back to Bavai had been completed, all the impedimenta had been sent back, and everyone knew how and when to withdraw.

The German blow was in great part delivered in the air, and though, as will be seen, the British cavalry and Fifth Division on the left did not escape scatheless, the greater part of French's Army was withdrawn from the sweep of the avalanche which threatened to overwhelm it, without material loss to themselves, leaving the battlefield strewn with the new field-grey uniforms which a few weeks before had been drawn from the mobilisation stores in Germany.

The retreat from Mons had begun.

CHAPTER 6

Pursuit and Retreat

(For the operations up to and including the Battle of Le Cateau see Map 2; for the retreat from Le Cateau see Map 1)

Ten miles south of Mons lay the northern forts of Maubeuge. This was not a fortress of the value of Verdun or Toul, for the French Governments, slow to believe that even Germany would violate her own pledge by forcing a way through Belgium, had never lavished on the defence of French Flanders anything approaching the sums which had been spent to safeguard the frontier where it marched with the German Reichsland. Still there had not been wanting thoughtful French soldiers who kept an anxious eye on the northeast, and plans for making the best of the defences of Maubeuge were ready when the storm burst.

The first sounds of war heard by the British Army as it assembled to the south of the fortress were the constant explosions telling that General Fournier was busy clearing the woods and buildings which obstructed the fire from his works, and as we marched northwards and saw the well-dug trenches and thick entanglements which formed an *enceinte* some twenty miles in extent connecting the permanent works, it seemed as if here was indeed something solid upon which we could in emergency rely for support. Fournier with a garrison of about 35,000 Territorials and reserve troops barred the main roads leading southwards from Mons and the railways both from Mons and Charleroi; Maubeuge therefore influenced immediately both the British retreat and the German pursuit.

The north-eastern forts of the place lay five miles south-west of Sir Douglas Haig's right, and the roads to the east of these forts were blocked by the retreat of the French Fifth Army; so, the first movements of the British Army were perforce in a south-westerly direction. Von Kluck had evidently been ordered to continue to move in the same direction with his whole army and to leave Maubeuge to be dealt with by von Bülow, for we find him on the 24th setting all his columns in motion on lines taking them west of the fortress, which was invested by the Seventh Reserve Corps of the Second German Army, brought up with the siege artillery from Namur, and, as we know, the place fell on September 7 just at the time when the crises of the Battles of the Ourcq and of the Marne were approaching.

Von Kluck had, as we have seen, made his plans for a general attack for the morning of the 24th on the front and flanks of the British Army, and it is a difficult matter to change plans quickly in the presence of an enemy. News dribbles back slowly from the fighting front to Headquarters, and orders are long in reaching troops once they are scattered over the battlefield, while the troops themselves, when they have once paid such a penalty for approaching rashly an occupied position, as had the Germans on the 23rd in their advance to the Mons Canal, are very cautious in drawing near to lines which they know to have been held, even long after they have been abandoned.

Many times in this war withdrawals both by ourselves and the enemy have only been discovered after a surprising lapse of time. In this case the retirement of the British right flank was covered by Maubeuge, and the guns of the forts gave the Germans an added reason for caution. This probably accounts for the fact that neither the considerable force of cavalry which von Kluck had on his left, nor his Ninth Corps moving forward from Binche, interfered with the retreat of Sir Douglas Haig's corps, which at nightfall reached positions between Maubeuge and Bavai. Even our 5th Cavalry Brigade, which covered this movement, was hardly molested.

Nor was the Third German Corps, after its morning repulse to the south of Mons, more successful in getting into touch with the Third Division, which formed the right of Sir Horace Smith-Dorrien's Corps, but the Fourth and Second Corps, forming, with an ample force of cavalry, von Kluck's right, had a different story to tell. On this side the German plan seems to have been to use the Fourth Corps in pressing the front and flanks of Smith-Dorrien's Fifth Division, while the Fourth Cavalry Division, with the help of part of the Second Cavalry Division, attacked the British cavalry, and the Second Corps marched southwards from Condé to get well round the British left flank and encompass its destruction.

In the area on both sides of the canal between St. Ghislain and Condé, von Kluck cannot have had, on the morning of the 24th, a superiority of less than four to one over the British, but he had waited too long to use his strength. It is a comparatively simple problem to defeat an enemy who accepts battle in ignorance that he is opposed by overwhelming force; it is quite another matter to snatch victory from an enemy who has prepared his plans for retreat. Between dawn and dusk on this day there ensued between the southern limits of the mining villages and the Bavai-Valenciennes road a running and unequal fight, in which the masses of German infantry and cavalry, always working round the British left, were delayed and hampered in a series of desperate actions throughout the long hot August day by the devotion of Allenby's and Ferguson's men.

Some of the battalions of Ferguson's Fifth Division suffered heavily in actions as honourable to the British infantry as any in their long and glorious history, and the Germans picked up not a few prisoners; but the columns of von Kluck's Fourth Corps in their efforts either to break the resistance of the British, or to hold them until the Second Corps could come round and cut them off, again gave both our foot and artillery such targets as, in the words of one of our battery commanders, they had prayed they might see before they died, and the Germans could never find a chance of using effectively their weight of numbers.

In fact, the bulk of the Fourth Corps suffered so heavily in the fighting in the morning amidst the mining villages, where it was attacking the main body of the Fifth Division in front, that it appears to have been too exhausted to continue the pursuit, and it was upon a flank guard of two battalions and a battery of our Fifth Division, aided by a brigade of Allenby's cavalry, during the remainder of the day that the brunt of the fighting fell, as the advance of that part of the Fourth Corps which was engaged in the turning movement, steadily reinforced by the Second Corps, became more and more menacing. Dramatic incidents were crowded into this series of Homeric combats, and must be left to the historian with all the records at his disposal to describe, but two at least may be mentioned as typical of the kind of fighting of this day.

Both of them occurred near Audregnies, a name to be for ever famous in the history of the British Army. At the time when the flank attack of the German Fourth Corps had reached its full development a column of German infantry, almost certainly not less than a regiment of three battalions, was just debouching to attack, when "L" Battery, R.H.A., came into action behind a hedge 2,000 yards from them, and, almost unaided and under heavy and continuous fire from not less than four enemy batteries, kept them at bay for nearly three hours, finally withdrawing without the loss of a gun, when almost all its ammunition had been expended.

The second incident is of a single company of the Cheshire Regiment, which by some mischance did not receive orders to retire, and with the aid of a machine-gun held up until dusk a second German column, also, of about three battalions. When at last this little band of heroes was overpowered and captured, the Germans found only some forty unwounded men to stand up and hand over the arms which they had used until, in the words of one of them, they were weary of slaughter.

Evening found the harassed British left flank, shepherded by Allenby's cavalry, who this day taught the Germans what can be done by men who know how to use the horse and rifle in combination, safely in line with the remainder of French's Army on a front extending from La Longueville, through Bavai toward Jenlain, that is, along the main road from Maubeuge to Valenciennes.

It will be remembered that the Eighty-Fourth French Territorial Division was at Valenciennes. There it was attacked by a column of the Second German Corps, and, being without any means of replying effectively to the German field howitzers, it fell back in the direction of Cambrai; while patrols of the Second German Cavalry Division occupied Douai, the general line of defence of d'Amade's Territorials being thus drawn back to between Douai and Cambrai. On the right of the British Army the German Second Army had during the day forced General de Lanrezac back farther south, and in the evening his left corps, the Eighteenth, was near Solre-le-Château, twelve miles southwest of the British right; while the Fifty-Third and Sixty-Ninth Reserve Divisions had halted inside the circle of the forts of Maubeuge, but had orders to continue the retreat at dawn.

General Sordet's cavalry corps, which was intended to assist in checking the threatened envelopment, had been unable to get across to our left flank owing to the congestion of the roads and to the exhaustion of his horses, so that, except for the friendly shelter of Maubeuge, the British Army still lay isolated and within cast of the net which von Kluck was spreading.

Just as in the first day of the retreat the fortress of Maubeuge had influenced the movements both of Sir John French and of von Kluck, so now the great forest of Mormal, which lies to the south of the fortress, settled in great measure the direction of the marches of the second day. This forest, stretching for ten miles from north to south, with a width of about six miles, is traversed only by the roughest tracks, unsuitable for vehicles. Were the whole British Army to attempt to pass to the west of it there would be created a very dangerous gap between the British right and the French Fifth Army, while the British left would be pushed out into the very arms of the German columns which were seeking it.

There were not sufficient roads for the whole army to pass to the east of the forest, so it was divided, Sir Douglas Haig marching by the east on Landrecies, Sir Horace Smith-Dorrien moving by the west on Le Cateau. From the prisoners captured on the 23rd and 24th—for parties of our men had been cut off and a considerable number of our wounded had of necessity been left in Mons and the neighbouring villages—von Kluck must by now have been well informed of the strength of the British Army, and as von Bülow can hardly have failed to send him news of the continued retreat of the French Fifth Army, he should have appreciated that his chance of annihilating the little force which was falling back before him depended upon swift and energetic pursuit.

Yet, though von Kluck had the whole of the Fourth and Ninth Cavalry Divisions and the greater part of the Second to follow up the retreating British, who moved off from their bivouacs about Bavai before dawn on the 25th, much of this mass of cavalry appears to have been employed in searching to the west for the Allied left flank, so that it might be enveloped when found, instead of being concentrated upon the task which lay at hand.

Some of the German cavalry became engaged with Allenby's men, very early in the day, to the south-east of Valenciennes, but made very slow progress against them in another running fight at long range, and were unable to get through to attack the flanks of Smith-Dorrien's infantry columns, which were marching to positions just off the Le Cateau-Cambrai road. Towards evening, however, the German horse, supported by some of their infantry, caught up and attacked an infantry rearguard of our Third Division holding a position just north of Solesmes. At that time the British cavalry was endeavouring to move south-eastwards towards Le Cateau, to fill the gap between the British First and Second Corps caused by the movement on either side of the Mormal Forest.

The village of Solesmes, which lies in a hollow, was, just at the time when the German cavalry attack became threatening, packed with the waggons of French refugees fleeing before the German advance, with the transport of the British cavalry, and with parties of French Territorials who had been cut off in the retreat from Valenciennes. It was a chance of turning retreat into wild confusion such as has rarely fallen to cavalry, but the German horsemen, ignorant of what was going on behind the British front, and wearied with long days of marching, were in no mind to push an attack home late in the evening against infantry who showed a bold front.

So, the little British rearguard, composed of two battalions, the Wiltshires and South Lancashires, and a battery of artillery, stoutly holding its own till after dark, gained time for the congested roads to be cleared. It then fell back to its billets at Cawdry, which it did not reach till midnight, having started its day's work at three o'clock that morning. The German cavalry appear to have gone off to find billets and water at nightfall, and made no further efforts to find out what the British were doing. Von Kluck's Third and Fourth Corps seem to have spent the morning in reorganising after the confused fighting of the day before, and then to have continued their march south-west, the Fourth Corps by Le Quesnoy and Solesmes, the Third Corps moving some time after the Fourth by the road just west of the Mormal Forest.

Between the right of the Fourth Corps and the Second Corps, which marched through Valenciennes towards Cambrai, now appears for the first time since the Germans marched south from Brussels an addition to von Kluck's Army in the shape of the Fourth Reserve Corps. Whether this corps had followed by road from Brussels or been brought up by train it is not yet possible to say, but it certainly fought next morning on the battlefield of Le Cateau, and it was marching with the First German Army on August 25.

Eastward of the Mormal Forest von Kluck's Ninth Corps, which had not been seriously engaged since it met the Belgians on August 18, followed up Sir Douglas Haig's First Corps with more vigour, as its advanced guards at dusk attacked the British at Maroilles and Landrecies just as they were settling into their billets. Some stiff village fighting lasted well into the night, our 4th Guards Brigade in particular earning distinction at Landrecies, which the Germans attempted to enter after dark, under cover of the ruse of dressing the leading ranks in French uniforms and answering our challenges in French.

Both attacks failed, but they had at least the effect of breaking the well-earned rest of our weary men. Had his troops everywhere displayed the same energy, von Kluck might in a short time have completely exhausted the British troops, upon whom the tension of a retreat, the reasons for which they could not understand, days of fighting followed by long marches under a hot August sun, ending usually in a hard spell of entrenching, want of sleep, and the strain of constant readiness to meet some vague unknown danger, had begun to tell. Luckily for us the strain was not confined to one side, for though they had the incomparable moral fillip of success, of penetrating each day farther and farther into the enemy's country, of picking up broken-down stragglers and the debris of an army in retreat, yet physical weariness was affecting the German troops too.

The supply arrangements were not working smoothly, for Maubeuge blocked the railways which might have fed von Kluck's army, and many of the bridges over the Mons Canal had been destroyed. It was therefore difficulty for the supply columns to keep pace with the continuous advance, and many of the German troopers whom we captured complained that neither they nor their horses were properly fed; so, on the night of the 25th August two weary armies faced each other.

It had been Sir John French's intention to continue the retreat on the 26th with his whole army, and Sir Douglas Haig's First Corps did, in fact, march southwards in the direction of Guise in close touch with the two reserve divisions of the French Fifth Army, but late in the night of the 25th-26th, Sir Horace Smith-Dorrien found that many of his troops had only just come in after over twenty hours of continuous and heavy work, that the enemy were close along his front, and that it was out of the question to continue the retirement at dawn. He therefore issued orders to stand and fight on the ridge which runs just south of the Le Cateau-Cambrai road.

Soon after daybreak on the 26th the leading men of a German advanced guard entered Le Cateau and discovered that the little town was full of British troops. In fact, in and around the place was the 19th Infantry Brigade, and a great part of the British cavalry division was not far distant, both having come in from the left flank and settled down after dark in complete ignorance of their surroundings; while some battalions of the British Fifth Division were also just outside the town. The confused fighting which followed was enough to supply the Germans with the information that the British were in force, and were not retiring, for the German batteries which came into action drew an immediate response from British guns on the ridge south-

Le Cateau

west of the town.

At an early hour the leading troops of the Fourth German Reserve Corps attacked Caudry, and found it held and the British entrenched and supported by artillery in position on either side of the place, while the *Jägers* and armoured cars of the German Cavalry Corps discovered that British infantry were in position between Caudry and Wambax. When these reports reached von Kluck his emotions must have been very similar to those of Napoleon on the morning of June 18, 1815, when he found the British in position at Waterloo. The commander of the First Army would be aware that his Ninth Corps was in touch with Sir Douglas Haig's First Corps, which was falling back, and that there was a big gap between it and Sir Horace Smith-Dorrien's right, and his cavalry would have told him that Cambrai was held by a French force, but that there was an interval of several miles between that town and the British left, which had apparently been reinforced.

After making all allowances for this reinforcement, it was out of the question that the British could oppose any but very inferior numbers to the four corps and three cavalry divisions which he had within reach of the battlefield. Even assuming, as is possible, that the whole of the Fourth Reserve Corps did not reach the battlefield on the 26th, he cannot have had less than 130,000 men to oppose to Sir Horace Smith-Dorrien's 55,000 and to some 4,000 French in Cambrai, while his superiority in guns was not less than three and a half to one. His plan was a repetition of that which failed to mature at Mons on the 24th; that is to say, he proposed to make a frontal attack, mainly with his artillery, followed by enveloping attacks on both flanks.

The Fourth Corps and Fourth Reserve Corps were to make the attack on the British front from the west of Le Cateau towards Cattenières. The Third Corps, of which the main body seems to have been at some distance from the field when the battle opened, and the Ninth Cavalry Division were to attack and envelop the British right. The column composed of the Second Corps and Second Cavalry Division were to work round the British left, while the remainder of the Second Corps moved on Cambrai.

Sir Horace Smith-Dorrien had the greater part of Allenby's cavalry on his right between Le Cateau and the Sambre, then came the Fifth Division, which, after its hard day on the 24th, had crossed the line of march of the Third Division and moved to the inner flank, and now held the front from the southern outskirts of Le Cateau to Troisvilles, with the 19th Brigade in Support. The Third Division held the centre as far as Caudry, and on the left lay the Fourth Division, which had just arrived, not quite complete, from England, and had moved forward north of the Le Cateau-Cambrai road the day before to protect the retirement of the Second Corps. The artillery and one of the infantry brigades of the division had moved back at dusk to the south of the Warnelle Brook, expecting to continue the retirement, but the remaining two brigades only arrived at a very late hour at Beauvois and Haucourt, where they still were at dawn on the 26th. The 4th Cavalry Brigade took position to the left rear of the Fourth Division and watched the flank.

Just as on the right the battle opened at an early hour with some indiscriminate fighting about Le Cateau, so that part of the infantry of the Fourth Division which was about Beauvois and Haucourt came into collision soon after 1 a.m. with German cavalry and the Fourth Reserve Corps advancing through and on either side of Cattenières. The intention was that the Fourth Division should take up its battle position with its right flank near Caudry and its front along the north bank of the ravine formed by the Warnelle Brook towards Esnes. Before they could establish themselves on this line the two infantry brigades, which could not at first be supported by artillery, as the guns were moving to their posts along the Warnelle, became involved in an unequal fight with German cavalry and infantry in greatly superior numbers supported by a strong force of artillery.

Our men fell back slowly, and the front of battle was formed roughly along the Warnelle Brook between 8 and 9 a.m. The Fourth Reserve Corps, which had not fought at Mons and was perhaps less cautious for that reason than its neighbour, had probably started in the morning expecting to follow up an enemy in full retreat, an expectation which would be confirmed by the withdrawal of the first British infantry they had met. Its somewhat premature advance was brought rudely to a standstill by the steady rifle fire of the British infantry and the accurate bursts of shrapnel from our guns.

These events must all be regarded as preliminaries, for von Kluck's orders for battle can hardly have reached his troops at the time when they took place, since he would not have been aware, until the first reports from his advanced troops came back to him, that the British meant to stand and fight. Certainly, judging from his subsequent procedure, an attempt to rush positions held by British infantry formed no part of his plans. His method of attack was in fact exactly that described by the German officer whose letter I have quoted in the last

British guns at Le Cateau

chapter—to reduce the wasps' nests by the fire of the guns. The battle proper opened with a heavy bombardment, which steadily developed in intensity as the artillery of his four corps came into action.

A series of villages formed supporting points either on or close behind the British front, and Troisvilles, Audencourt, Caudry, Ligny, Haucort, and Esnes, all standing prominently along the ridges which formed the main position, each with a church spire rising from its centre, made fine targets for the German howitzers. We had not then learned that while a village cam be turned into a small fortress if there is ample time, material, and labour to prepare it for defence, it is a trap when exposed, without such systematic preparation, to the pounding of high explosive shell. The supports, the headquarters of battalions and brigades, and the collecting stations for the wounded which had been established in the churches and more solid buildings, were all sooner or later forced to leave by the constant rain of projectiles.

Our own artillery, though inferior in numbers and in weight of metal, found itself much more favourably placed than at Mons, and attempts by the German infantry to come forward and test the strength of our entrenchments repeatedly withered away under our searching and accurate shrapnel fire. Only on the right flank was part of the artillery of the Fifth Division unable to find covered positions, and there the gunners, shelled simultaneously from the north and the east, suffered heavily, but though a number of their guns were damaged and the enemy seeing them in the open could concentrate upon them an apparently overwhelming fire, yet to the very last such guns as remained serviceable were kept in action.

For the most part, however, both the enemy's artillery and our own devoted their attention to the infantry, the Germans trying to drive our men from their entrenchments by weight of shell and our artillery seeking to prevent the development of an infantry attack.

After the check administered by our Fourth Division to the German Fourth Reserve Corps on the left, the enemy's infantry, except at two points, made few attempts to press in, but waited, enduring our shelling and watching the effect of their own. These two points were the extreme right flank near Le Cateau and the village of Caudry. Near Le Cateau the ground was more broken than elsewhere on our front, and the German infantry, covered by the fire of their guns, established in great numbers in a semicircle round our flank, were able to work forward and keep up a constant fire, mainly from machine-guns, throughout the forenoon upon the infantry of the Fifth Division, which had to stand a heavy and continuous shelling, and could not receive the same support from their artillery as was given by our guns more comfortably established on other parts of the line of battle.

Thus, it happened that the Fifth Division, which had been moved to the inner flank, that it might be less exposed after the severe trial it had endured in the withdrawal from Mons, had again by the fortune of war to bear the brunt of this day's fighting. By a curious mischance the other point of danger, the village of Caudry, was also held by troops which had been sorely tried. Its garrison was found by the 7th Infantry Brigade, which had formed the rearguard of the Third Division on the previous day, and having been engaged in a stiff fight until well after dark near Solesmes, a great part of the brigade had only reached Caudry at a very late hour and in a state of exhaustion.

As already described, the first troops of the Fourth German Corps struck the village at an early hour, before there had been time to establish a complete defence, and some of the German infantry succeeded in entering the place. When a little later our Fourth Division drew back to its battle-line along the Warnelle, Caudry was left a salient jutting out like a bastion from the angle of the British front, and became a target such as the German loves.

Just as at the opening of the Battle of the Sambre the enemy's first blow fell on Namur at the angle of the Allied line, and on the 23rd he first pressed against the salient to the north of Mens, so now he followed up the early efforts of his advanced guard with repeated attempts to get hold of Caudry, and kept up against it throughout the forenoon constant infantry attacks varied by spells of heavy shelling. It was the German guns which drove the British out of the village about noon, but a counter-attack at once regained a part of it, and the enemy's infantry were prevented from making any substantial progress.

At 1 p.m. the British front, which had for seven hours been in contact with forces in greatly superior numbers, was still everywhere intact, and Sir Horace Smith-Dorrien's courage in accepting battle had been justified; but he knew that his right would become more and more exposed by the retirement of the First Corps, and that columns of German troops, which in the morning had been at some distance from the battlefield, were still converging on his men. He was also aware that it would take time to get the heavier impedimenta out of the way, and for the orders to retire to reach his troops, so that when they began to move back the afternoon would be well advanced and darkness would before long cover the retreat. He therefore decided that, as the stubborn resistance which had everywhere been offered to the enemy afforded a chance of withdrawal, and any chance of plucking his men from the danger of envelopment which hung over them must be seized, the orders to fall back should go out.

This decision was no less bold than that of the previous night to stand and fight. The orders for the retreat from Mons had been prepared before dawn on August 24, and had reached the troops ere they had become engaged on that day, so that the army generally knew beforehand what to do and how to do it, but a withdrawal in broad daylight, when the battle was at its height, and the troops in close touch along the whole front with an enemy who had in position an overwhelming preponderance of guns belching high explosive shell and shrapnel, was an operation which most soldiers before the war would have regarded as involving complete and irremediable disaster.

Yet it was very nearly accomplished with entire success, of which it just failed because the left of the Fourth German Corps, apparently considering that even British infantry would be unable to stand the pounding of its guns from front and flank, and assured of the support of the main bodies of the Third Corps, which by now had reached Le Cateau and was ready to fall on our right flank, began an assault upon the war-worn Fifth Division before the orders for retreat had been fully circulated. This to some extent precipitated the retirement, which, as far as concerns the extreme British right, the Germans might claim was not voluntary. But the Fourth Corps did not realise its success, or it was slow in communicating the news to the remaining German Corps, for these did not begin to press in.

The withdrawal of most of the British infantry was covered with great skill and devotion by the artillery, and was effected with astonishingly little loss after the trenches had been evacuated, a result to which another and unforeseen cause largely contributed. I have mentioned that the retreat began before orders could reach all the troops. The consequence of this was that at a number of points along the front parties of our infantry, varying in size from several companies to quite small detachments, remained in the front trenches in ignorance that their comrades had withdrawn.

Most of these were eventually captured by the enemy and spent long years in German prisons, but it must be some consolation to them to know that by holding on as they did to the last, they completely deceived the enemy as to what was going on and prevented an immediate pursuit of their comrades. In no other way is it possible to account for the inaction of the enemy, who was seen to be still bombarding our front trenches to the east of Caudry at a time when the main bodies of our infantry, rapidly re-formed after the first disorder of the withdrawal, were crossing the ridge near Elincourt, six miles to the south.

Sir Horace Smith-Dorrien marched his columns partly through St. Quentin, and partly by roads to the west of that town, straight for the Somme, at and near Ham, and had got his whole force safely across the river at an early hour on the 28th. The cavalry covered their retreat with great skill, and only occasionally were parties of German cavalry able to come in contact with the infantry columns, which beat them off without difficulty. None the less for infantry which had taken part in a long day's fighting and endured hours of shelling from the enemy's massed batteries it was an exhausting effort. All the columns marched day and night, relieved only by brief halts, which gave little opportunity for sleep, some covering in thirty-eight hours as much as forty miles, in many cases without food.

Fortune had a second time presented von Kluck with the chance of inflicting an annihilating defeat upon the British Army, and a second time he had failed to take the chance when it came. Obsessed as he was with the idea that by a wide envelopment alone could decisive success be won, the detours of his flanking columns brought them too late to the battlefield, and this, combined with the respect for British rifle fire and British shrapnel with which his infantry was imbued, and with the cool leadership of Sir Horace Smith-Dorrien, enabled our Second Corps to escape from what, on the morning of the 26th, appeared to be certain destruction.

Had von Kluck been a great commander he would, as soon as he had discovered that the British had been forced to accept battle in greatly inferior numbers, have prepared not only for success on the battlefield, but for such a pursuit as would have converted retreat into rout. For this he had an ample force of cavalry at hand, and it should have been carefully rested, watered, and fed, while the infantry and artillery were employed in driving the British from their positions, in order that it might be ready to follow up retirement promptly and energetically. An attack by a fresh cavalry division upon our weary and exhausted Fifth Division on the afternoon of the 26th might have been decisive in its effect.

Certainly, cavalry is never likely to obtain a more favourable opportunity than was presented at that time, but the German cavalry never appeared at all. They had been wearied by employment throughout the day on enterprises which had no influence on the result of the battle, and in the evening were seeking food and water when they should have been pressing hard upon our men. Pursuit cannot be improvised, for the limits of human endurance are reached even by those who have taken part in a victorious battle; it must therefore be prepared beforehand, and this von Kluck, though time and means were available, neglected, for he was thinking of other things.

The Battle of Le Cateau was the last important engagement of the retreat from Mons, which was not again seriously molested. The Germans entirely failed to appreciate either the opportunities which it presented or its results, and, as will be seen, this misconception led to vital change in their plans; but before coming to that change the story of the events on either side of the battlefield must be completed.

First, as to the left flank: the French troops which have been mentioned as holding Cambrai on the 26th August consisted of part of the Sixty-first Reserve Division. This division and another reserve division had been detached from the garrison of Paris, and had just joined General d'Amade. These troops had been attacked during the Battle of Le Cateau by the main body of the German Second Corps and had fallen back on Bapaume, whence they had marched to Peronne in touch with General Sordet's cavalry corps. The French cavalry had at length been able to cross the roads congested by the retreating columns of the French Fifth Army and of the British Army, and on the 26th were to the south of Cambrai. On the 28th, that is, on the day on which the British Second Corps crossed the Somme at Havre, Sordet's cavalry and the two reserve divisions were attacked on the Somme near Peronne, and again compelled to fall back, the reserve divisions retiring on Amiens, followed by the enemy.

Meanwhile a much more important development had taken place just to the south. General Manoury had arrived at Montdidier, and following him from the Alsace front came the Seventh French Corps, part of which had already detrained. Manoury had been ordered by Joffre to form and take command of a Sixth French Army, consisting of this Seventh Corps and of other troops to be sent north from Alsace, of Sordet's cavalry corps, very much reduced by the exhaustion of its horses, and of d'Amade's two reserve divisions. Thus, a force which was destined to play a great part in the campaign was gradually forming to meet von Kluck's envelopment and to cover the threatened British left.

It was the beginning of the formation of a new mass of manoeuvre to take the place of Joffre's original reserve, the Fourth Army, which was heavily engaged in the Ardennes. As we shall see, this Sixth Army was steadily increased during the next few days, while yet another army, the Ninth, under the command of General Foch, was being formed behind the French centre by the withdrawal of corps from other armies. Thus, Joffre's measures for seizing the opportunity, which was to present itself before very long, were taking definite shape.

On Smith-Dorrien's right Sir Douglas Haig's First Corps had retired on the 26th due south from Landrecies, where it had been engaged during the previous night with von Kluck's Ninth Corps; but the First German Army, for reasons which will appear, seems to have been ordered to continue to move south-westwards. Accordingly, on the 27th, while the Second British Corps was retiring from Le Cateau, the Ninth Corps turned off from following up Sir Douglas Haig, and moved in the direction of St. Quentin, leaving our First Corps to the tender mercies of the Guard Cavalry Division and the Seventh Corps of von Bülow's Second Army. Troops of these formations engaged a rearguard of the First British Division, and succeeded in isolating a battalion of the Munster Fusiliers, which, after a desperate and gallant fight against very long odds, was surrounded near Etreux, where the Landrecies-Guise road crosses the Sambre, and lost more than three-quarters of its effectives, the remnant being rescued by the plucky intervention of a squadron of the 15th Hussars. The noble stand of this unfortunate battalion enabled the remainder of the corps to complete its march without difficulty.

The 28th was chiefly remarkable for the first real attempts of the German horse, chiefly of their Second Army, to follow up the British retreat in force, attempts which were checked by our cavalry, who again showed themselves to be the better men whether in mounted attack (the 12th Lancers had this day the satisfaction of getting home with the lance) or in dismounted action, and, thanks to this friendly screen, the weary infantry completed their marches without molestation. On this evening the First Corps lay between the Gobain Forest and the Oise to the south of La Fère, the Second Corps to the north of the Oise about Noyon, both corps being covered by the cavalry.

CHAPTER 7

Von Kluck Changes Direction
(For von Kluck's marches see Map 1)

The British Army owed its immunity from pursuit after the battle of Le Cateau to a variety of circumstances, chief amongst which were von Kluck's failure to appreciate the results of the battle, and the effect of this failure upon von Moltke at German Headquarters. The German official reports of this period give the impression that the British Army had been completely defeated and was in disorderly retreat. Now it is notorious that official reports are frequently highly coloured, for other than military reasons, and that they do not necessarily represent the real opinions of the military authorities by whom they are prepared and issued; but when the actions of these authorities accord with the general tenor of their reports it is fair to assume that the latter reflect their real views. The German official report of August 27 ran as follows:

> Nine days after its concentration the German Army has advanced victoriously into French territory from Cambrai to the southern Vosges. The enemy has been beaten on the whole front, and is in full retreat. In view of the enormous extent of the field of battle, which runs through wooded and in some parts, mountainous country, it is not possible to give exact figures as to the enemy's losses in killed and wounded, nor of the number of colours captured.
> The army of General von Kluck has driven back the British Army near Maubeuge; and by means of a turning movement attacked again on August 27 to the south-west of Maubeuge. The armies of General von Bülow and von Hausen have completely defeated about eight French and Belgian Army Corps between the Sambre, Namur, and the Meuse. These battles last-

ed several days. Our armies are pursuing the enemy to the west of Maubeuge, and Namur has fallen into our hands, after two days' bombardment. We are now attacking Maubeuge.

It will be noticed that this report exaggerates the strength of General de Lanrezac's Army, which is said to consist of 8 French and Belgian corps, whereas we know that there was only 1 Belgian division in Namur, and the French Fifth Army consisted of 4 corps, with 5 attached divisions. This exaggeration is perhaps excusable, but it is not easy to understand why the date of the Battle of Le Cateau is given as August 27. Further particulars as to this battle followed soon afterwards. The next reports said:

> The English Army, to which three French territorial divisions were attached, has been completely defeated to the north of St. Quentin; it is in full retreat through St. Quentin. Several thousand prisoners, seven batteries of field and one battery of heavy artillery have fallen into our hands.
> To the south of Mézières our troops, fighting their way forward continuously, have crossed the Meuse on a wide front. Our left wing, after nine days' fighting in the mountains, has driven back the French Alpine troops to the east of Epinal. Our cavalry is advancing victoriously.

This was followed by two semi-official reports from German Headquarters. The first, dated August 29, runs:

> The latest defeat of the English near St. Quentin has been brought about by the fact that our masses of cavalry, pursuing the English in their retreat towards St. Quentin, forced them to stand, and thereby enabled our army corps to intervene a second time in a decisive manner. The defeat of the English is complete. They are now completely cut off from their communications, and can no longer escape by the ports at which they disembarked.

The second semi-official report, dated the 31st, says:

> The English Army is retiring on Paris in the most complete disorder, and its losses are estimated at 20,000 men.

All this information, which was sent off from the German Headquarters at Coblenz, must have come from von Kluck, and it is evident that he believed that he had inflicted an annihilating defeat upon Sir

John French's Army. No doubt the reports sent back to him by his troops of the condition of our lines at Le Cateau, after we had abandoned them, encouraged him to believe that we had fled in great disorder. As Sir Horace Smith-Dorrien had, until a late hour of the 25th, intended to continue the retreat, and the orders to stand and fight did not reach all his troops until the early hours of the 26th, there had not been time to send back much of the light transport needed with the troops on the march, and this having been drawn up in and around the villages on our battle-front, had been smashed up by the enemy's artillery fire, the debris being scattered over the battlefield.

A considerable number of guns had suffered the same fate and had to be left behind when we withdrew, while many exhausted stragglers, who had lost their way in the withdrawal, had fallen into the enemy's hands. Further, in the early days of the retreat, when we were marching day and night without regular halts, and when all the transport had been sent back as far and as quickly as possible, the troops could not be supplied with food by the ordinary methods of distribution, so Sir William Robertson, the quartermaster-general, had adopted the expedient of dumping alongside the roads by which we were retreating, sides of beef, flitches of bacon, piles of cheese, and cases of biscuit, so that the troops might help themselves as they passed.

In distributing the supplies in this way, the lorries of the Army Service Corps were sent right forward, and on more than one occasion came into contact with the enemy's cavalry, A portion of a supply column being cut off by a party of German horse, and the officer in charge summoned to surrender, his answer was to put on full speed and burst, like Norman Ramsay's guns, through the enemy's ranks, a glorious baptism of fire for our modern transport.

Much of the food deposited in this way had to be left where it was placed, sometimes because it was not found in the darkness, sometimes for lack of time to use it or of means to carry it away, and this, combined with the inevitable litter of packs and greatcoats abandoned by exhausted men, no doubt presented to the enemy a picture of disorder and rout which, as he took no steps to investigate the facts, he did not realise was not a fair representation of the state of our army.

The news spread among the German troops of a succession of overwhelming victories had raised them to a high pitch of excitement and jubilation, and disposed them to exaggerate grossly indications of disaster and disorder in the ranks of their enemy. They had been taught to expect a rapid and complete victory over the French, and they were persuaded that the intervention of Belgium and Britain had been of no effect in staying the triumphant progress of their arms. I was in Germany at the time of the Agadir incident, when war with France seemed very near, and the Prussian regimental officers were then openly boasting that the campaign would be for them a military parade; and now that the great war for which they had been ardently longing for years had come, they were, it appears, convinced by their first successes that the military parade had come too.

It seems all but incredible, now that four years of terrible experience has taught the world the meaning of modern war, that any men who had devoted their lives to Its study could have desired to bring about such a calamity, but there is no question that this is so. The German military system had raised the corps of officers to the position of an autocracy, but had failed to provide them with the means of maintaining the exalted role they were asked to play in the national life. The great majority were very poor, and they saw around them the commercial and manufacturing classes steadily growing in wealth and setting a standard of living with which they could not compete. Promotion was slow, the work hard and monotonous, and discontent with their straitened circumstances was rife.

A very large number of German officers made no attempt to conceal their longing for a war, which they were certain would be a German triumph, and in moments of expansion spoke of the loot to be had in rich France. This being so, it is not surprising that the events of August 1914 appeared to them to be the realisation of their fondest hopes, and produced an intoxication which bemused their military judgement.

Here are two extracts from the diaries of two German officers of von Kluck's Army bearing on this period; the first is as follows:

August 23.—We receive news that we have gained a great victory near Metz.

24.—We hear that the British cavalry has been annihilated, and that six English divisions have been exterminated as they were detraining.

25.—A telegram from the emperor, expressing his delight at the fabulous marches of the Second Corps, has been made known. We have covered about 78 miles in the last three days. The enemy is retreating fast and we are not yet in touch. There are reports of another great victory. It is said that we have taken

20,000 prisoners and 150 guns.

The second, dated August 28, runs:

> This evening we had news of victories gained by von Bülow's Second Army; our souls were filled with joy when the regimental bands played the Hymn of Praise by the light of the moon and of the bivouac fires, and the tune was taken up by thousands of voices. There was general rejoicing and jubilation, and when the next morning we resumed our march, it was in the hope that we should celebrate the anniversary of Sedan before Paris.

In reality Sir Douglas Haig's First Corps had not been seriously engaged at all. The men were wearied with marching day and night, and puzzled by continual retreating, for which they could not understand the reason, but a short rest and, above all, some sleep was all that was necessary to make them as fit for battle as they had been on the day on which they marched towards Mons. The cavalry had more than held their own whenever they had met the enemy, and though both they and their horses were tired their moral was high. The Third and Fifth Divisions of the Second Corps had indeed been highly tried: their losses had been heavy, they had fought two severe battles against great odds and a number of engagements during the retreat, they had endured long hours of continuous shelling, they had lost much equipment, and were not fit in the days which followed immediately on the Battle of Le Cateau to fight another serious engagement.

But both at Mons and at Le Cateau they had been withdrawn from their positions by order, and had not been driven from them by the enemy, on whom they had inflicted far heavier losses than they had suffered. They knew that whatever the reasons for the retreat might be it was not due to any failure on their part to hold the positions they had been asked to defend, and therefore their spirit was very different from that of a routed army, so that they too only required rest and sleep and the replacement of their lost equipment to make them again an effective fighting force; while the Fourth Division and the 19th Brigade, which had been formed into a Third Corps under General Pulteney after they had crossed the Oise, had been less severely tried than Sir Horace Smith-Dorrien's two divisions, and needed an even shorter rest to make them ready for anything.

It was the physical strain of the constant marching by day and by night, with such brief halts as left the men no time to prepare a hot

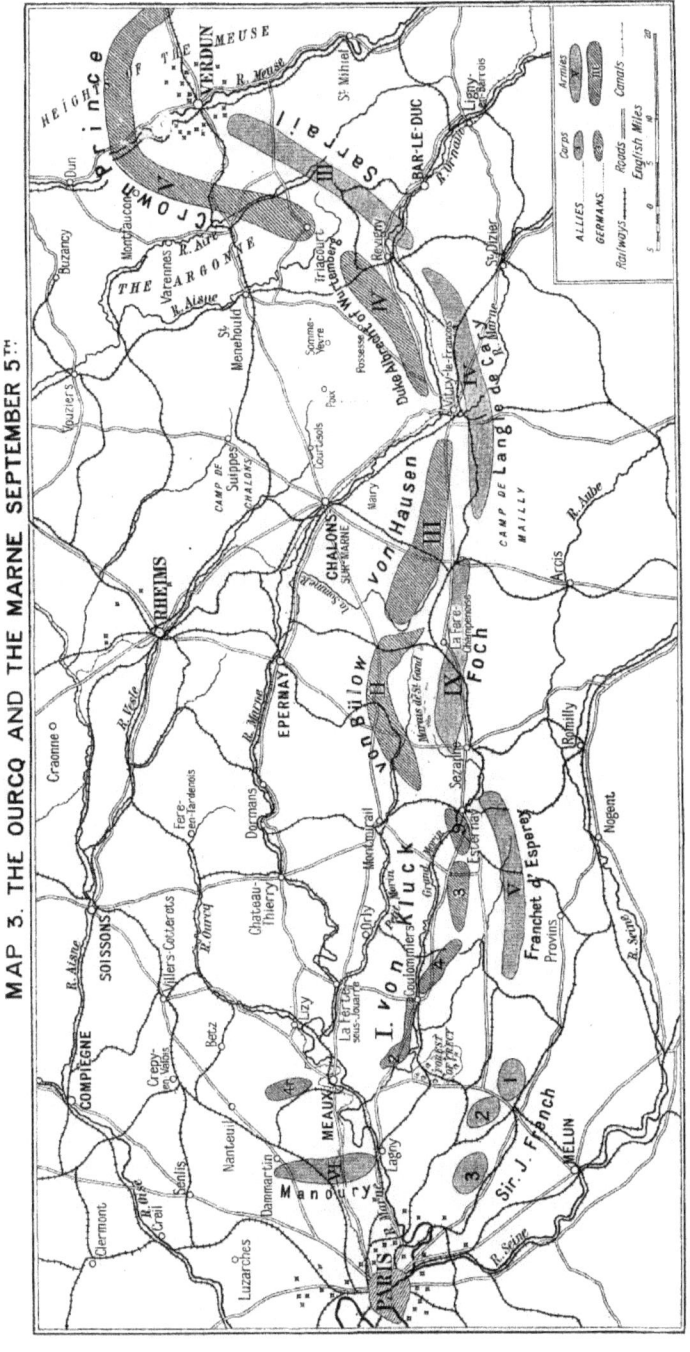

MAP 3. THE OURCQ AND THE MARNE SEPTEMBER 5TH

meal, to wash, or to take off their boots and tend their blistered feet, much more than the fighting which told on the troops. At each halt, even at each short check, in the march the infantry dropped where they had stopped and were instantly snoring, so that the equally tired officers and non-commissioned officers had to rouse each man when the time to resume the weary tramp came. The days under a blazing August sun, when the long straight stretches of the white dusty highroads of France burned their sore and bleeding feet, were even more trying than the nights with their added sense of some vague unknown danger, to avoid which we were retreating, always retreating.

But the bombardments of those days, heavy as they appeared to troops meeting for the first time a rain of high explosive shell in what today would be considered mere apologies for trenches, are not comparable with the tornadoes which now herald an attack, nor had the Germans added the barbarity of poison gas to the horrors of war, so that the mental and nervous exhaustion caused by these early battles was not as great as is produced by the prolonged struggles which have followed the establishment of trench lines from the Channel to Switzerland, and the recovery from bodily weariness is much more rapid than from nervous strain.

The restorative effect, upon troops who have undergone extraordinary physical exertion, of a hot meal and good night's rest and a bath is little short of marvellous, and these were what our army chiefly needed during the first week of the retreat to enable it to take the field again. The general condition of the British Army immediately after the battle of Le Cateau was in fact such that if our Second Corps had been followed up and forced again to fight against superior numbers it is difficult to see how it could have escaped disaster, and in that case Sir Douglas Haig's position would have been precarious; but, if the pursuit were not pressed, it was certain that the army would quickly regain its fighting power if the enemy was kind enough to give us the one chance we needed.

From the evening of August 26 Sir John French's retreat had been directed due south to the Aisne, between Soissons and Compiègne , and the river was safely crossed by the whole army during the forenoon of August 31. From then on it became possible to reduce the length of marches, to halt at night so that the weary men should have some rest, and to begin replacing the lost equipment of the Second Corps, so that the army as a whole steadily recovered from the effects of the severe strain through which it had passed. Its losses up to the end of the Battle of Le Cateau, estimated by the enemy at 20,000 men, amounted to little more than half that number, and reinforcements were available to replace at least a part of these.

Now what was von Kluck doing that he allowed our little army to escape? It would appear that his general instructions were to march south-west until he had overlapped the Allied left, and so south-westwards he went without regard to the direction of our retreat or to the opportunity which the fortune of war had presented to him. There were French forces on the British left, and it was, in the main, against these that he directed his march on August 27. On the 26th he had been fighting on the front Le Cateau-Cambrai, and from the latter place he had driven back a part of d'Amade's Sixty-First Division.

Two days later, on the 28th, that is, the day on which our Second Corps, marching due south, had reached the Oise near Noyon, he was attacking French troops at and to the north of Peronne with his right, while his left was just west of St. Quentin; so that in effect only his extreme left, consisting of his Ninth Corps, which was well to the east of Le Cateau during the battle and had been in touch with Sir Douglas Haig, crossed the line of march which Sir Horace Smith-Dorrien had followed in his retreat.

There was therefore no pursuit at all of the British by the German troops which had fought at Le Cateau, for the whole of them were marched off in a direction which took them away from the retreating British. It was left to von Bülow to use such of his Second Army as he could spare from following up General de Lanrezac to pursue the British, with whom, as we have seen, his Guard Cavalry Division and part of his Seventh Corps came into contact on the 27th and 28th, when they were engaged with Sir Douglas Haig and with our cavalry. On the 29th von Bülow had other things to think about, for on that day the French Fifth Army turned round, and advancing between Vervins and Ribemont attacked and inflicted a severe reverse upon von Bülow's Guard and Tenth Corps in the neighbourhood of Guise.

This most welcome diversion came at a very opportune moment for us, and effectively prevented von Bülow from taking up the pursuit which von Kluck had neglected, but it was unfortunately not powerful enough to put a stop to the progress of the German left wing, and in fact de Lanrezac's Eighteenth Corps immediately on our right was heavily counter-attacked by the Germans and forced back. It was necessary to get our own army as quickly as possible out of the enemy's reach, so that it might be rested and reequipped, and Manoury was still far from ready, for less than a half of the troops whom he expected had detrained, and only a portion of this half had arrived at the actual front. Therefore, the retreat had to be continued.

Von Kluck having captured Peronne on the 28th, on the 29th moved forward in the general direction of Amiens with his extreme right extending as far north as Albert and his left in the neighbourhood of Ham. On this day he attacked d'Amade's two reserve divisions, and such part of Manoury's Army as was ready for action along the Somme, with his Second, Fourth, and Fourth Reserve Corps and two cavalry divisions, and secured the passages over the river. On the 30th he drove d'Amade back through Amiens and, after some delay in getting his columns across the Somme, had, by the evening of the 31st, forced Manoury across the Avre and halted north of that river, his front facing south and extending from Amiens through Roye towards Guiscard.

Manoury, perceiving that it would be hopeless to attempt to complete the concentration of his army in face of an enemy in superior force, fell back, in constant touch with von Kluck's right, southwards on St. Just, and thence through Creil towards the northern defences of Paris, where we shall find him later; but it is important to remember that his army began its existence on August 26 on the Somme, where it played an important part in drawing von Kluck from our retreating army, that it grew steadily both as it retired and during the fierce struggle on the Ourcq, and that it did not, as has often been supposed, issue from Paris like Minerva from the brain of Jove and fall, fully equipped for battle, upon von Kluck's flank and rear.

August 31 saw von Kluck attain the extreme westerly point of his enveloping movement. The reports of the Battle of Le Cateau and of the British retreat had by then reached von Moltke, who seems from the information he received to have come to the conclusion that the British Army had ceased to exist as a fighting force. The ease with which d'Amade's reserve divisions had been driven back from Cambrai and Peronne, and the passages of the Somme forced against Manoury's troops, led apparently to the equally hasty deduction that these were of little value.

On the other hand, the French Fifth Army had been making itself unpleasant, and by actually moving forward on the 29th instead of continuing to retreat had brought itself within the grasp of von Kluck's envelopment, provided always that neither Manoury nor Sir John French interfered, and judging from von Kluck's reports they were both incapable of interfering.

Away down in the south on the extreme left of the German Armies everything was progressing well. The French had been driven back as far as the outer forts of Epinal, and if they were fighting stubbornly in front of Nancy and Verdun this would show that they still had large forces heavily engaged on their right, and could not therefore spare reinforcements for the menaced left. The time appeared to have come for the pincers to be closed on the French Armies. September 2, the anniversary of Sedan, was approaching, and dreams of a greater Sedan than had ever before been conceived by man began to kindle the thoughts of the emperor and his advisers to an extent which clouded their military judgement, and made them, in order to follow a will-o'-the-wisp, turn away from the solid advantages which they might have gained by destroying the British Army, by scattering Manoury's force before it had time to concentrate, and by occupying Paris, which lay at their mercy.

This was the consequence of a pedantic adherence to theory. The German General Staff had absorbed the principle that the first object in war is the destruction of the enemy's main forces in the field, and that this achieved all else follows: fortresses fall like ripe plums from a shaken tree, capitals can be occupied at will, and complete and decisive victory is attained. They had learned from the study of past wars that when this principle had been neglected, when fortresses and capitals have proved too attractive, the penalty has been severe, and they were determined that nothing should tempt them from following the precepts of their gospel.

The "contemptible" British Army was flying in disorder; its advanced base at Amiens lay at von Kluck's mercy and could be occupied at once and without difficulty, while cavalry could cut communication with the Channel ports, and this done, neither reinforcements nor stores could reach Sir John French; the hastily collected French Territorials and reserve troops on the British left had proved of little value; the French Fifth Army was the left of the main French forces and was closely engaged with von Bülow, so that if von Kluck's masses could be brought down upon its flank, the whole French line would be rolled up and Paris entered after a victory such as history had never yet recorded.

So, von Kluck is told to send a detachment to occupy Amiens, to leave a flank guard to watch the British and the French forces on their left, and to change the direction of his main columns so as to bring them down upon de Lanrezac's flank. The fallacy of this reasoning lay in the assumptions that the British Army had been defeated so decisively as to be incapable of interference, that Paris had only a moral and not a military value, and that Manoury could be safely neglected. On the first point the German Headquarters were apparently misinformed by von Kluck, but it should have been realised that an army which is not pursued recovers rapidly and cannot be left alone with impunity. The chief responsibility for the failure to pursue us must rest with von Kluck, who was the man on the spot, and who ought, whatever his instructions were, to have adapted them to the changes of the military situation as they occurred.

To continue to march south-west when the enemy is retiring due south is as curious a manoeuvre as is to be found in military history. War is very unforgiving of mistakes, and rarely offers a second time opportunities which have not been accepted, while of all the opportunities which it can present the retreat of an enemy from a battlefield is the most favourable if it is promptly seized, and the most pregnant of unpleasant consequences if it is neglected. Napoleon failed to pursue Blücher after he had defeated him at Ligny, and this failure led directly to his downfall at Waterloo; von Kluck failed to pursue Smith-Dorrien after Le Cateau, and paid the penalty in the retreat to the Aisne.

It may be assumed that the Germans obtained early information that we were abandoning our main base at Havre, and they may have deduced from this that our army would be unable to receive from England reinforcements, stores, and supplies for a long time to come. If they were influenced by this consideration (and it would appear from the semi-official report which I have quoted that they were), then they had forgotten that our sea-power would allow us to open a new base upon the French Atlantic sea-board and to establish a line of communications not exposed to the predatory raids of their *Uhlans*.

As to the second point—the value of Paris—it is perfectly true that its occupation would not have ended the war in the West, and that this result would only be attained by inflicting a crushing defeat on the Allied Armies. The French Government, ready for any sacrifice, had made all preparations for transferring the seat of government to Bordeaux, and was prepared even to abandon the capital to the enemy if the need arose; but Paris, besides being the capital of France, was her most important railway centre and a large military depot. The great city was ideally placed for the assembly and maintenance of a force to counter just such a movement as von Kluck was now ordered to make, and the purely military advantages to be gained by denying to Joffre the use of the railways converging on Paris were very real.

D'Amade's hastily formed second-line divisions had not proved capable of resisting first-line German troops in superior numbers; and Manoury, who had been met at a time when only a small portion of his army could be placed in the field, had not been able to oppose von Kluck effectively on the Somme; but it was a hasty assumption that if he were left alone, and had the free use of the Paris railway junctions, he would not be able to increase and organise his forces, and the wise and prudent course was to strike at the weak enemy who was in reach and to allow him neither time nor opportunity to become strong. Instead of doing this von Kluck repeated on the 30th his manoeuvre of the 27th, and just as he marched south-west from the British, who were retiring south from the battlefield of Le Cateau, so after driving in Manoury's advanced troops on the 29th, he next day turned southeast, while the French like ourselves fell back southwards.

If on the 30th von Kluck could leave a flank guard to watch both French and Manoury, he could certainly have detached a sufficient force on the 27th to keep the latter from interfering with him while he fell with his main body upon the British Army, and either defeated it completely or drove it south of Paris. He could then have prevented the French from using the railways through Paris, have cut off Manoury and the French troops in the north from Joffre, and have drawn from the city the supplies of which he was running short. All these substantial gains were sacrificed in favour of a grandiose and ambitious scheme which, as events proved, could not be realised.

It is true that by continuing to march south-west after the Battle of Le Cateau von Kluck prevented Manoury from concentrating behind the Somme, but that result would have been obtained with no less certainty if the British Army had been effectively pursued, for Manoury could not have remained in the neighbourhood of Amiens with von Kluck's Army advancing past his right, threatening to interrupt his communications with Paris and to isolate him from the remainder of the Allied forces.

There must before the war have been many anxious discussions in Germany between the military party, who believed in the power of Germany to carry through to a speedy and triumphal issue their vast programme of conquest, and the more moderate and enlightened, who foresaw something of the feeling which the policy of blood and iron would arouse. Bethmann-Hollweg's intense depression on hearing the news of Britain's intervention is an indication of the anxiety of the latter party, It is easy to imagine that the shouts of the extremists at the news of the first German victories silenced all doubts. One can almost hear the Crown Prince and his friends saying, "We told you so. The German Army is irresistible. Our enemies are soft and degenerate. We cannot be too bold. Forward with God and *Kaiser* to a German triumph!" In short, Prussian conceit and self-sufficiency marred the execution of a well-laid plan.

It has been reported that the emperor, eager for an early and triumphal entry into Paris, strongly opposed the change in the direction of von Kluck's march, but the evidence as to this is very vague, and I cannot but think that the probabilities are that he was on the side of those in favour of deferring the advance on the French capital until a greater Sedan had been consummated. His versatile and erratic mind was doubtless deeply impressed by the great successes which the surprise engineered for him by his generals had won, and he must have seen visions of taking prisoners by the hundred thousand, guns by the thousand, and colours by the hundred, in short, of a victory which should completely overshadow for all time the memory of the elder William and of the elder Moltke. Even the glory of riding through the Arc de Triomphe would be a small matter compared with so stupendous a *dénouement* to a campaign of thirty days.

Von Kluck was not alone in failing to appreciate the difference between a retreat undertaken to avoid a trap and a retirement following upon defeat in a battle which has been fought to the last. The French Armies had been worsted in the first engagements, but they were not broken, and many of them had not as yet been completely engaged. It was the menace of von Kluck's advance and not the complete defeat of the French Armies which had forced Joffre to swing back his line.

He had been surprised and had to pay the military penalty of surrendering the initiative to the enemy and of being forced to change his plans in haste, but it is to his eternal glory that, amidst the collapse of his first schemes, and with a burden of responsibility on his shoulders which would have appalled an ordinary man, he never lost his grasp of the situation, never wavered in his determination to return to the attack at the first opportunity, and in circumstances of extraordinary difficulty assembled at the right time and at the right place the forces necessary to enable him to seize the opportunity when it came.

If Joffre stood the test of early failure, the German commanders did not stand the test of early success. For generations they and their forebears had laboured at perfecting their military machine, until in organisation, discipline, and equipment the German Army was admittedly the first of the Armies of Europe, and they firmly believed that to this catalogue of its superiorities might be added valour and generalship. After more than forty years of strenuous effort in time of peace the machine was now being tested in war, and everywhere their enemies were fleeing before its blows.

The bulletin of August 27 announced that "the enemy has been beaten on the whole front," in the circumstances a perfectly justifiable announcement to make to the German people, but not an appreciation of the position upon which military plans should have been based. Yet it appears clear from the emperor's perfervid telegrams to his family, to his people, and to his Allies, and from the action of his military advisers that at this time he was convinced that the shining sword was irresistible, that the war in the West was already won, and that any risk might be taken in order to reap the full harvest of victory.

Having given his Imperial sanction to the orders which were to go out to von Kluck, and being confident that all was going well in the North, the emperor shortly after went off to see that his left, which was preparing an attack on Nancy, did not lag behind his brilliant right.

It has generally been assumed by French writers on this period of the war that the decision to give up the march on Paris and to move against the flank of the French Fifth Army was not reached till much later, the date generally given being September 4, but it is quite evident that on the 30th von Kluck's Army was engaged with Manoury between the Somme and the Avre, that on the 31st he was wheeling southwards, and that from then on his infantry columns were marching south-eastwards as fast as the limits of human endurance would permit, while his cavalry and his left corps were crossing the Oise at and to the south of Noyon on the 31st, and moving towards the forest of Compiègne and Villers-Cotterets.

This makes it probable that the conversion from the south-westerly movement, which had been continued without deviation ever since Brussels was left on August 20, to a march south-eastwards was ordered on the 30th by von Kluck, in accordance with instructions received from von Moltke, and quite certain that the change was not made later than the 31st, for from then his columns continued to move, not towards Paris, but towards the flank of the French Fifth Army, right up to the time when they were brought to a standstill by Joffre's manoeuvre.

Von Kluck ordered his Fourth Reserve Corps to move by St. Just-en-Chaussée to cover the right rear of his march from any interference by Manoury, the French having quitted that place the previous day and moved back towards Creil. Von Marwitz's cavalry protected the outer flank of the movement, and marching south-eastward through the forest of Compiègne, came on the evening of August 31 again into contact with the British Army, while on the evening of September 1 von Kluck's main body, which, now that the Fourth Reserve Corps had been detached on a separate mission, consisted of the Ninth, Third, Fourth, and Second Corps, in that order from left to right, lay with its left a few miles north of Vic-sur-Aisne, and its right on the main Amiens-Compiègne road about twelve miles north-west of the latter place.

The British Army crossed the Aisne during the 31st and lay that night with its right, Sir Douglas Haig's corps, to the south-west of Soissons; the centre, Sir Horace Smith-Dorrien's corps, between Villers-Cotterets and Crépy; and the left, General Pulteney's Corps, to the west of Crépy and to the south of the forest of Compiègne, the cavalry being disposed partly in the gaps between the corps and partly on the left flank. Here while our army was still in this position a curious incident marked the dawn of September 1. For some days past such pressure as the enemy had brought to bear upon us had come from our right front, that is, from von Bülow's Army, but now von Kluck's change of direction was bringing his cavalry into touch with us from a new direction upon our left front.

The German Fourth Cavalry Division appears to have crossed the dense forest of Compiègne, which would shield them effectively from the observation of our aeroplanes, during the late afternoon of the 31st, and to have halted close to the village of Nery, hoping to surprise early the next morning our Fourth Division, which they had located. Our 1st Cavalry Brigade had arrived at Nery after dark, and had, unknown to the enemy, come between them and the Fourth Division, so the next morning opened with a mutual surprise. Our men were engaged as day broke in watering their horses when two German batteries opened fire upon them. The situation was at first an anxious one for us as the German shells fell among our horse-lines.

Only three of the six guns of "L" Battery could be placed in action, two of these being almost immediately silenced, but the one remaining gun continued firing to the last. The men of the 1st Cavalry Brigade rallied from their surprise, and they were promptly supported both by the 4th Cavalry Brigade and by the 19th Infantry Brigade of General Pulteney's corps, which had halted for the night in the immediate neighbourhood and had sprung to arms at the sound of the guns. The German cavalry, who had apparently been in complete ignorance that they were in the presence of so considerable a force, fell back, leaving eight guns and a number of prisoners in our hands, and cannot have felt proud of the circumstances in which they renewed acquaintance with our troops.

About the same time that this combat was in progress the Fourth Division successfully repulsed another attack by German cavalry near Verberie, and the Fifth Division beat off an even sharper attempt by the enemy to get through what he believed to be our broken front. Yet another surprise collision occurred later in the day in the forest of Villers-Cotterets, north of the town of that name. Sir Douglas Haig's corps was marching south-westwards through the forest so as to close finally the gap which had separated his troops from those of Sir Horace Smith-Dorrien ever since August 25. The 4th and 6th Infantry Brigades of Haig's Second Division became engaged with German cavalry and the usual escort of *Jägers*, which were marching south-eastwards on Villers-Cotterets to clear the road for von Kluck's Third Corps.

Some confused fighting ensued in the dense forest, in which the Germans were repulsed, and our men were able to resume their march, but not until the Irish Guards, who were here seriously engaged for the first time in their history, had suffered somewhat heavy losses.

At the end of this march the whole of Sir John French's Army was once more united, Sir Douglas Haig's corps lying between La Ferté Milon and Betz, Sir Horace Smith-Dorrien's between Betz and Nanteuil, with General Pulteney's corps and the bulk of the cavalry just to the west of the latter place. Directly parallel to the British front von Kluck's main bodies were halted about eight miles to the north on a line running eastward from the southern edge of the forest of Compiègne, so that the opponents of Mons and of Le Cateau were again face to face. General Manoury's Army had on this day fallen back from the Oise near Creil and Pont Ste. Maxence to and to the south of Senlis, a movement which sensibly diminished the gap between the British and the French on this flank.

On September 2 there occurred an even more curious development than those which had resulted on the previous day from von Kluck's zigzag marches. It appears that on the 1st considerable bodies of the Second and Ninth Cavalry Divisions penetrated between Manoury's right and General French's left, occupied Chantilly, the Newmarket of France, which lies west of Senlis and fifteen miles north of the northern suburbs of Paris, pushed patrols up to the outer defences of the French capital, and were actively at work with armoured cars and parties of horsemen well to the rear both of the French Sixth Army and of the British Army.

During the night of September 1-2, they seem to have suddenly become aware that we and Manoury were closing in upon them from left and right, and to have moved off in a great hurry to avoid being caught in a trap. Our cavalry during their march of September 2 found four guns abandoned by the enemy's horse in the forest of Ermenonville, while parties of our infantry in the course of their march southward came upon equipment, lorries, and waggons which had evidently been abandoned in great haste.

When von Kluck's men had parted with the British Army after the Battle of Le Cateau they had left it a very exhausted and to some extent disorganised force. While it would be absurd to pretend that the Third and Fifth Divisions in particular, which had lost a high proportion of their experienced officers and non-commissioned officers, a number of guns and machine-guns, and a quantity of transport, of which little had been replaced, had recovered altogether from the fiery trial through which they had passed, yet the Germans of the First Army on meeting us again found us with order completely restored and ready to reply at once and sharply to any attack, a discovery which caused an important modification in the German plans.

At the time of the Battle of Le Cateau they had been in close touch with our front and consequently well informed as to our movements, but now they found that they were no longer opposed, as they expected, to an army marching almost continuously day and night to escape their clutches, but to one moving in its own time and not in the least perturbed by their activities. Having dropped the threads which had once been in their hands, they appear to have been at first completely in the dark both as to our condition and to our movements, and to this fact must be ascribed the curious chance collisions and still more curious marches and counter-marches which took place at this time. Nor was this the only result of the orders which had sent the First German Army at first westwards away from the enemy whom they had been fighting and then brought them back hastily eastward into the presence of the same enemy.

This manoeuvre had compelled von Kluck's men to march round two sides of a triangle, while the British had been moving along the base, and had put upon them a strain which, in the hot August days, proved wellnigh unendurable. An interesting picture of the state of von Kluck's Army during these days is given in the diary of a German officer taken prisoner by the French, who have translated and published his record of events. Writing on September 2, he says:

> Our men are done up. For four days they have been marching 24 miles a day, (*i.e.*, since the change of direction on the 30th. The object of this rapid marching being probably to catch the Fifth French Army in the act of crossing the Marne.) The country is difficult, the roads are in bad condition, and barred by trees felled across them, the fields are pitted with shell-holes. The men stagger forward, their faces coated with dust, their uniform in rags, they look like living scarecrows. They march with their eyes closed, singing in chorus so that they shall not fall asleep on the march. The certainty of early victory and of the triumphal entry into Paris keeps them going and acts as a spur to their enthusiasm. Without this certainty of victory, they would fall exhausted. They would go to sleep where they fell so as to get to sleep somehow or anyhow.
>
> It is the delirium of victory which sustains our men, and in order that their bodies may be as intoxicated as their souls, they drink to excess, but this drunkenness helps to keep them going. Today after an inspection the general was furious. He wanted to stop this general drunkenness. We managed to dissuade him from giving severe orders. If there were too much severity, the army would not march. Abnormal stimulants are necessary to make abnormal fatigue endurable. We will put all that right in Paris. There we will prohibit the sale of alcohol, and as soon as the men are able to rest on their laurels, order will reappear.

I would remark with reference to this candid picture of the state of discipline of the German Army that the fatigues and privations of our Second Corps during the first marches after Le Cateau were certainly greater than any which von Kluck's men had had at this time to undergo, and that our men had not the delirium of victory to sustain them, yet I never saw nor heard of a single case of drunkenness amongst them. As the wine districts of France were entered by the enemy and wine was obtainable everywhere this drunkenness in the German Army increased to an extraordinary extent, and when the Germans were in retreat to the Aisne whole parties of officers were captured because they were too intoxicated to move. Writing on September 3, the diarist says:

> We are leaving Paris on our right and are going to concentrate toward the south-east against the debris of the Franco-British Army, which is vainly endeavouring to reunite its scattered fragments along the Marne.... Our men have no idea that we are giving up for the time being our march on Paris. They are counting so much on finding themselves at the gates of Paris tomorrow or the day after that it would be cruel to undeceive them. They would at once lose all their spring.

Von Kluck would not communicate to his subordinates more of his plans and intentions than it was necessary for them to know in order that they might carry out intelligently their daily tasks, therefore it is not at all astonishing that an officer of one of his formations should only discover on September 3, from the direction of the marches, that Paris was not the goal. The movements of the 3rd, which would have been ordered on the evening of the 2nd, took von Kluck's left through Neuilly-St. Front, his centre through La Ferté Milon and Betz, and his right through Nanteuil towards the Marne between Château-Thierry and La Ferté-sous-Jouarre, obviously away from Paris.

Indeed, the two left corps, the Ninth and the Third, must have realised when they crossed the Aisne on the 1st and moved south-east to the forest of Villers-Cotterets that they at least were not marching directly on Paris; but the two right corps of the main group, the Fourth and Second, apparently still had hopes until they moved across the main Soissons-Paris road. This statement therefore shows that von Kluck's decision to leave Paris for the time being could not have been taken later than the evening of the 2nd, and as there was no perceptible change in the direction of his marches between August 31 and September 4 it is much more probable that, as I have suggested, the vital decision was reached on August 30. The officer describes how he saw von Kluck on September 4, and had a conversation with one of his staff, who told him that the general had no doubt that the Germans would quickly crush the French Army.

"The reports of spies who had seen the enemy in retreat are very satisfactory. They are a disorganised and discontented horde, and there is no chance of their being able to do us any harm. The general fears nothing from the direction of Paris. We will return to Paris after we have destroyed the remains of the Franco-British Army. The Fourth Reserve Corps will have the honour of the triumphal entry into the French capital."

On the date of this last entry in the diary, September 4, von Kluck's main body, continuing its march south-eastwards, had, for the most part, crossed the Marne, and was disposed along the Petit Morin between Montmirail and La Ferté-sous-Jouarre, with the Fourth Reserve Corps watching his left rear about half-way between Nanteuil and Meaux, some eight miles west of the Ourcq, and his cavalry across the Petit Morin in touch with our troopers. Sir John French, who had continued a now leisurely retirement, had on the 3rd crossed the Marne and halted to the south of that river between La Ferté-sous-Jouarre and Lagny.

While we were still in this position the Fifth French Army on our right was attacked and pushed back, and as Joffre, whose plans were now beginning to take definite shape, required more room for this army, which had to take ground rather farther to the west owing to the intervention on its right of his new Ninth Army under the command of General Foch, the French commander-in-chief requested Sir John French to fall back yet once more, and so on the night of the 4th-5th we marched to the south of the forest of Crécy, and halting there on September 5 brought the long and adventurous retreat to an end.

CHAPTER 8

The Ourcq and the Marne

It is now time to see what had been happening on the rest of the front while von Kluck's march was in progress. Up to the afternoon of August 23, when the enemy's plan stood revealed to him, Joffre had, it will be remembered, hoped to strike the flank of the German Armies moving through Belgium by sending his Fourth Army, which had formed his original reserve, forward through the Ardennes. This movement had already developed on August 23, by which time General Langle de Cary, who commanded the Fourth Army, had crossed the Semois and come into collision with the German Fourth Army; but he had found himself hampered in the wooded and mountainous country, and was unable to make his weight felt before von Kluck's turning movement had taken effect.

This was what the Germans had calculated on, and they proved right, for their envelopment, which by August 27 had driven the Franco-British left to the south of St. Quentin, was then considerably nearer to Paris than was the French Fourth Army; and Joffre had been compelled to draw back his whole line north of Verdun, pivoting on the fortress, in front of which General Sarrail, who had now succeeded General Ruffey in command of the Third Army, was successfully holding the German Crown Prince. So, Langle de Gary had by September 4 retired slowly, through Rheims and Chalons, to a position astride the Marne south of Vitry le François, with his right in touch with Sarrail's left, which had swung back through the Argonne to the south-east of Verdun.

Joffre's second offensive plan had therefore failed to mature, but in no wise discouraged he immediately set about preparing a third. As early as August 25 he issued the following order:

As it has not proved possible to carry out the offensive manoeu-

vre which had been planned, the object of the future operations will be to reconstitute on our left flank, with the Fourth and Fifth Armies, the British Army, and new forces drawn from our right, a mass capable of resuming the offensive while the other armies containing the enemy for the time necessary.
A new group will be formed in the neighbourhood of Amiens between August 27 and September 2.

This was the birth of Manoury's Sixth Army which Joffre had hoped would be able to take the offensive from the Somme. But von Kluck had intervened too quickly, and Manoury, compelled to retire towards Paris, had become separated from d'Amade's two reserve divisions, the Sixty-First and Sixty-Second, which had retired westward through Amiens while Manoury was falling back on Creil. From then on the task of completing the formation of the Sixth Army was entrusted to General Gallieni, the Governor of Paris, who set himself to increase Manoury's forces by reassembling and transporting to Paris d'Amade's two divisions, by constituting a new Forty-Fifth Active Division of troops which had been drawn from Algeria, and by expediting the detrainment and despatch of other troops which Joffre was sending north from his right, the most important of these reinforcements being the Fourth Corps, which was detached from Sarrail at Verdun.

On the evening of September 4 Manoury was covering Paris on the north-east, with his right just north of the Marne at Lagny, and his left through Dammartin. He then had with him the Seventh Corps (which had been withdrawn by Joffre from the Alsace group, had detrained near Amiens, been partly engaged with von Kluck on the Somme, and had then retreated towards Paris), the Fifty-Fifth and Fifty-Sixth Reserve Divisions, a brigade of Moroccan troops, and some marines, and with these forces was in touch with von Kluck's Fourth Reserve Corps to the west of the Ourcq.

The new Forty-Fifth Division would be ready to join Manoury on the 6th, the Fourth Corps had begun to detrain in Paris on the 6th, and d'Amade's Sixty-First Division was also assembling near the capital. Therefore, Manoury was not only considerably superior to the German force immediately in front of him, but was certain of receiving reinforcements, while von Kluck had the greater part of his army across the Marne, well to the south-east, and was deeply committed. The time was ripe for Joffre's counter-stroke.

The French commander-in-chief had not been content with the

formation of a Sixth Army, for his principle, in accordance with the whole trend of modern French military thought, being to manoeuvre, not on a fixed plan, but in agreement with the development of the situation, he required to have in his hand as large a reserve as possible, so that he might either take advantage of opportunities as they presented themselves or be ready to parry an unexpected blow.

Therefore, on August 29, when it had become clear that Manoury would have to fall back from the Somme, he had ordered the formation of the Ninth Army, under General Foch. To create this, he drew partly upon his right and partly upon the Fourth Army, which had been the least tried of any of his forces.

By this means he obtained for Foch an army of eight infantry divisions, and a cavalry division, and, as soon as it became evident that the German south-easterly movement was bringing the enemy's main weight to the south of Rheims, he interposed this new army between the Fourth and Fifth Armies, so that the Fifth Army, taking ground to its left, might be able to intervene more effectively in the attack upon von Kluck, and the centre of his line between Paris and Verdun might be held safely while that attack was maturing. Accordingly, on the evening of September 4, Foch had taken his place in the line to the south of the St. Gond marshes with his centre about La Fère Champenoise.

With these dispositions completed Joffre was ready, and on September 4 he issued the following order:

> It is necessary to profit by the dangerous situation in which the First German Army has placed itself, by concentrating against it the efforts of the Allied Armies on the extreme left. During September 5 all arrangements will be made to begin the attack on the 6th.

Then follow the tasks of the different armies. Manoury was to drive the Germans over the Ourcq; the British Army was to advance northeast and attack the Germans on the Grand Morin on either side of Coulommiers, while the Fifth Army on the British right advanced due north. Farther to the right Foch was to hold the weight of the enemy in the centre of the new battle-front and cover the offensive of the Fifth Army. This was the order which turned retreat into advance, and at the moment when a complete triumph for the German arms appeared to be in sight changed the whole course of the war in the West.

It is important to notice the role assigned to the British Army, because it has been hinted that we did not give Manoury all the assistance which he was entitled to expect. We were to advance in a north-easterly direction between the Fifth and Sixth Armies and were not to swerve either to the right or left to take part in battles which might be raging on our flanks. The wisdom of Joffre's choice of the line on which we were to advance will appear. But before following out the consequences of this order we must look for a moment to the extreme right, which had furnished so large a part of the troops of which Joffre had formed his two new armies.

The weakened Alsace group had, as the German *communiqué* of August 29 announced, been compelled to fall back on the fortresses of Belfort and Epinal, while farther to the north Castelnau, by constant local attacks in front of Nancy, covered the withdrawal of French troops from the right flank, and successfully kept the enemy under the delusion that Joffre's main forces were still in this part of the field.

The great success achieved by their heavy howitzers at Namur had inspired the Germans with a hope that it might be possible to complete the destruction of the French Armies by bursting through the formidable barrier of fortresses which line the eastern frontier of France. On September 4 we find the German *communiqué* saying:

> The mobile heavy batteries which have been sent to us by Austria have rendered us valuable services at the capture of Civet and Namur. The mobility and the effect of the fire of these batteries are remarkable. The forts of Hirson, Ayelle, Condé, La Fère, and Laon have been taken without fighting, and all the forts in northern France are now in our possession, except Maubeuge. The enemy is in retreat to the Marne before the armies of Generals von Kluck, von Hausen, von Bülow, and of the Duke of Würtemburg. The Armies of the Crown Prince of Bavaria and of General von Heeringen have still in front of them strong enemy forces holding entrenched positions in French Lorraine.

This pronouncement shows that up to the very eve of the battles of the Ourcq and the Marne the Germans believed that the Franco-British left had been beaten, and that the French right was still in great strength. The *Kaiser*, under the conviction that von Kluck and von Bülow on the right had only to go forward to turn retreat into disaster, had come out to witness the defeat of the main French forces in the south and to make his entry into Nancy. So, while Joffre was completing his preparations for the counter-stroke against von Kluck,

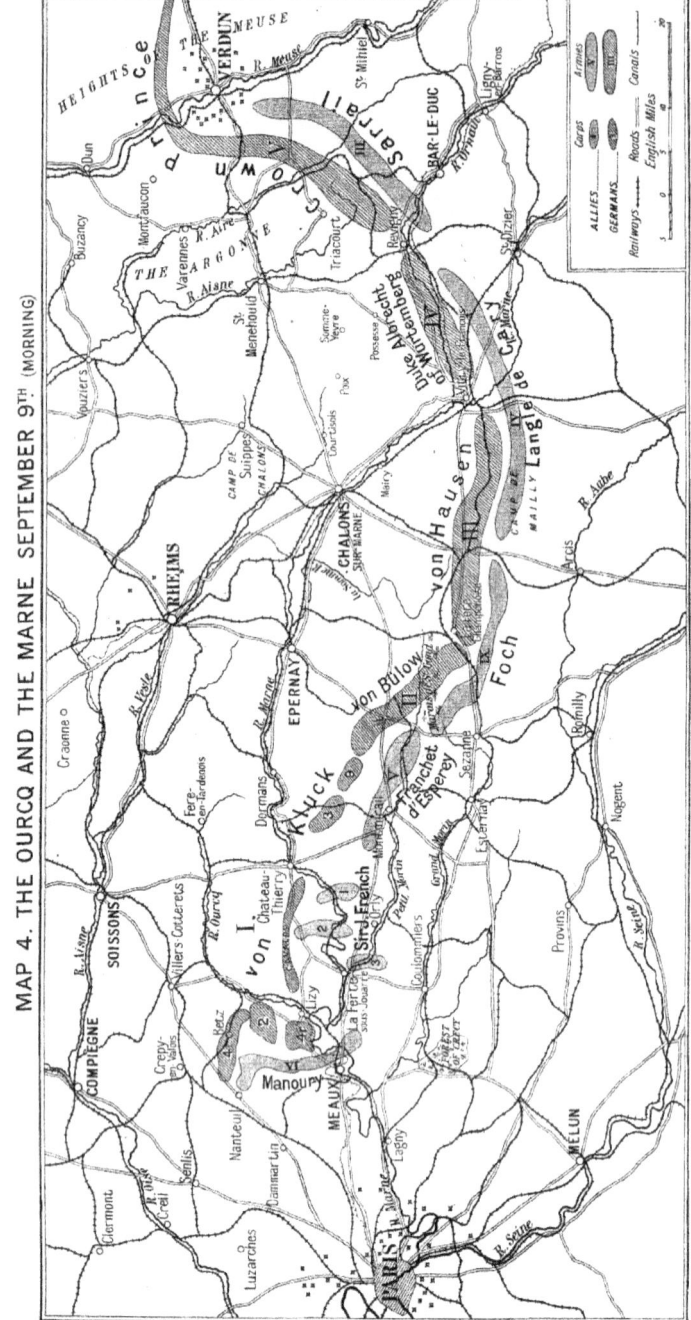

MAP 4. THE OURCQ AND THE MARNE SEPTEMBER 9TH (MORNING)

Castelnau was fighting in front of Nancy against the Armies of the Crown Prince Rupprecht and von Heeringen a battle very similar to our first Battle of Ypres. From September 3 onwards Castelnau was with his reduced forces incessantly attacked by overwhelming numbers, the effort of the Germans culminating in a *Kaiser* battle on September 6, in which they were completely repulsed.

As at Ypres this was followed, after the climax had been passed, by a number of spasmodic attacks probably intended to keep in the south the large forces which the Germans falsely believed to be in front of Nancy; these attacks finally dying away on the 11th, when the Germans in the north were in full retreat to the Aisne. This splendid resistance of Castelnau's men in face of great odds undoubtedly confirmed the Germans in their overestimate of the French strength in the south, and the resultant underestimate of the Allied strength in the north; for von Kluck continued to commit himself deeper and deeper, and on September 5 (for the position on September 5 see Map 3), we find him still moving southwards from the Petit Morin across the Grand Morin, ready to strike at the French Fifth Army next day.

But by the evening of the 5th unexpected news had reached him. His Fourth Reserve Corps had reported to him that they had been attacked by French forces in superior numbers and had been driven back towards the Ourcq. He then became suddenly aware that Manoury, so far from retreating or passively protecting Paris, was a serious menace to his rear.

The orders conveying the news that we were to turn about and go forward reached the British Army on the afternoon of September 6, and were received with the deepest joy and thankfulness. To all but the few who were in the confidence of Sir John French the advance was just as inexplicable as the retreat had been, but now no one bothered his head with searchings for causes—something had happened and we were to move north. "Why, it's better than Corunna. Moore had to take to his ships, he did not advance again," said one beaming brigadier when he received his orders.

Many of our battalions did not know when they turned out of their billets on the morning of September 6 whether they were not to march to the Atlantic, and a spontaneous burst of cheering welcomed the discovery that they were heading northwards. The news, in fact, supplied the moral fillip which was the one thing needed to make the army forget its troubles, and complete the good work begun by sleep and regular food. The Second Corps was still woefully deficient in experienced officers, and owing to the delay caused by the change of the base and to the congestion of the railways around Paris, by the movement of troops from the south to reinforce Manoury, it had proved impossible to replace much of the lost equipment, and the Fifth Division in particular was far short of its proper complement of guns. Still the ranks had been partially refilled with drafts, and we marched at dawn of a beautiful September morning back across the forest of Crécy in a very different spirit from that in which we had moved south through the same forest some thirty hours before.

Von Kluck had decided that he must, to save himself, stop his advance and reinforce his Fourth Reserve Corps so as to defeat Manoury, and he therefore ordered his cavalry under von Marwitz to delay the advance of the British Army, while he marched his Second Corps, which on the night of the 5th-6th had halted at and about Coulommiers, back across the Marne. A little later he also withdrew his Fourth Corps, which had been opposite our right and the left of the Fifth French Army, and sent it too northwards to fight Manoury, thus leaving a very large gap to be filled by his mounted troops.

His general plan appears to have been at this time to assemble behind his Fourth Reserve Corps, which should draw Manoury on, a large force to fall upon and destroy the bold Frenchman, while his cavalry screen held up the British Army, and his left in conjunction with von Bülow's right stopped the Fifth French Army. This, unfortunately for him, they entirely failed to do, for Franchet d'Espérey, who had now replaced de Lanrezac in the command of the Fifth Army, steadily gained ground throughout the day, and the German cavalry, after resisting the British progress for some time in the forest of Crécy, finding that our advance on a broad front threatened their retreat, fell back to the Grand Morin, which was reached by the British centre in the evening.

While this was going on, the Germans farther to the south were heavily attacking Foch and Langle de Gary, and both these armies were compelled to give some ground.

It is not my purpose to attempt a detailed description of the great battle which raged during the next three days over a front of 150 miles from the Argonne almost to the outer defences of Paris, but it is necessary to understand its broad lines in order to follow what happened to von Kluck, and how his situation reacted on the other German Armies engaged. From the time when it became clear that von Kluck in spite of his strenuous marches would not be able to cut off the French Fifth Army on the Marne, and that the British Army, again in being, was on Franchet d'Espérey's flank, some modification of the German scheme had become necessary.

The outer flank of the British Army rested upon the defences of Paris, and an immediate envelopment of the Allied left was no longer in question, so instead, the German aim became to break through the French centre to the south of Epernay, sweep the debris of the western half into Paris, which would then be invested, while the eastern half was also broken in front of Nancy and driven towards Verdun, which was already partially enveloped on the north and west. The German Crown Prince's left was already well round Verdun, and if his Bavarian colleague and von Heeringen played their part the bulk of the forces on the French right could be locked up in the fortress and kept out of harm's way, while the German Second and Third Armies with von Kluck's help herded the Allied centre and left into Paris.

Some such decision as this was apparently reached about September 2, that is, after von Kluck had again come into contact with the British Army, and found that it was not quite such a rabble as had been supposed. The attack upon Nancy, which had been planned as part of the original programme of envelopment (it was in fact to have been the left arm of the pincers), had not then developed, and could be fitted into the new programme. The Allied centre was sagging badly, and might snap if it was pressed hard, while von Kluck advancing across the Marne would not only lend a hand to von Bülow by keeping the British Army and the French Fifth Army fully occupied, but would act as a pivot upon which the German centre would wheel to its right as it drove the enemy opposed to it across the Seine in a westerly direction.

It is only possible to explain the attacks upon Nancy and on Foch's Army, and von Kluck's advance across the Marne on September 4, on the basis of some such general plan as I have indicated, for all these must have been prepared at a time when it was clear that the First German Army had not succeeded in getting round the Allied left, and before the Germans were aware of Manoury's counter-threat. This new programme of breaking through the centre apparently runs counter to the principles on which the original German plan was based, if my reading of the German mind is correct.

They had, I have suggested, in the first instance avoided the attempt to get a decision by breaking through the front as being slow and costly in comparison with an envelopment of a flank. But I believe that all the evidence points to the conclusion that the Germans, at this time, regarded the Allies in the West as substantially a beaten foe, and it is justifiable to adopt methods against a beaten foe which would be quite out of place against a more formidable opponent. It is true that the Germans had found the British Army more capable of resistance than they had expected, but it had not attempted to attack, and the Allies as a whole had been retiring for nearly a fortnight, and had been losing very heavily, so they may well have argued that the time had come to break down the enemy's last powers of resistance, and that meticulous adherence to theories which had been formed to meet quite other conditions was no longer in place.

One part of this ambitious programme had some success, for very shortly after the great attacks on Nancy were begun the German Crown Prince started an offensive against General Sarrail's right, which was gradually driven back across the Heights of the Meuse between Toul and Verdun, and so was produced in the French front the beginning of that curious indentation with its head on the Meuse near St. Mihiel which the Germans maintained until driven from it in September 1918 by the First American Army. But without the remaining concomitants of the plan this success proved harmless, and as early as the eve of September 6 the Germans had discovered that their castle in Spain was tumbling about their ears.

The left arm of the encircling movement had definitely failed before Nancy, and the right was found to be in a very dangerous position. Being good soldiers, far from holding up their hands in despair, they immediately shaped a plan to meet the situation. The greater part of the Second and Third Armies were, as arranged, to unite in a desperate effort to overwhelm Foch and burst through the French centre, and von Kluck, as his reinforcements from the south came into play, was to defeat Manoury, while the British and the French Fifth Army were kept occupied by comparatively weak forces.

This was a bold effort to retrieve the situation, and it promised, if successful, to give the Germans such a victory as would shatter the Franco-British left wing and leave Paris at the mercy of the conqueror. If Foch could be broken and driven back to the Seine, Sir John French and Franchet d'Espérey enticed slowly forward, while von Kluck, working round Manoury's northern flank, enveloped him and drove him back into Paris, then the British and the French Fifth Army, already sorely tried by hard fighting and a long retreat, would be caught between von Kluck and von Bülow and compelled either to fly precipitately or to accept battle under most unfavourable conditions.

There were no half-measures in this plan, but it could not be carried through unless Manoury were driven back into the defences of Paris and rendered harmless, for it must have been clear to the German leaders that if the French Sixth Army had been reinforced once it might be reinforced again, and that therefore a temporary check to Manoury would leave the danger to their rear unscotched. To strengthen the Fourth Reserve Corps with sufficient force to allow of the Ourcq being held against Manoury would have meant weakening the remainder of the First Army to an extent which would have compelled it to abandon attack, and to stand on the defensive along the Grand Morin against the British and the French Fifth Army. This would have had the effect of handing over the initiative on the western flank to the Allies, an alternative which nothing in the general situation, still apparently very favourable to their arms, would have been likely to justify in the minds of the German High Command. Accordingly, it was decided that Manoury should be crushed, and that, if necessary, such part of von Kluck's Army as was not required for this purpose should give ground before the British and the French Fifth Army.

For the realisation of this bold scheme, it was essential, first, that Foch should be smashed, and secondly, that the British Army should be held off long enough to allow von Kluck the time necessary to defeat Manoury thoroughly. Of these two essentials the second was the more important, for even if the plan to defeat Foch failed, von Kluck could, provided he overthrew the French Sixth Army, escape from the critical position in which he was placed, more troops could be brought south from Belgium and Maubeuge, which was on the point of falling, and the attack on the Allied left could be resumed after an unfortunate but by no means fatal delay. On the other hand, if the British were to come down upon von Kluck's flank and rear while Manoury still held the field then there would be nothing for it but retreat.

Von Kluck no doubt weighed the chances carefully, but he was apparently still under the influence of his early impressions of our army, which he regarded as a defeated and all but negligible force. He was also unaware of the extent of the reinforcements which Joffre and Gallieni had prepared for Manoury, and he seems to have counted upon having sufficient time to defeat the French Sixth Army if he struck hard with every man he could collect. He therefore sent both his Second and Fourth Corps northwards on the 6th from the British front, a decision which was evidently reached in great haste, for on the forenoon of the 6th our First Corps, advancing towards the Grand Morin, became aware of a column of German infantry moving southwards towards them. This column suddenly turned about and marched northwards without firing a shot, and it would seem that it had only then received information of the change of plan.

The British troops very naturally supposed that the enemy in front of them was in full retreat. They were destined to bring about the retreat of the First German Army, but these first backward movements of the enemy were, though we did not then know it, rather an alteration in the dispositions of the Germans on the battlefield than a retreat. Only von Marwitz's cavalry corps of three divisions was at first left to hold us back. But the German horsemen were not trained to fight on foot and to use the rifle to the same degree as our cavalry, and the small force of *Jägers* who accompanied them could not be everywhere, so von Marwitz was not able to delay us as von Kluck had hoped, which meant there was less time for the defeat of Manoury.

Not only was this so, but Manoury's Army was growing in strength, so that more and not less time was required to accomplish its defeat. We therefore find von Kluck continually adopting expedients to stay the British advance, now reinforcing von Marwitz with such stray infantry as he can get together, now sending him additional artillery, and towards the end borrowing more cavalry from his neighbour von Bülow.

The course of the battle is then that Manoury becomes more and more heavily engaged as von Kluck develops his strength against him, but being continually reinforced by the troops sent out from Paris is just able to hold his own. The British and the French Fifth Armies drive the Germans opposed to them steadily northwards, while Foch in the centre, fighting desperately and counter-attacking whenever he gets an opportunity, is slowly pushed back to the south of La Fère Champenoise.

September 8 was a critical day on the left flank. Manoury, very hard pressed throughout the morning and the afternoon, was forced to give ground, some of his troops, especially his gallant Seventh Corps which had been fighting since the beginning of the battle, were becoming exhausted, while his left was in danger of envelopment as Von Kluck deployed more and more troops upon his northern flank. During the day the Germans captured Betz and pressed forward towards Nanteuil, attacking at the same time the whole of Manoury's front as far south as the outskirts of Meaux. But the stream of reinforcements from Paris was flowing steadily north-east.

The Forty-Fifth Division had arrived on the 6th, as had one division of the Fourth Corps, which had gone to support the British left south of Meaux. The first of d'Amade's divisions came into action on the 7th, and now on the critical 8th the remaining division of the Fourth Corps, which had been rushed out of Paris by Galliéni in motor-buses and taxis the day before, was brought into line. Thus, the French Sixth Army was holding on gallantly, while the advance of the British and the Fifth Armies was now beginning to tell.

We entered Coulommiers early on the 7th, and found that von Kluck's Second Corps had left it in great haste the previous day. The little town had been thoroughly pillaged by the enemy, who had stolen such provisions and liquor as they could lay their hands upon, carried off any portable valuables, and ruthlessly smashed such as were guilty of the crime of being too large or too heavy for a German haversack. Throughout the day there were a number of engagements at various times along our front with the enemy's cavalry, who were everywhere thrown back. On the 8th we continued our advance northwards to the Petit Morin, where von Marwitz's cavalry, supported by infantry and some heavy artillery, made another stand in order to hold us up.

The Guard Rifles, (consisting of parts both of the Guard Jägers and Guard Schützen Regiments), brought up hastily in lorries, had entrenched a position along the river at Orly, and were told to hold it to the last, orders which they carried out to the letter when deserted by the German cavalry, for in the end we either killed or captured almost the whole of the force. Throughout the forenoon the enemy made resolute attempts to hold the line of the Petit Morin from Montmirail to its junction with the Marne at La Ferté-sous-Jouarre, but by noon after a stiff fight Allenby's cavalry with the help of Haig's infantry, had forced the passages of the river about ten miles to the west of Montmirail, and the German cavalry, fearing to be cut off on the Marne, retired, leaving their infantry, who were closely engaged with the heads of our infantry columns, to look after themselves.

The day ended with our troops well across the Petit Morin, having taken several hundred prisoners, and a few guns, while Franchet d'Espérey on our right also crossed the river with his left and drove back the Germans from Montmirail.

This first considerable capture of German prisoners had a most inspiriting effect upon our men, and the infantry, who a short time before would barely support the weight of their packs, now with the British soldier's passion for souvenirs merrily loaded themselves with the shakos of the Guard Rifles, with captured rifles and even with the heavy German greatcoats.

Von Kluck, on hearing that we had forced the Petit Morin, gave orders for the bridges over the Marne to be destroyed, but he was too late, and his cavalry could only blow up those at La Ferté-sous-Jouarre.

It was with great joy that our main columns advancing at dawn on the 9th found that not only were the bridges to the west of Château-Thierry intact, but that the enemy had made no attempt to hold this part of the Marne. (For the position on September 9 see Map 4.) The river here runs through a deep gully, the cliffs on the north bank being crowned with thick beech woods, from which the roads winding down to the bridges on the south side are in full view, and had the enemy posted a few guns and machine-guns in these woods it would have been a matter of great difficulty either to locate them exactly or to judge of his strength. The position was, in fact, admirably suited for delay, but von Marwitz's horses were exhausted, he had been given a bigger task than he could carry out, his men had been roughly handled the day before, and he was no longer capable even of attempting to close all the doors which opened upon von Kluck's flank and rear.

It was not until we were well established on the heights north of the river that the German guns opened upon us, and as early as 9 a.m. on the 9th our Second Corps had not only crossed the Marne, but the leading brigade of the Third Division was established more than four miles beyond the river, on the Château-Thierry-Lizy road, where it was well north of the latitude of von Kluck's left flank, which was fighting hard with Manoury across the Ourcq, twelve miles to the west. Had we then been able to press forward on the whole front we might well have cut off a considerable part of the German First Army.

But unfortunately, the First Corps on the right was delayed for some little time by a threat of attack on its flank from Chateau-Thierry, which was still held by the enemy, and was unable to come into line until the afternoon, and the Third Corps on the left, which was endeavouring to cross at La Ferté-sous-Jouarre, was checked at that place, both by the destruction of the bridges and by the enemy's defence of the line of the Marne at this point. The delay enabled the Germans to patch up some sort of defensive line across the bend of the Marne between Chateau-Thierry and Lizy. Von Richthofen's cavalry from the German Second Army came from the east to help the hard-pressed von Marwitz, while von Kluck reinforced his horse with hastily assembled infantry detachments, and swung round some of his heavy artillery to support them.

During the afternoon there was heavy fighting with this new German screen, in which the 1st battalion of the Lincolnshire Regiment had the honour of capturing the first battery of German howitzers which fell into our hands in this war. But long before this the presence of the British forces north of the Marne had taken effect. Von Kluck had at an early hour begun to press his envelopment of Manoury's left flank in a last attempt to complete the defeat of the French before we could intervene, and advancing from the direction of Betz had occupied Nanteuil.

It was a question of hours only whether this part of the German plan succeeded or not. Von Kluck's men were very near exhaustion, and for some days past, partly owing to the constant changes in the position of his troops, and partly to the fact that, while Maubeuge held out, the forwarding of supplies to the German right by rail was complicated and difficult, his supply arrangements had not worked smoothly, his men had not therefore been receiving their rations regularly, and many of the prisoners we captured complained that they were hungry.

More important still, Germany, like every other power engaged in the war, had under-estimated the enormous expenditure of ammunition which the prolonged battles of these days entail, and the supply of shells, which had been heavily drawn upon during the four days' struggle on the Ourcq, was running low. On the other hand, reinforcements in the shape of *Landstrum* and *Landwehr* troops sent south from garrison duty in Belgium were on their way to von Kluck, and some indeed had actually arrived, Manoury's troops were as exhausted as his own, he was making real progress round the French left, and a few hours more of resolute effort might yet give him such a victory as would banish all the troubles in which his rash advance across the Marne had involved him.

This was the situation when two pieces of news reached him. Gallieni, again collecting in Paris all the motor-buses, taxis, and lorries which the city could furnish, had sent out in them at an early hour to strengthen Manoury, and to assist in covering the retreat which the evening before had appeared to be inevitable, every soldier he could make available. So, his aviators reported to von Kluck that along the roads leading north-east from Paris convoys of motor vehicles of every conceivable type were streaming towards Manoury, at about the same time as he heard that the British had crossed the Marne and were threatening his rear. This combination was too much for him.

In less than three weeks the situation had been completely reversed, and he now found himself in very much the same position as that in which Sir John French had been placed by the arrival of Joffre's telegram at 5 p.m. on August 23. Before 11 a.m. von Kluck had thrown up the sponge, and ordered the retreat of his left and centre, an order extended a few hours later to his right, which in the interval was attacking fiercely, in order to cover the withdrawal of the remainder of the army.

Meanwhile on our right the French Fifth Army, steadily pushing before them the two corps which von Kluck had left behind when he marched against Manoury, at the same time overcame the right of von Bülow's Army and forced it to retire. These successes enabled Franchet d'Espérey to detach his right corps to the help of Foch, who throughout this period had been enduring the heaviest attacks from the left of von Bülow's Army and from von Hausen's Third Army. The arrival of this welcome help enabled Foch to draw back his Forty-Second Division, one of the two divisions of the "Iron Corps" which he had commanded and trained before the war, and to place it in reserve under his own hand.

Throughout these strenuous days he had been keenly watching for a chance to strike back at the enemy, and now the chance was forthcoming, and he had the troops to make use of the chance. On the morning of the 9th the Germans renewed their attacks both on Foch and on Langle de Gary, still in the hope of retrieving the situation by breaking through the French centre. But von Kluck's difficulties had been gradually pulling von Bülow more and more to the right, until at last he had not sufficient troops both to help his embarrassed comrade and to continue his attacks upon Foch.

Still, he had been steadily gaining ground against the French Ninth Army, and a little more might give him all he wanted, so that it was worth taking some risk to keep up the pressure. Therefore, to get the necessary troops von Bülow left a gap in his centre between La Fère Champenoise and the marshes of St. Gond.

The situation on the afternoon of the 9th was then that Franchet d'Espérey's Tenth Corps, coming at the critical time to Foch's help, had attacked and was slowly pushing back von Bülow's right, whose flank had become exposed by the retirement of von Kluck's left before the French Fifth Army; the left of Foch's Ninth Army was holding its own south of the marshes against portions of the Prussian Guard.

Then came the gap between the marshes and La Fere Champenoise, south of which von Bülow's left of the German Guard and the right of von Hausen's Army were pressing hard on, and gaining ground against, Foch's centre and right. Thus, the issue still hung in the balance, but Foch had his Forty-Second Division ready, and between 5 and 6 o'clock in the afternoon he flung it into the gap against the exposed flank of von Bülow's left wing.

This in one glorious charge it smashed to pieces, while at the same time the whole of Foch's line advanced to the attack. Under this double pressure from front and flank the German centre broke, turned, and streamed northwards, pursued far into the night under a deluge of rain, as a thunderstorm burst over the battlefield, by Foch's eager infantry. The Battle of the Marne was over, and by this crowning mercy the whole German line from Verdun westwards was compelled to follow the example of von Kluck's Army.

Much has been written about the miracle of the Marne, and I yield to no one in my admiration for Foch's generalship and the cool judgement which, after days of almost intolerable strain, he displayed in seizing at once upon the weak spot in the enemy's line and aiming at it, at exactly the right time, a blow which changed what would otherwise have been a limited success into complete victory.

Contemporary opinion has already done justice both to Foch's leadership and to the endurance and valour of his troops. Nor has there been any failure to recognise either the splendour of Manoury's resistance in face of von Kluck's desperate efforts, or Gallieni's resource and enterprise which contributed so much to the final victory. But nowhere yet, so far as I am aware, has justice been done to the part played by the British Army in this glorious episode. Our men were not called upon to fight as they had fought at Mons and at Le Cateau, nor as Foch's and Manoury's men had had to fight in this battle.

But I am convinced that history will decide that it was the crossing of the Marne in the early hours of the 9th by the British Army which turned the scale against von Kluck and saved Manoury at a time of crisis. At the time when we were crossing the Marne the French Sixth Army was very near the limits of its endurance, and, as I have already indicated, Gallieni had begun to take the measures necessary to prepare for a retreat. Manoury on the morning of the 9th had been forced to act defensively along his whole front, and though it is probable that von Kluck had realised by then that he could not overcome the gallant Frenchman in the time left to him, yet it cannot be maintained that an army on the defensive, however stout its resistance, can of itself compel an enemy to retire as fast and as far as did von Kluck's Army.

The left of the French Fifth Army did not reach the Marne until the evening, and therefore it can hardly have affected the German general's decision of the forenoon. Foch's blow at La Fere Champenoise was not struck until late in the afternoon, and it is impossible that the news of von Bülow's defeat could have reached von Kluck until late in the night; yet he had evacuated Betz as early as 11 a.m. and by 4 p.m., that is, before Foch's orders for his master-stroke had taken effect, both our cavalry and our airmen reported the German columns on our front were streaming northwards. It is therefore not possible to arrive at any other conclusion than that it was the menace of the British advance to his flank and rear which precipitated von Kluck's decision, caused the Germans to begin their retreat, and saved Manoury at a time when he was in grave danger.

The retreat from Mons is already a glorious page in the history of the British Army, but the advance after the retreat is certainly no less remarkable. That an army, which on August 23 had been all but surrounded by an enemy who outnumbered it by two to one, should have fought its way out, retreated 170 miles, and then immediately turned about and taken a decisive part in the battle which changed the course of the campaign of 1914, is as wonderful an achievement as is to be found in the history of war.

Amidst all the feats of endurance, courage, and (devotion which marked these memorable days, feats of which we have as yet heard but a very meagre tale, for many of the finest were performed by men who have spent long years of heart-breaking captivity in German prison camps and their stories have not been heard, there is nothing of which we may be prouder than of the behaviour of the men, and of the devotion to them of their officers and non-commissioned officers, not in the days of battle only, but in the far more trying days and nights of weary tramping in retreat.

At first the bonds of discipline were of necessity relaxed, small parties became separated from their own battalions and joined up with others which they did not know and where they were not known, individual stragglers who had dropped behind from exhaustion or had lost their way were frequent, and rations, despite the exertions of the Army Service Corps, could not always be got to the troops. There was every opportunity and excuse for excess, yet there was none, and it is not only in the rapid change from retreat to advance that the story of the retreat from Mons may challenge comparison with that of the retreat to Corunna.

I well remember on the morning of August 28 meeting in a small French town the commander of a company of a famous regiment, who, to my certain knowledge, had not in the previous sixty hours had more than a few odd snatches of sleep, and had passed the whole of the previous night tramping with his men. He had been told that he would have three hours' rest, and he spent the greater part of it in driving round the town in a light cart he had borrowed buying any food he could discover, and paying for it out of his own pocket such prices as the inhabitants liked to ask. This is one small example, but it is typical of the spirit of the British Army. It did not occur to this officer that he was doing anything out of the ordinary; his men had had no food since the previous morning, and his first duty was to look after his men.

The food might have been taken by force, and no one would have been the wiser, for the Germans would be in the town in a few hours and would help themselves without payment, but for the honour of Britain—I will not say of England for my friend was a Scot—and for the honour of the Army all things had to be done in order. He had told his men that he would get them a breakfast, so while he went marketing, they tightened their belts and waited patiently in the midst of comparative plenty, for the German advance had come like a bolt from the blue and the inhabitants had had little time to remove their stocks.

The Germans boast loudly of the iron discipline of their army, but when we compare the behaviour of their soldiers in retreat with that of our men in like circumstances, we may thank God that British discipline, which depends first and foremost on the relations between officer and man, is of a very different type, and rejoice that it stood better than the enemy's rigid rules the severest test which war can bring. Everywhere as we advanced, we found a trail of wanton destruction—the wine shops gutted, the village streets littered with broken bottles, household treasures too heavy to remove wantonly destroyed; and this time it was not the organised and systematic brutality which had ravished Belgium as part of a military plan, but the dissolution of order which left the German soldiery free to follow their natures and rob and pillage at will.

Before I close this chapter there is one criticism of our advance which must be met. Von Kluck took two whole corps away from the front which the British Army was directed by Joffre's order to attack, to fling them against Manoury, and it has been hinted in some quarters that the German was only able to do this because we failed to play our part. This is an assumption which is in no way warranted by the facts. On the afternoon of September 4 Joffre had requested Sir John French to move his army to the south of the forest of Crécy, because the French Fifth Army had again been compelled to fall back, and he required more room to the south of the Grand Morin to combine the operations of his Fifth Army with those of the new Ninth Army, which had come into line on Franchet d'Espérey's right.

So, it came about that on the morning of September 5, after marching all night, our main bodies were some fifteen miles southeast of Coulommiers. Now von Kluck became aware of his danger on the evening of September 5, and began to march his Second Corps northwards from Coulommiers at an early hour the next day. It was therefore clearly out of the power of the British Army, placed as it was, and with a strong screen of German cavalry between it and the Grand Morin, to have prevented this movement. It was, as I have said, unfortunate that we could not get more troops across the Marne in the early hours of the eventful 9th, for, could we have done so, we might have utterly smashed von Kluck's embarrassed left.

But Sir Douglas Haig, who was at the time well in advance of the French Fifth Army, was delayed by von Richthofen's movement from the east to support von Marwitz, just as the Third Corps was delayed by the broken bridges of the Marne. It was known that there were large German forces on our right, and an attack upon our right flank while our main bodies were in the act of crossing the Marne was just such a manoeuvre as the enemy might be expected to attempt in order to get himself out of his difficulties.

Had Sir Douglas Haig known that von Kluck had decided on retreat and that the force reported to be moving west from Château-Thierry was composed of cavalry coming to cover the retreat, he probably would not have checked his march, but he knew none of these things, and until he was more certain of the situation it would obviously have been the height of imprudence to risk the passage of an important river. Of such are the accidents of war. Neither Sir John French nor his corps commanders had, or could by any possibility have had, at the moment the knowledge of the situation which we now possess, and it is from the standpoint of what he knew at the time and how he acted upon his knowledge that a commander in war should be judged, not from the standpoint of knowledge collected after the event.

It needs small skill to be a general when all the enemy's plans and dispositions are exposed. Therefore, it is not in the light of what might have been achieved had the circumstances been different that the effect of the advance of the British Army must be judged, but rather by what was actually accomplished, and this, as I have tried to show, was no mean thing.

CHAPTER 9

The Higher Command in War

My object in the foregoing chapters has been to explain the part taken by our original expeditionary force in the first phase of the war, and to display the strong and weak points in the German armour. Owing to the surprise achieved by the German General Staff, Sir John French's Army had to meet the full weight of the instrument which the enemy had designed to be the chief means of carrying to complete victory his campaign in the West—von Kluck's Army. Our officers and men had been taught in peace time that decisive results in war can only be obtained by attack, and that the defensive is the refuge of the weak.

Looking hopefully to the relief of Belgium by an offensive campaign, they had been thrown at once upon the defence, and their first experience of modern European war was hurried retreat. They saw at once something had gone very wrong with the Allied plans. Moreover, when Joffre, pivoting on Verdun, was compelled to swing back the northern section of his line, we on the outer flank had to carry out the longest retreat, in the most exposed position, and in face of an enemy of not less than twice our strength. It is the highest possible tribute to the quality and training of the Old Army that in these circumstances it not only retained its moral and cohesion, but played a leading part in bringing to naught the enemy's dreams of a rapid conquest of France.

It saved the French Fifth Army from destruction, when, standing alone at Mens, it drew upon itself von Kluck's attack. If the First German Army had been able to come down upon de Lanrezac's flank when he was retreating before von Bülow from the battlefield of the Sambre, the Germans might well have succeeded in their ambition of rolling up the French line from the left.

Looking back now at the situation in which we were placed on the morning of August 24, it seems almost incredible that we should have escaped destruction. No less marvellous is it that Sir Horace Smith-Dorrien's force should on the 26th have been able to break off in broad daylight a battle with an enemy of more than twice its strength and five days later have been in a condition to fight again with effect. That the German leaders misjudged the situation and missed chances which now appear obvious does not detract from the achievement of our men. The chances were missed because the enemy's plans were upset by cool leadership in almost desperate circumstances, and by the dogged and skilful fighting of the British soldier, who surprised the enemy, first by the unexpected vigour of his resistance, and then by his no less unexpected recovery.

The German plan of envelopment was finally foiled when von Kluck, after changing direction and making forced marches southeastwards from Amiens to cut off the French Fifth Army from the Marne, came upon us on September 1 an organised and formidable force. The enemy's plan of campaign was fundamentally changed by that encounter with an army which he thought he had completely defeated. The march round had become impossible, and its place had to be taken by the break through, and so the first Battle of the Marne was brought about. Our army had in the interval helped to gain time for Joffre to prepare his scheme of counter-attack after his first offensive plans had collapsed. When the counter-attack came we saved Manoury, as we had saved de Lanrezac, were the first of the Allied forces to cross the Marne in pursuit of the enemy, and were one of the main factors in bringing about von Kluck's retreat to the Aisne.

I have in discussing the events of the retreat from Mons tried to make clear where and how the German leaders failed in the execution of their plan. There was nothing in the way in which von Kluck turned to account the position of overwhelming superiority in which he was placed on the morning of August 23 to compare in paint of generalship with Sir John French's extrication of his army from the jaws of destruction. Armies have in the past been placed in situations almost equally perilous, but I can recall no instance in which they have escaped with so little damage to themselves and so much loss to the enemy, nor any in which they have passed so quickly from retreat to an advance against their pursuers.

There was nothing in Moltke's manoeuvring of his armies, when once battle was joined, which bears comparison with the manner in which Joffre, with the fate of his country and of Europe on his shoulders, quietly and calmly picked up the broken threads of his first plans, and wove them afresh into a formidable and successful scheme of attack. There was no German general who, in these opening battles of the war, showed a glimpse of such inspiration as Foch displayed in his counter-stroke at La Fère Champenoise.

No, it was not by generalship in the field and by the way in which their generals dealt with the daily changes in the military situation that the Germans won their initial advantage in the West, and yet they did win such advantages as all the efforts of the Allies from the beginning of 1915 until the summer of 1918 failed to wrest from them.

They carried the war into the country of their enemies, overran Belgium, occupied the rich industrial districts of Northern France, and while doing this held off the Russian hosts. In population, wealth, manufacturing capacity, and even in the strength of their naval and military forces, the Central Powers were, at the outbreak of war, in the aggregate inferior to their enemies. If their generals were not superior to the Allied commanders in qualities of leadership, and their troops in no way pre-eminent in valour, how did they gain the preponderating position which they held for so long?

The Germans schemed for this war, devoted long years to preparation for it, and entered it thoroughly organised for a struggle of nations. That is universally recognised. We have more than paid a just tribute to the capacity of our chief enemy for organisation. Yet, save in one respect, we have proved ourselves to be at least his equal. Given the fact that we had never grasped the meaning of a war for national existence, that we did not want war at all, and were in no way ready for it, our achievements in organisation are in no way inferior to his. We have done what he believed to be impossible, in raising and placing in the field new armies many times as strong as the forces which we maintained in time of peace. We have kept open for ourselves and our Allies the sea communications of the world.

Our financial organisation has from the first been superior to his. In our arrangements for the control of our food supply we have notably improved upon the methods of Germany. The enemy has produced no weapon or device applicable to modern war which we have not at least equalled, and in most cases surpassed. We have often been lamentably slow in getting to work, but in all these cases we have shown no lack of organising power when the matter was really taken in hand. The one respect in which we have failed has been in the organisation of our Higher Command. By this I do not mean merely the arrangements for the control of our naval and military forces, but rather the machinery for the co-ordination of policy with naval and military strategy, machinery which I may call, in short, the government of the war.

The elder Moltke was, as the result of his experiences in 1870, the first to perceive that Napoleon's aphorism "in war men are nothing, the man is everything" did not apply absolutely to the nation in arms. He realised that the importance of organisation in times of peace had enormously increased, and believed, as his successors have believed, that the nation which was best organised could obtain such a start as no efforts made during the course of a war by laggards in preparation could make good.

He saw that armies numbering millions could not be influenced by the personality of their general-in-chief in the way in which Napoleon influenced his armies, that there would be less scope for the intervention of the Higher Command on the battlefield, and more need for careful planning before battle was joined. Lastly, he grasped the essential fact that in a war for national existence it would no longer be a question of employing military force to the best advantage but of combining the whole power of the nation, the whole political, diplomatic, naval, military, financial, and industrial strength of the country for the defeat of the enemy. Such a burden could not be borne by any one man, and therefore he designed to assist and, in some measure, to replace the man by a system.

It is unnecessary for me here to describe in detail the constitution and organisation of the German General Staff. This has long ago been admirably done by Professor Spenser Wilkinson in his little book *The Brain of an Army*. My purpose is to sketch briefly the working of the system in relation to the supreme control in time of war. The basis of the system is the separation of administration from command, that is, of responsibility for what I may call the business side of war from responsibility for the planning and conduct of military operations. The planning side presents to the business side its estimate of what is needed to ensure the success of any given campaign or operations in men, transport, supplies, munitions, and material of all kinds.

If the bill cannot be met the plan is bad, and has to be modified to fit in with the available resources. The planning side is so organised that there are selected and trained experts to deal with the details of any particular problem which may arise. The work of these experts is co-ordinated by higher authority and presented to the head of the whole organisation in a reasoned form. It is then the business of the chief to see that plans so prepared in accordance with his instructions are made known, as far as may be necessary, to such other departments of state as may be affected, and to present to the supreme authority of the state a complete proposal as to military policy, for the execution of which he is responsible when it has been accepted. The chief point of the system is that one man and one man only is in a position to advise the supreme authority in this manner, and he is the Chief of the General Staff, who alone has at his disposal the machinery for preparing considered advice, and for supervising the execution of the approved policy.

Moltke said of his system towards the end of his career that it would aid a genius if Germany were so fortunate as to possess a genius in time of need, and could be worked effectively by a man of ordinary capacity who had been trained to understand and use it. He held that no system of control in war could be sound which depended for success on the accident of a genius being at hand when required, and that modern national life was so complex that no genius could, without the help of a complete and scientific organisation, make full use of its potentialities for war. In an outburst of complacence he said, in reviewing his life work, that he had left his country a system of command which no other nation could equal.

He has proved to have been very nearly but fortunately not quite right. He did not foresee the evils which result from placing in the hands of an autocratic authority such an instrument as an all-powerful and highly organised General Staff. He did not foresee that Prussian Junkerdom would use the instrument which he had created to further its own base ends. Both he and Bismarck, neither of them unduly troubled by conscience, as the piece of trickery by which they brought about the war of 1870 shows, must have turned many times in their graves at the stupidity of their successors in ranging the rest of the civilised world against the Central Powers.

He did not foresee a war of such length as would give the enemies of Germany time to make good their defects in preparation. He did not foresee that his system, too rigidly applied by ordinary men, brought up in blind faith in its efficacy, would limit their power of dealing with the unexpected and weaken their initiative in the field. The German system of command has not escaped the evil which has affected the whole national life of Germany, the evil against which we are fighting, but its underlying principles are none the less sound, and despite all the errors which our enemies have made in its application, it remains a terribly effective instrument for the conduct of war.

If we turn our minds back to what we expected Germany to achieve when she forced the world into war, and compare this with what she actually accomplished in 1914, if we reflect that it was not fighting or generalship in the field but careful planning and organisation which placed the German Armies in the position of overwhelming superiority in which they found themselves when they first met the Allied forces in the West, if we consider that it was again planning and organisation which were near giving Germany complete success in the spring of 1918, when she once more sought to decide the war in the West, we must admit that a system which can produce such results at least merits respectful consideration. (It was the planning and preparation during the previous winter, as much as the transference of troops from the Eastern front to the Western, which led to Germany's success in March, 1918.)

We have, as I have already pointed out, learned much from the enemy in this war. Where his weapons proved superior to our own, we have copied or improved upon them. We have carefully studied his tactical methods and gained by the study. It is therefore logical that we should also study his methods of conducting war, taking from them for our use what is good and rejecting what is evil. Yet in this respect we have lagged behind, and constructed slowly and painfully a machinery of our own without sufficiently profiting by the experience we have gained or by the example which the enemy has set us.

All European Armies, and ours among the rest, have adapted the German General Staff's system in one form or another, to their own special conditions, but we have not yet succeeded in welding the General Staff system into the machinery of government in time of war. We still as a nation are unable to distinguish the essential difference between the military opinion of individual soldiers and the military opinion of the responsible head of a scientific organisation. We still confound command and administration, to the detriment of both. We began in August 1914 with the mistaken notion that we could go into European war with a limited liability. For a war of limited liability our preparations were adequate. The mobilisation and despatch to France of our little Expeditionary Force were completed smoothly and efficiently, thanks to devoted work at the War Office, carried through in face of great difficulties.

Owing to the labours of the Committee of Imperial Defence the

Departments of State knew what they would be required to do in such a war. But it occurred to no one in authority that our system of government in time of peace would require profound modification in time of war, and no one had thought out what form such modification should take. Relying on the individual rather than the system, the nation placed at the head of its military administration the soldier in whom it had the greatest confidence, and was for a time content.

Fortunately for ourselves and for Europe Lord Kitchener proved himself at once to be a man of wider vision and sounder judgement, on the broad issues of the war, than any other statesman either in our own, in Allied, or in enemy countries. He at once scouted the theory of limited liability, and set to work to organise the Empire for a prolonged struggle, thereby saving both us and our Allies.

Unfortunately, almost the whole of Lord Kitchener's military and administrative career had been spent in the outer parts of the Empire, He was unfamiliar with our methods of government, and had not been brought into touch with the modern General Staff system. He had placed upon his shoulders the intolerable burden of administration and of command. He had at one and the same time to undertake the tasks of raising us to the rank of a first-rate military power and of acting as the supreme military adviser to the Government on the conduct of the war. He did not himself realise until after he had been for some considerable time in office that this system was wrong, and by the time he did realise it, it had already broken down. The Dardanelles Commission puts the matter clearly and tersely in the following words:

> We are of opinion that Lord Kitchener did not sufficiently avail himself of the services of his General Staff, with the result that more work was undertaken by him than was possible for one man to do, and that confusion and want of efficiency resulted. (Dardanelles Commission, First Report, 1917.)

The Commission might have added that on the principle of limited liability the General Staff at the War Office, considering that there would be no scope for its energies in London, had been transferred almost in a body to France.

Lord Kitchener had, owing to his reputation and strength of character, a commanding position in the councils of the State, and this had the unfortunate result that many who realised that something was wrong came to the conclusion that the fault lay in giving a soldier too much authority rather than in the defects in the machinery of government. Our principle of government in time of peace has always been to place authority in the hands of men who are not experts, to leave them free to consult such experts as they wished, and to draw their own conclusions after hearing the opinions of these experts.

This will not work in time of war, because, as I have explained, under any properly organised system of military command there can only be one expert who is in a position to give authoritative and responsible military advice to the Government. Our troubles in this war have arisen, not because our governments have neglected to take military advice, but almost invariably because they have not confined themselves to the right kind of military advice. If Ministers seek advice on the conduct of war from a number of soldiers, taking this man's advice on one point, and that man's on another, they are impressed chiefly by each individual soldier's power of expressing himself, and of urging his views, and not by the one consideration which gives his advice value, namely, whether it is the result of careful and detailed examination of all the factors involved in the problem in question.

Only the soldier with the machinery at his disposal to enable him to conduct such an examination can, the conditions of war being such as they now are, give advice as it should be given; the others may occasionally be right, they will more often be wrong. Under any other system Ministers have themselves to piece together a mosaic of military policy, and this they have not the necessary technical knowledge to do, while they are tempted almost irresistibly to select from each adviser that advice which suits best their preconceived ideas and policy.

An extreme instance of the weakness of our system of conducting war is the manner in which the decision to advance to Baghdad in the autumn of 1915 was reached. The Government had before them the opinion of the general on the spot, who looked at the matter from the local point of view, but who was not adequately equipped with the means of forming an opinion as to the forces which the enemy could bring to his theatre of war from elsewhere. They consulted the Commander-in-Chief in India, who was not responsible for the collection of information about the Turkish forces, which was the business of the General Staff at the War Office. They consulted the General Staff at the War Office, which was not responsible for the conduct of these operations, and was not fully informed of the condition of the troops or the state of the transport. They consulted the Military Secretary at the India Office, who was not responsible in any way for the conduct of the campaign. In all this galaxy of advisers there was not one in a position to review the whole problem, and to propose a plan which took all the factors into account.

The Mesopotamia Commission summed up the matter as follows:

> The dual system under which London and Simla tried to conduct the campaign in Mesopotamia has obvious drawbacks. The chain of responsibility is greatly lengthened by the number of authorities who had necessarily to be consulted, and who had a voice in the direction of affairs. We will enumerate the various authorities who had to be consulted with regard to the Mesopotamian Expedition: first the General Officer commanding on the spot in Mesopotamia, then the Commander-in-Chief in India, then the Viceroy, then the Secretary of State for India, with his Military Secretary, then the War Council, with the Imperial Staff, and finally the Cabinet Such a subdivision of authoritative control must weaken the sense of responsibility of each authority consulted, and it certainly has made it very difficult accurately to apportion blame or credit. It was under the dual system of control that the administrative failures took place during 1915 in Mesopotamia, and it was not until London took over sole charge that there was any marked improvement in the management of the campaign. The improvement and success since effected are a striking illustration of the all-importance of unity of control in time of war. (Mesopotamia Commission, Report, 1917.)

We have travelled some distance since those days, but still not far enough. We have solved the complex problem of unity of command in France, with results which are patent to everyone, but we have still to accept the principle of unity of advice at home. I doubt if there is any responsible British statesman today who would not say that it is not only his right but his duty to call in a second opinion when he is in doubt. As recently as May 1918 a Member of the War Cabinet said that in this very case of the Mesopotamian campaign the cause of our troubles lay in placing too much authority in the hands of the soldiers, and if this statement represents the views of the Government, it shows that the Commission has laboured in vain.

★★★★★★★★★★★★

I myself had bitter experience of it in India, and anyone who had read the Mesopotamian Report would see the results of setting up a military administration practically independent of civil control. (Lord Curzon speaking at Caxton Hall, May 19, 1918).

★★★★★★★★★★★★

Ministers feeling deeply their responsibility and their ignorance of strategy are naturally loth to place themselves unreservedly in the hands of a soldier. Yet the acceptance of the principle of unity of advice does not debar the Government from obtaining any opinions or any views which it may desire to hear; it merely ensures that all opinions and views are presented to it through one channel, so that they may be tested, examined, and criticised in relation to other plans and proposals. It means, in short, system and organisation.

System and organisation will not eliminate the human factor, but they will reduce, if they cannot abolish, the chances of error. The most perfect General Staff will make mistakes in war, because the conduct of war still depends largely upon guessing what the enemy is thinking and planning, and the best generals or the best staff can only hope to guess right more often than they guess wrong. Any human organisation depends for efficiency on the character and personality of its chief, and none more so than an organisation for the conduct of war.

Further, it is of the very first importance that there should be the most complete trust and confidence between the Government and their military adviser, and if they should be limited to one consultant at a time there should be no limit to their choice of that consultant. If the Government is not satisfied with the advice which they receive, the remedy is to change the adviser, not to seek a second opinion. In one important respect we have drifted backwards, since the Secretary of State for War has again been made responsible to the Government and to Parliament both for the administration of our military forces and for the conduct of the war. This change has been made on Constitutional grounds.

But surely the principle of our Constitution is that Ministers should be responsible to Parliament, and it cannot be a serious subversion of this principle that the Chief of the Imperial General Staff should report directly to, and be responsible to, the War Cabinet, who in turn are responsible to Parliament. There is nothing of militarism in such an arrangement, which strengthens rather than weakens the authority of the Civil Government: there lurks behind it no peril to our liberties.

Either the Secretary of State for War's responsibility for the conduct of military operations is real, in which case he is overburdened, just as Lord Kitchener was overburdened, for the supervision of the administration of our huge armies and all that it involves is more than sufficient to occupy the energies of the veriest glutton for work, or it is nominal, in which case it is a farce. From a military point of view there are very real advantages in placing the commanders-in-chief in the field in direct communication with the military adviser to the Government. Such a system defines responsibility and would avoid so absurd a situation as that in which Mr. Chamberlain was placed by the report of the Mesopotamia Commission. Mr. Chamberlain was held to be responsible for the conduct of operations in Mesopotamia, but it is quite obvious that, under the system as it existed, he did not and could not exercise any real control, and that he could not have acted otherwise than he did act. He was the victim of our neglect to organise on scientific, lines a central control of the war.

At the present time this central control is vested in a War Cabinet, which is concerned not only with war policy but with the domestic policy of the whole Empire. We have been told that this Cabinet meets on an average more than once a day throughout the year. It is often concerned with the gravest social and political problems which have no direct bearing on the conduct of the war, and in these circumstances, one wonders what time the members can have for quiet thinking about the essential question, how to obtain victory in the shortest possible time. The War Cabinet is composed of ministers without portfolios, not in direct touch with the great War Departments of State, and it is necessary that its members should be kept constantly informed upon all naval and military questions.

This entails the attendance of their naval and military advisers at almost every meeting, and therefore seriously curtails the time which those advisers are able to give to the consideration of the problems of naval and military strategy which are their special province. In fact, just as responsibility is over-centralised in the Secretary of State for War, so it is over-centralised in the War Cabinet. What we require is a Great General Headquarters for the Empire, charged wholly and solely with the conduct of the war, and responsible for the co-ordination of political, naval, and military effort for the defeat of the enemy.

Such a body, composed of the heads of the various War Departments, with the Prime Minister in the chair, and with the chiefs of the naval, military, and air staffs directly responsible to it, would not require to meet daily, for its members, being, for the most part, ex officio conversant with the course of the war, would not require to meet for the purpose of keeping abreast of events, but solely for the purpose of deciding on important questions of war policy and strategy. Such questions do not arise daily, and they should, if the organisation is sound, be questions rather concerning the distant future than current events. An organisation which has time to think, plan, and prepare should rarely be surprised, and there is no surer indication of defective government in war than the need for hasty measures to meet unforeseen emergencies.

We have come to regard "muddling through" as an inevitable factor in our conduct of war, and after each war we tinker with the army and hope that things will be better next time. We have consistently failed to recognise that the cause of our failures is defective machinery for control of affairs, in the widest sense, in time of war. Occasionally some statesman has grasped this fact, and said with a sigh that the British Constitution cannot be adapted to the conduct of war. This is not the case. If it were we might well despair of the future of the British Democracy, for a system of government which is incapable of dealing with war as it would deal with pestilence or any of the great social evils stands condemned.

The plain fact is that no British statesman had before this war ever given his mind to the conduct of a national war, and when national war came our rulers have been too busy in meeting the emergencies of the day to give time to the solution of this by no means insoluble problem. To solve it we do not require any revolution half so drastic as that which placed the whole government of the country in the hands of a committee of six, but we do require to meet an organised enemy by counter-organisation.

Everything that I have said here as to the conduct of military operations applies with equal force to naval operations, and still more to the combination of both. We, the greatest sea power in the world, have made but one attempt in this war to employ naval and military force in co-operation, and that, owing to the neglect of the first principles of organisation in war, was a failure. Military strategy is to the amateur more fascinating than a chess problem, and in appearance not more difficult to grasp. Naval strategy is too technical, too closely affected by the mighty forces of nature to be congenial to the dabbler. The maintenance of the vast land forces of these days touches every aspect of national life, and five voters are personally affected by a national army to one whom a national navy concerns.

So, the army is subjected to a perpetual inquisition; the plant is continually being pulled up to see how the roots are growing, while the navy is left to itself, and the combined power of the navy and army is neglected. We shall never make the best and fullest use of our whole power either for war or for peace until those responsible for its direction have time to think, and the means to translate their thoughts rapidly and effectively into action. The whole of the War Cabinet and most of its servants are overworked, and an organisation which is overworked is defective. We have in the end gained complete victory, but we could have gained it more quickly had our governments been organised for war.

We alone of the Allies have conducted campaigns in three continents. No other of the nations engaged in this world war has been confronted by naval and military problems of such variety and complexity as we have been. None, therefore, needed a more carefully-thought-out organisation, and none has one which is so ill-adapted to the waging of war. We owe it alike to the men who have fallen, to those who have fought and won, and to posterity to put this matter right. If we learn from our experiences in the war to appreciate the value of scientific organisation, we shall not have fought in vain. If we do not, we shall not establish such a peace as we desire.

The Last Four Months

Contents

Preface	143
What Went Before	145
Foch *Versus* Ludendorff	176
The Preparation for Armageddon	198
Armageddon	222
Ludendorff Tries to Rally	258
The Last Push	273

Preface

Who won the war? is a question that has been often asked. In the countries of all the great Allied Powers there have been found those who answered it to their own satisfaction as patriots, because it is easy to demonstrate that the war would not have been won, as and when it was won, had any of those countries failed to do what it actually achieved. Most of us, however, are agreed that victory was the result of combination, and I am convinced that that opinion will grow stronger the better the story is known. During the struggle the news we received of the doings of the Armies of our Allies was naturally even more limited than was that of the doings of our own men, and it was not easy to allot to each its place in the general scheme.

In this book I have sought to give a picture of Foch's great campaign and to sketch in due proportion the parts which went to make up the whole. The splendour of the achievements of our army is, I believe, enhanced when they are given their proper place in the frame. I have reduced my descriptions of the battles to the simplest terms, because my object is to explain the broad causes of success and of failure, and there is danger in entering into details of operations on so vast a scale of losing sight of the wood for the trees. As no story of a campaign can be complete unless it describes the intentions, aims and feelings of the enemy, at least at the most critical periods, I have collected the best information available on these points from captured documents or from publications in Germany.

Fortunately, there has in that country been considerable public discussion between Hindenburg, Ludendorff and their critics as to the conduct of the former during the period with which I am here chiefly concerned, and material has not been lacking. Ludendorff's Reminiscences have appeared while this book was in the press. I have throughout referred to the German edition, as at the time I write the English translation has not been published. I owe grateful thanks to

Captain C. T. Atkinson for kindly reading the proofs and for many valuable suggestions.

F. Maurice.

London,
August, 1919.

Chapter 1

What Went Before

In Europe 1917 was a year of disappointment for the arms of the Allies; only in Asia, where our earlier ventures had failed, did fortune smile on us. At the beginning of that year Ludendorff and Hindenburg brought off their first *coup* on the Western Front, when they withdrew the German forces from the awkward position in which they were placed as the result of the first Battle of the Somme, and retired behind the Hindenburg line, which then first became famous. By this manoeuvre they checked the plans of the Allies and brought about the failure of General Nivelle's great offensive upon which such high hopes had been set. The result of this failure had been to throw a great strain upon the British Army, which had to obtain for the French the time to recover.

In the Battle of Arras, we had won the greatest success yet gained by British arms in France, but Haig had been forced to continue that battle to the stage when, the enemy having recovered from his first shock, progress was slow and losses were heavy. In June Plumer had brilliantly cleared the Messines Ridge and obliterated the Ypres salient, which for nearly three years had been a sore spot on our front; but the French still needed relief, and at the end of July the long, slow struggle which ended on the Passchendaele Ridge had begun. (*Vide* also *Plumer & Messines* by Sir Charles Harington, John Buchan & Francis Dodd; Leonaur, 2023.) Then, just at the time when the German forces had been so weakened by that battle that there was good prospect of reaping at Cambrai the fruits of the year's campaign, there had come the surprise of Caporetto, the collapse of the Italian Army on the Isonzo, its retreat with very heavy losses to the Piave, and the dispatch of large forces from France to the help of our Ally.

In this year the Germans committed one of their cardinal blunders in proclaiming unlimited U-boat warfare, which added decisively to the number of their foes; but the consequences to themselves of that blunder were not immediate, while we at once saw our sea communications endangered and our people threatened with very serious privation if not starvation. In Mesopotamia Maude overcame the Turkish Army at Kut and drove their beaten troops through Baghdad, while Allenby ended the year's campaigns with a triumph at Gaza and Beersheba and with the capture of Jerusalem. (*Vide* also *Mons, Anzac & Kut* by Aubrey Herbert; Leonaur, 2010.) But history will certainly count the entry of the United States of America into the war and the Russian Revolution as the two outstanding events of 1917, the two events which exercised the most far-reaching influence upon the course of the war.

Early in the year it had become apparent to the military authorities of the Allies that the results of the Russian Revolution would be felt before the military power of the United States could become effective on the Western Front. In short, it was clear that the Germans were going to get a start in the race, just as they got a start in 1914, and that consequently the Allies would be faced with a period of danger in which they would have to stand on the defensive.

At a meeting of the Allied Commanders-in-Chief and chiefs of staff held in Paris in June, 1917, to consider the military policy of the Allies in these circumstances, it was recommended that some machinery should be established to ensure "unity of command." This was by no means the first time that this question had been mooted. In quite early days in the war various tentative proposals had been put forward with the object of ensuring better control and greater unity of action amongst the forces of the Allies, but the political difficulties had always proved insuperable.

Soon after Mr. Lloyd George became Prime Minister of Great Britain, a serious attempt was made to reach a practical solution at a conference between the French and British Governments at Calais in February, 1917, and for the great offensive campaign planned for the spring of that year on the Western Front the French Commander in Chief, General Nivelle, was given complete control. Unfortunately, the failure of General Nivelle's campaign gave a setback to "unity of command," and encouraged those who were opposed to it in the belief that it was not desirable to place the army of one nation directly under the command of the general of another. It was not then recognised that there was a very important difference between entrusting the supreme command to the commander-in-chief of one army, whose mind and thoughts must necessarily be chiefly concerned with his own men and his own front, and placing it in the hands of one man who could stand back and look upon the front as a whole, free from the burden of the special charge of any one part of it.

Also, there was the question of finding the one man. Nivelle had failed, Joffre was on the shelf, and Foch was still under the shadow of his failure to take the Vimy Ridge in 1915. Thus, in spite of the recommendations of the Allied generals, nothing was done until the disaster to the Italian Army at Caporetto produced a crisis.

Mr. Lloyd George, with his usual energy in an emergency, then proposed that a conference should be held between the British, French and Italian Governments for the purpose of establishing an Allied organisation for the better control of the war. That conference was held in November, 1917, at Rapallo, on the Italian frontier, and it was then that the Supreme War Council, commonly known as the Versailles Council, was established. One of the objects of that step was to put the conferences of the Allied statesmen on a surer and more business-like basis than had up till then existed. Before the Versailles Council was instituted the Allied Governments used to confer at irregular intervals when they had important questions to discuss, but there was no organisation available to prepare beforehand the business for such meetings or to supervise the execution of the decisions which were reached.

For these reasons the Versailles Council supplied an obvious need and was a step in the right direction; but it did not and could not provide the means of exercising effective military command. In the first place the Council had no executive authority; it could only advise. In the second place the military representatives who formed the main part of the permanent organisation of the Council were each of them responsible to their own Governments, and had to refer back all important questions for the instructions of those Governments. Therefore, decisions could only be reached slowly and after discussion, whereas in war it is essential that military decisions should be taken quickly and in accordance with one clear policy.

The military side of the Versailles organisation was of value in collecting and bringing together information from each of the Allied Armies. This enabled it to tender general advice as to the policy to be followed several months ahead, but it was quite incapable of dealing with day-to-day emergencies or of issuing orders to the Allied Commanders-in-Chief.

After the Versailles Council was established at Rapallo Mr. Lloyd George came home through Paris, where he made the famous speech in which he commented scathingly on the conduct of the war by the Allies. He asserted that each of the weaker members of the Alliance had been sacrificed in turn, while France and Great Britain were knocking their heads against what he termed the impenetrable barrier in the West. This speech aroused a great deal of criticism. That criticism was mainly of two kinds. There were those who realised that the Versailles Council did not provide for the danger which was facing us, that it did not, in fact, produce effective "unity of command." These critics were not opposed to "unity of command," but were opposed to what they regarded as an inadequate measure.

The second group of critics was opposed to the Versailles Council because they were suspicious of any weakening of the control of Parliament over the army, and they regarded an attempt to place the military forces of the Allies under an international organisation as a blow at the sovereign rights of the people. This group may be regarded as composed of out and out opponents of "unity of command" in any form. A good deal of confusion was caused by lumping these two bodies of critics together and by classing the many soldiers who desired "unity of command," but refused to recognise the Versailles Council as a practical military organisation, with those who were opposed to "unity of command" mainly for political reasons.

While these discussions were going on the Germans were acting, and from the beginning of November onward they were moving troops from the Russian to the French front as fast as their trains could carry them. It was calculated that the Germans would be able to increase their strength on the Western Front between the beginning of November and the end of April by not less than a million and a half of men, and that they would be able to bring over a very large number of aeroplanes and heavy guns which they would no longer require on the Eastern Front. In these circumstances the military authorities of the Allies began pressing their governments for more effective measures to meet the coming blow, and amongst those measures there was a demand for something better calculated to ensure "unity of command" than the Versailles Council.

Keen observers in the United States of America, standing at a greater distance from the war and able to take a calmer and more general view of the whole vast conflict, had long been insisting on the need for really effective unified control, and at the time of the

Rapallo conference the United States Government had proposed that the Versailles Council should be vested with executive authority. The French Government was frankly in favour of the appointment of a *generalissimo*, but as this office would naturally fall to a French general there was some reluctance to appear to force it upon an Ally, and Mr. Lloyd George was not ready to go so far.

This, then, was the direction in which matters were moving at the beginning of 1918, when a conference was held at Versailles to consider the Allied plan of campaign for that year. At that conference it was decided to form an Executive Military Council, composed of a French, a British, an American and an Italian general, with General Foch as chairman, and that this body should be given authority to co-ordinate the strategy of the Allied commanders-in-chief, to create a general reserve to be under its control, and to employ that reserve in accordance with the needs of the situation.

The institution of this body produced another crisis, for the British Chief of the Imperial General Staff, Sir William Robertson, objected that no committee could exercise effective command, and he asked to be permitted to resign rather than to work with it. The British Government offered him the alternative of becoming the British representative on the Executive Council or of remaining as Chief of the Staff and working with the Executive Council. Sir William Robertson replied that, as he did not believe that the Executive Council could be an efficient military organisation, he could not work with it in either capacity, and his resignation was accordingly accepted.

These various events all produced the impression that British soldiers were in general opposed to "unity of command." In fact, however, many of them Had long been working hard to find some solution of the difficulties which stood in the way of the realisation of what they regarded as a necessary measure. The majority of them were, however, certainly opposed to what they considered to be an ineffective compromise. The history of war teaches that committees have never been able to command, that they lead invariably to delay and compromise, and these things are fatal in war. The Austrian Aulic Council and the Dutch Field Deputies of the War of the Spanish Succession have been deservedly held up to ridicule by all history, and most soldiers were whole-heartedly opposed to proposals which appeared to savour of the repetition of such ill-advised measures.

However, the length of the war, its enormous cost in life and treasure, the many failures of the Allied generals, and the fact that the hopes which they had expressed had been very rarely fulfilled, all tended to confirm the statesmen in their view that what was needed was more effective political control. A single commander-in-chief would naturally possess a position of far greater authority even in his own country than would a committee, while the influence of a foreign government upon the commander-in-chief who commanded their troops would be very limited indeed.

When to those who held these views was added the influence of those who looked with suspicion upon "unity of command" as constitutionally an unsound measure there were very strong forces arrayed on behalf of the compromise. So, as the crisis approached, the supreme direction of the military forces of the Allied and Associated Powers in the Western theatres of war was in the hands of a polyglot committee, each member of which was responsible to a separate government, and immediately this committee set to work its clumsy machinery began to creak.

Then suddenly the blow came. On March 21 forty German divisions were flung against the fourteen divisions of the British Fifth Army, which was driven back. By March 25 there appeared to be great danger that the Germans would succeed in capturing Amiens and in separating the British from the French Army. By that time almost the whole of the British reserves had been drawn into the fight, and Sir Douglas Haig did not feel that he was strong enough to ensure the safety both of Amiens and of the Channel ports, while General Pétain was doubtful whether he could send Sir Douglas Haig sufficient troops to make Amiens safe and at the same time secure his own front and cover Paris.

It was a grim crisis, probably the most serious of all the many crises with which the Allies had been faced in the course of the war. It happened that at this time Lord Milner, the Secretary of State for War, and General Sir Henry Wilson, the new Chief of the Imperial General Staff, were in France, having gone there to report to the British Government and to concert with the French Government upon such measures as seemed best in the emergency. Sir Douglas Haig and his generals were naturally fully occupied with the military situation, and it was arranged for their convenience that a conference should be held on March 26 at the little town of Doullens. That conference was attended by M. Poincaré, the President of the French Republic, M. Clemenceau, the Prime Minister of France, M. Loucheur, the French Minister of Munitions, who represented the French Government,

Lord Milner, who represented the British Government, Sir Douglas Haig and the four Army Commanders of the British Army, Sir Henry Wilson, General Pétain, and General Foch.

When he was presenting the *bâton* of Marshal of France to General Foch M. Poincaré told us that a conversation held in the garden of the house at Doullens in which the conference was held had convinced him that the *bâton* was coming to Foch. The Executive Council of generals had, as had been anticipated, proved to be too slow and cumbrous to deal with a real emergency, and already at this early stage it was in a state of suspended animation and had to be replaced promptly by something more adequate. In fact, the situation was so serious that immediate action had to be taken. There was no time to refer back to the Allied Governments for authority and approval, and in that day of stress common sense prevailed. Political difficulties vanished, and General Foch was given authority to co-ordinate the action of the Allied Armies on the Western Front.

Even then our government was a little frightened of calling a spade a spade, and was at pains to explain that Foch had not been appointed *generalissimo*; but both the soldiers and the public hailed the Doullens decision with such enthusiasm and with such complete disregard of the niceties of official terminology, that after some further discussion and some skilful and tactful handling of the position by M. Clemenceau, Foch, on April 14, was nominated Commander-in-Chief of the Allied Armies in France and Belgium.

It has often been asked who was mainly responsible for the appointment of General Foch. There is no question but that Mr. Lloyd George worked for "unity of command." The difficulty with him was that he did not understand fully the essential conditions of military command, and that for the sake of political considerations he was prepared to be content with something which fell short of military necessity. It is also certainly the case that the Government of the United States desired to achieve "unity of command," and that their influence was a most potent factor in bringing about the result which was eventually achieved.

The conference at Doullens had been assembled in such haste that there was no time to obtain the presence of General Pershing, who was down in the south at Chaumont. Immediately General Pershing heard of the decision of the conference he wrote to General Foch his well-known letter of March 28 offering the new *generalissimo* every man he had available. There never was any doubt but that the decision would be cordially welcomed and approved both by the statesmen and the generals of the United States, though in point of fact neither were represented when the decision was reached. This decision was probably mainly due to the influence at the conference of March 26 of M. Clemenceau, who had been quietly preparing the way for the appointment of a *generalissimo*, Lord Milner and Sir Douglas Haig.

There were rumours flying about at the time that Sir Douglas Haig and the British generals looked askance at the appointment of General Foch, but these were absolutely devoid of any foundation in fact. General Foch's appointment was welcomed immediately by both Sir Douglas Haig and his army commanders, and there has been no better example of loyal co-operation in war than that between Sir Douglas Haig and Marshal Foch.

But, when all is said and done, the man who brought about "unity of command" was Ludendorff. It was the emergency created by his great drive upon either side of the Somme which produced clear thinking and prompt decisions. Boswell once remarked to Dr. Johnson that few people allow themselves to think clearly about death, but that when a man is threatened with death he usually behaves with resolution. And so, it was at Doullens on March 26. Ludendorff had dealt a deadly blow to the Allies, and under the menace of that blow the gentlemen assembled in the little town of Doullens concentrated their minds, behaved with resolution, and took what was probably the most momentous decision made during the course of the great war, while those who had been hesitating on the bank found when they had taken the plunge that the waters were not so cold as they looked.

I have spoken of Ludendorff as the controlling mind at German Headquarters. In the middle of the campaign of 1916 Falkenhayn, whose plans for the capture of Verdun had failed ignominiously, was removed from his position as Chief of the Great General Staff, and Hindenburg, with Ludendorff as his first assistant, was brought over from the Russian front to succeed him at Great Headquarters. The pair had not been there very long before it became clear that Hindenburg was little more than a figurehead and Ludendorff was *de facto* chief of the German war organisation. Hindenburg had gained the deep gratitude of the Berliners by his great victory of Tannenburg, won at a time when they were trembling in their shoes at the Russian invasion of East Prussia.

We built high hopes upon the Russian "steam roller," and during the first months of the war the German public regarded it as being as formidable as we did. They were never easy in their minds until the Russians were driven back, and when this result was achieved, they contrasted Hindenburg's performances—with armies composed at first largely of second-rate troops—and the manner in which he restored the military efficiency of their feeble Austrian Ally, with the failure of their generals in the West, who, though they had the pick of the German Army at their disposal, had not achieved victory.

Hindenburg's square head, his burly figure, his strong character, his contempt of the arts of peace, of which many stories were in circulation, made him an admirable embodiment of Prussian militarism, a living exponent of the gospel of might is right which the German people had adopted with enthusiasm. He provided the *Kaiser* with just the personality needed at Great Headquarters to keep the war fever in the Fatherland at boiling point. Ludendorff, who did his work at the office desk and was first and foremost a military thinker, could never make the same appeal to the popular imagination as did his chief. The pair, therefore, made an excellent combination. The Germans have always been good at such combinations, at providing the strong personality or the royal personage with just the right brain.

The classic example is that of Blücher and Gneisenau in the closing years of the Napoleonic wars. Blücher was then the personality, Gneisenau the brain. Both of them came to England for the fetes which followed the peace of 1815, and it is told of Blücher that he then made a bet in a London drawing-room that he was the only man in the room who could kiss his own head. He won his wager by walking up to Gneisenau and giving him a smacking kiss on both cheeks. I doubt if Hindenburg were ever so frank as Blücher, but the relations between him and Ludendorff were very much those of their predecessors of one hundred years before.

By placing the supreme control of the Allied Armies in the West in the hands of Foch, one of the essential preparations to meet the German menace was completed just in time to prevent disaster, but it was already too late to take those others which might have saved us from such shocks as caused us to tremble for our safety. At the end of 1917 the man power of France, in the fourth year of the fierce struggle in which she had, until the summer of 1916, borne the brunt of the fighting, was approaching exhaustion, and the French Government was no longer able to keep up its forces on the Western Front at full strength. The British Army was wearied by the campaign in Flanders, and was grievously disappointed that the brilliant promise of the tank attack at Cambrai in November had ended in one more check. Both we and our French Allies had had to weaken materially our forces on the Western Front in order to bring help to our friends in the Southern theatre of war.

The collapse of Russia was definite and complete, and German divisions were streaming from the Eastern to the Western Front. It had become a certainty that early in 1918 we should be confronted in France and Flanders by almost the full military power of Germany. The one bright spot in the picture was the arrival of the first American divisions in France, but there was little prospect that America would be able to solve the vast problem of creating armies and transporting them three thousand miles across the Atlantic in time to make her strength felt in France before the late summer.

Prudence therefore demanded that we British should do everything that was possible to increase our forces there, Allenby's victory at Gaza and Beersheba and his brilliant pursuit ending in the capture of Jerusalem had disorganised the Turkish Army preparing near Aleppo under German leadership for the recapture of Baghdad, and had made our position in Asia secure. Two British divisions had been moved from Salonika, and a third, composed largely of Territorial battalions brought from India, had been created in Egypt, to reinforce Allenby for the campaign in which he broke through the Turkish lines on the southern frontier of Palestine. His artillery and aircraft had also been increased, and later a veteran Indian division had been moved from Mesopotamia to Egypt, while the Indian cavalry regiments which had been serving in France were also sent there.

Allenby's force was, therefore, very considerably stronger than that which had for a long time protected Egypt by covering the routes across the Sinai desert. North of Jerusalem, in the hills of Judaea, it was much better placed than it had been opposite Gaza. On one flank lay the Mediterranean, on the other the Dead Sea, while east of the Dead Sea spread the desert, of which our Arab friends were daily gaining more effective control. In March, 1918, Allenby had under his command an army of three mounted divisions, one mounted brigade, and eight infantry divisions of an approximate strength of 170,000 men, of whom about 150,000 were white troops and 20,000 native troops. (*Vide* also *The Great War in the Middle East* volumes 1 & 2 by W. T. Massey: Leonaur, 2009.)

In India Sir Charles Monro's expansion of the Indian Army was well developed and a steady stream of Indian troops for service in

Palestine was assured. We should, therefore, have incurred no risk whatever in the East by sending Haig at the beginning of 1918 a considerable reinforcement of white troops from Palestine. Not a man, however, was moved from the East to reinforce Haig until after the German blow had fallen and our armies had suffered the most serious reverse which befell us during the whole course of the war.

In January, 1918, the fighting strength of our army in France had been much diminished as a result of the prolonged fighting which had begun at the end of July, 1917, in the attack on the Flanders ridges, and had not ended till the German counter-attack at Cambrai had been checked, well on in November. Hardly a battalion, a battery, or a squadron had its full complement of men. This had been expected, and indeed it was a normal experience of the war on the Western Front, for while great battles were in progress the losses exceeded the flow of drafts from home. The period during which hard fighting took place on the British front normally lasted from March to November, and consequently at the beginning of the year the fighting strength of the army was usually at its lowest.

During the winter and early spring conditions of weather and of ground put a stop to operations on a grand scale, with the result that the losses were comparatively small; this then was the time to bring the army up to strength in preparation for the campaign which might be expected in the spring. It was necessary that the preparations for filling the gaps in the ranks should be made a long time ahead, for it took from four to five months to train a recruit to take his place in the ranks in France, and the process of calling him up often took as long as from two to three months from the time he received his first notice. Therefore, arrangements for filling up the ranks during the early months of the year should have been well in hand by the previous summer.

In December, 1916, the ranks of the fighting troops had been heavily depleted by the long and bitter struggles of the Somme and the Ancre, but by April, 1917, on the eve of the Battle of Arras, the ranks were again full, and Haig had been provided with considerable additional reinforcements; in fact, at that time the fighting strength of our army was almost at the highest point it ever reached. We then still had divisions at home which could be sent out to reinforce the army in France, and were able to bring back troops from Egypt, because by advancing into the Sinai desert and gaining control of the wells, which provided the only water available for a force advancing to at-

Canadian troops on Arras–Cambrai road 1918 Second Battle Cambrai

tack Egypt, we could defend that country much more economically than if we held the long line of the Suez Canal.

In 1918 we had in England no divisions which could be sent to Haig, and it was therefore the more necessary, in view of the danger which threatened us and of the fact that five divisions had been sent from our army in France to Italy, to bring back to France every man who could be spared from the more distant theatres of war, and to make our ranks up to their full strength. Yet none of these measures was taken. In March, 1918, Sir Douglas Haig's fighting strength was weaker by over 42,000 men than it had been on January 1, 1917; there had been some increase in artillery and a considerable increase in aircraft, tanks and machine-guns, and a very large increase in labour formations, both British and coloured; but unarmed labourers and Chinese *coolies* were not the kind of reinforcements Sir Douglas Haig needed to fight Germans, though they were invaluable to him for other purposes.

His deficiency of infantry—the essential arm, whether for offence or defence—was greater by more than 100,000 men than it had been at the beginning of 1917. A comparison of the strengths on the eve of the Battle of March, 1918, with those in January, 1917, is, however, misleading, for it is a comparison of a period when the ranks ought to have been full with a period when they were naturally empty; the only fair comparison is between the position in March, 1918, and in March, 1917. On the latter date the rifle and sabre strength of the army in France—that is, the number of men available for duty in the trenches—was greater by 180,000 men than it was at the former.

During the early months of 1918 the drafts sent out from home fell so far short of Sir Douglas Haig's requirements that it was impossible for him to maintain his army any longer at the strength at which it had been during the previous autumn. Accordingly, between the middle of January and the middle of February, three battalions out of the thirteen in each of the British divisions were broken up, and the men in them were used to take the place of drafts from home to fill up the ranks of the remaining battalions. This measure, which was the consequence of the failure of the Government to provide the drafts, caused a drastic change in the organisation and tactics of our infantry at a critical period when there was no time to accustom commanders and troops to the new conditions.

Worse still, it advertised our weakness to the army, and was the reverse of encouraging to men who were preparing to meet a great attack. Nor was this all. Owing to the decline of the strength of the French Army the French Government became more and more insistent that we should take over a longer stretch of the front. Pétain at this time thought it extremely probable that the German attack would be directed against him, and he did not feel himself able to meet such an attack unless we relieved some of his troops. When the length of front held by us and by the French was compared it appeared at first sight that France was bearing a very undue share of the burden; but the burden borne by troops in trench warfare cannot be estimated merely by the length of the line they hold.

The French, for example, held a very long line in Alsace and Lorraine, where for months on end a serious bombardment was almost unknown, and the trenches could be very lightly held, because the Germans on this front were not in strength and showed no disposition to attack. On the other hand, the enemy had always kept a large proportion of his troops in the West opposite the British front, while the climate and soil of Flanders made this, for many months in the year, one of the most exacting parts of the whole line. A still more important consideration was that only on a comparatively small part of the French front would loss of ground bring with it very serious consequences, while the British front north of the Somme covered so narrow a strip of country in front of the Channel ports that almost every yard of it was precious.

However, after prolonged negotiations between the two Governments, and after the question had been referred to the new Versailles organisation for examination, the French arguments prevailed, and Haig, in order to meet the wishes of the British Government, agreed with Pétain to take over an additional twenty-eight miles of front and to extend his front south of the Somme as far as the Oise. This extension made the length of our line 130 miles, the greatest length of front we had ever held, while the number of rifles available to hold it was approximately equal to that in March, 1916, when the length of our front was eighty miles and the Germans still had great armies on the Russian front.

The new front taken over from the French fell to our Fifth Army, which, though it was urgently in need of rest, had in the few weeks preceding the German attack to familiarise itself with fresh ground and to work incessantly at the erection of defences. Actually, then, our preparations for meeting the threat which the Germans held over us were that we had agreed with our Allies to invest the supreme command in the hands of an executive committee, we had abolished two of Haig's cavalry divisions, had reduced the number of infantry battalions at his disposal by close on 25 *per cent.*, had made an important alteration in the organisation of our infantry, and had at the same time increased our liabilities by taking over twenty-eight miles of new front, this new front being not less important than our positions in Flanders, for it covered the roads to Amiens and Paris.

It will naturally be asked how it came about that we did not do more to prepare for the great German attack, which was expected long before it took place.

Mr. Lloyd George was confirmed by the result of the third Battle of Ypres in his opinion that the position on the Western Front was one of stalemate. We and the French had made attempt after attempt to break through the German trenches when our numerical superiority over the enemy had been greater than his was expected to be when he had brought his troops across from Russia. In April, 1917, on the eve of General Nivelle's offensive, it had been calculated that the Allies had on the Western Front a superiority of 600,000 rifles and 5,000 guns. In the spring of 1918, it was estimated that the Germans might have a superiority of 300,000 rifles and that their preponderance in artillery would not be considerable. Mr. Lloyd George believed that the whole experience of the war on the Western Front had shown that the Germans would require a far greater numerical superiority than they appeared likely to possess in order to endanger our position.

He doubted if the Germans would make the attempt, but was quite certain that the Allied forces in France and Belgium were strong enough to stop them if they did. He believed that victory could only be won by taking the way round, by knocking down Germany's props. He had held this view from the early days of 1915, when the trench barrier was first established between the North Sea and the Swiss frontier. He had first advocated reinforcing Serbia with the object of attacking Austria and bringing in the other Balkan States on our side. Then, when he failed to carry his arguments in favour of that enterprise, he had proposed to attack Austria through Italy.

Both these operations were now out of the question; the Allied Armies in these theatres could only be reinforced to the necessary extent at the expense of the Western Front, and if he did not think it necessary to strengthen that front, he was not rash enough to weaken it; but by leaving Allenby the troops he had in Palestine, and by reinforcing him from India, he believed that it would be possible to defeat

Turkey, who was very shaky. Victories in Asia Minor would, he hoped, encourage the Allied peoples to hold on during 1918, while America was preparing her armies and shipping them to France, and it would be time enough to consider in 1919 whether it was worthwhile to defeat the German Armies in the West. He had to provide labour for the munition factories, for the coal mines, and for the shipyards to meet the submarine menace. He could only obtain the soldiers needed to keep our troops in France up to strength by raising the age limit for the draft, and he dreaded the political effect of doing this if he left Ireland exempt, while the problem of forcing conscription on Ireland was one which he did not care to face.

He considered that by instituting the Versailles Council and its later development, the Executive Military Committee of the Council, he had counterbalanced the advantage which the Germans had in the West in a single homogeneous army under one commander, and he refused both to meet the demands of the soldiers for men to fill the depleted ranks in France and to transfer troops from Palestine to France. He was, in fact, sincerely convinced that the barrier in the West was impenetrable alike by us and by the Germans.

Though the procession of German troops from East to West had begun in November and continued steadily throughout the winter and spring, it was not until March that Ludendorff's fighting strength on the Western Front was approximately equal numerically to that of the Allies. It is not possible, however, to estimate correctly the power of opposing armies merely by counting heads, and Ludendorff had many factors in his favour which added materially to his strength. For a long time before he opened the campaign of 1918 there had been little or no fighting on the Eastern Front, which became for him a vast rest camp and training centre in which his men could be prepared for work elsewhere. Thus, while our men and the enemy opposed to them were engaged in desperate and exhausting fighting, large German forces were quietly preparing elsewhere for their next effort.

The collapse of Russia and the failure of the 1917 campaign to yield any decisive results had thrown us on the defensive, and had given Ludendorff the opportunity, of which he skilfully took full advantage, of playing upon the fears of the Allied commanders and of keeping each of them under threat of attack. Further, in March, 1918, Ludendorff had large reserves of trained men still in the East, ready to come across. Actually, between March and the end of May, when his strength was at its highest, his forces were increased by sixteen divisions and a large amount of heavy artillery. Therefore, Ludendorff had an important reinforcement at hand in March, and the Allies had no corresponding reserve which could be ready until long after the German commander had his on the spot.

The extreme advocates of the policy of seeking victory by the way round failed from the first to recognise that the German forces on the Russian front were a potential reserve for their armies in France, and that at any time from the beginning of 1915 onwards the German leaders might have reversed the process which they carried through after their defeat in the first Battle of Ypres, have stood on the defensive in the East and sent all troops not necessary for defence there to the West. Even before the U-boats, Gothas and Zeppelins became as dangerous as they subsequently were, it was clear that, if the Germans reached Calais and Boulogne, Great Britain would be in danger of starvation and of invasion, and that her army in France would have a very precarious line of communications with the Motherland.

The importance of protecting Paris needed no discussion. In September, 1914, Joffre, backed by the French Government, had made all possible preparations for continuing the war even if the capital fell to the enemy, but the morale effect which the success of a second German attack on Paris might have had is incalculable, and the safety of Paris ought not in any circumstances to have been risked. It is an old and well-established maxim of strategy that before launching out upon an offensive enterprise a general must look to the safety of the vitals both of his army and of his country. The Channel ports and Paris were the vitals of Great Britain and of France.

The moment these were seriously threatened the Government perforce took in haste the measures which might have been carried through at leisure. The application of the Military Service Acts was extended, drafts were rushed out from home, and every British soldier who could be spared from the East was brought to France. Just as the Germans forced "unity of command" upon us, so they compelled us to discard the errors in our strategy. But it is now time for a word as to the events which brought these things to pass.

By the middle of February, 1918, it had become apparent that the Germans were pushing forward their preparations for a great offensive with all possible energy, and there were already indications that they intended to attack the British right, held by our Fifth and Third Armies. Ludendorff was, however, much too skilful to confine his preparations to one part of the front, and these pointed to the possibility that the attack on our right might be a preliminary to a greater blow against our line farther north, or against the French to the south.

The northern portion of our front was but fifty miles distant from Calais and sixty miles from Boulogne; therefore, in the north every yard of ground was of value to us, and if the Germans had broken through even to a depth of twenty-five miles we should have been in dire straits, for they would then have gained possession of the hill of Cassel which dominates the Flanders flats northwards to the coast on either side of Dunkerque, would have forced the Belgians to fall back, could have shelled and bombed the harbours, and have hemmed the Allied left flank into a position from which issue would have been wellnigh impossible. In the south we had more elbow room, for our front between St. Quentin and the Oise was over ninety miles from the coast, and could, in case of emergency, be more quickly reinforced by the French than could our line in Flanders.

Sir Douglas Haig, therefore, felt bound to keep the greater part of such reserves as he had at his disposal, north of the Somme. Gough's Fifth Army held the line from our point of junction with the French on the Oise not far from La Fère to Gouzeaucourt, south-west of Cambrai, a distance of about forty-two miles. On the whole of this front Gough had fourteen divisions and three cavalry divisions, eleven of his divisions being in the line, and the remainder in reserve, each of his divisions in the line holding on an average 6,750 yards of front. Byng's Third Army on Gough's left held a front of about twenty-seven miles with fifteen divisions, eight of them being in the line and seven in reserve, the average length of front held by each division being about 4,700 yards. Gough's liabilities, therefore, were very considerably greater than Byng's, and the reserves of the Fifth Army were much weaker than those of the Third, while, as it turned out, Gough had to bear by far the greater weight of the German attack.

Throughout the winter Ludendorff had been planning, with the method and care of a trained German mind, how to achieve his object and to solve the problem of breaking through the trench barrier, a problem to which all the generals on the West, on both sides, had hitherto found no answer. All were by this time agreed that the method of attack by means of a great and protracted bombardment, followed by an infantry assault pressed through upon one part of the front, was a failure. The immense and lengthy preparation which this form of battle involved made any surprise impossible, as sooner or later the defender's reserves came up, and the battle ended in a slogging match in which the assailant gained little return for very heavy losses.

Ludendorff probably realised that it would be out of the question to keep all his preparations for attack secret. No camouflage could altogether conceal from our air observers that something was afoot, and some information would certainly have been elicited from the prisoners taken in the daily skirmishes of trench warfare. But he conceived that it would be possible to deceive us as to the weight of the blow which he meant to deliver, and to achieve some measure of surprise by keeping the great part of his artillery and the bulk of his attacking divisions at a distance from the battlefield until the last possible moment. This method had the double advantage of keeping us in uncertainty both as to the strength of the attack and as to whether it would be made in more than one place, for, in the weeks preceding the battle, he placed his reserves so that they could be moved as readily against our northern front, or even against the French front, as against our right flank.

He decided, then, to have no long preliminary bombardment, which would have given us a definite indication of his plans, and, as we had found to our cost, would so destroy the surface of the ground and break up the roads and the railways, as to make it a matter of great difficulty to get the reserves forward when they were needed. He also decided to bring up his attacking divisions at the last moment by train and by rapid marches under cover of darkness. This was the essence of his plan and the feature in which it differed most from other attacks which had been tried in the West.

In the details of its execution there was also much that was new. Ludendorff and his staff had studied very carefully all the previous attacks which had been carried through both by us and by the French, and he found that opportunities had often been missed because parts of the attacking line had been checked at strong points held resolutely by the defenders, and the remainder had waited for these to be reduced; he also maintained that the progress of the Allied infantry had been delayed by too frequent reliefs.

He therefore determined that as a principle he would follow up success wherever it was won, driving in at such weak points as he discovered, and that he would not delay his advance in order to overcome centres of resistance against which his progress was checked. In order to develop this method of attack to the utmost he devoted the winter to selecting from his army the best and bravest of his soldiers and putting them through a special form of training. These men, whom he called "storm troops," were to lead his attacks, with orders to press forward as far and as fast as possible, while they were given the assurance that where they were successful, they would be immediately supported by the reserve. He impressed upon his infantry divisions that they must go forward to the utmost powers of their endurance without expecting relief, and practised them in making long advances, carrying food for several days.

By March 19 Haig's Intelligence Department had discovered that the German preparations for attack on the Third and Fifth Armies were nearly complete, and it was anticipated that the battle would begin on March 20 or 21. The attack actually opened shortly before 5 a.m. on the 21st with a bombardment of the greatest intensity against the whole front held by those armies, while in order to keep us in doubt till the last possible moment as to their intentions, the Germans simultaneously bombarded parts of our northern line and the French fronts on either side of Reims. For about five hours a perfect hurricane of shell was hurled against Gough's and Byng's defences, and it has been stated by German officers that the rate of fire was so rapid that many of their guns became red hot. Then, shortly before 10 a.m., the German infantry advanced.

This five-hour bombardment may be compared to our artillery preparation for the first Battle of the Somme, which lasted seven days. The battle had not been long in progress before it became clear that Ludendorff was throwing his whole weight against our right, and, therefore, though Haig had guessed accurately both the time and the place at which the attack would be made, Ludendorff had won the first move by getting all his reserves in motion first. This much was due to his skill, but he was also greatly favoured by fortune.

The early months of 1918 had been phenomenally dry, but March 19 had been a day of drizzle sufficient to damp the surface of the hard ground; on the 20th the sky had cleared and the sun had drawn up a dense blanket of fog which, on the 21st, enveloped the whole battlefield, with the result that in few places was it possible to see more than fifty yards. We often during the war created artificial fogs and blanketed successfully the enemy's deadly machine-guns by means of smoke clouds, the preparation of which had cost us much time and trouble. Ludendorff was provided by Nature with a more effective screen than we had ever been able to produce.

Our system of defence was an adaptation of that which had been used by the Germans with considerable success in the third Battle of

Ypres; that is to say, it consisted, in the first place, of an outpost zone covering the area which, as experience told us, would probably be most heavily bombarded by the enemy. This outpost zone was lightly held, and the troops in it were intended, after giving warning of the German advance and delaying it to the best of their power, to fall back on the battle positions behind. The strength of these battle positions depended greatly upon the cross fire of guns and machine-guns, and upon a series of elaborate strong posts so placed that the garrison of each could see under normal conditions both the enemy, at whom they were to fire, and the neighbours with whom they were to co-operate.

This system, which later more than justified itself when there was no fog, was unsuitable when guns, machine-guns and infantry were blinded. The only answer to the fog was to strengthen the infantry holding the trenches, but for this there were not men available unless they were taken from the already weak reserve. Nor was the fog the only stroke of fortune which favoured the Germans. Gough's front ran roughly north and south till it reached the River Oise, and then bent back south-eastwards along the northern bank of the river.

In this portion of its course the Oise runs through a wide and normally marshy valley, such as no great attacking force could cross in an ordinary spring. It had, therefore, not been expected that the German attack would include this sector, which was lightly held. In fact, one of the arguments which the French had put forward in order to induce us to extend our front so far south was that no large number of troops would be required to defend the Oise, where our line would be so strong naturally as to be impervious to attack.

The Oise line had always been regarded as a quiet sector. Being very short of troops, Gough had decided to hold this, apparently the least vulnerable part of his front, with a series of posts, and not to have a continuous line of defence. The dry weather, however, enabled the Germans to cross the marshes without difficulty, while the fog allowed them to penetrate between the posts, often unobserved. The result of this was that the enemy were able to get behind our defences further north and cut off the defenders.

It is not my purpose to describe the struggle in detail. My object is to make clear the causes which led to the defeat of the Fifth Army and to show that they were beyond the control of the brave men of whom that army was composed. From the first day of the battle Ludendorff flung sixty-four divisions against the Third and Fifth Armies. Of these sixty-four at least forty attacked the fourteen divisions and three cavalry divisions of Gough's Fifth Army, while the remaining twenty-four fell upon Byng's fifteen divisions. It is, therefore, in no way surprising that the Fifth Army was overwhelmed.

The news that it had been overwhelmed came as a rude shock to the public at home. It seemed inconceivable that the Germans should have been able to break so completely through such elaborate defences, manned by British troops, when we had, despite lavish supplies of guns and munitions and the incomparable valour of our men, only been able by continuous effort and at an appalling cost to achieve much smaller results. Wild stories were flying about of the breakdown of the Fifth Army, and it was whispered in the drawing-rooms of London that the men had not fought as they ought to have fought. In the confusion and uncertainty of retreat the true facts could not be discovered and made known, with the result that for long imputations rested upon the Fifth Army which were wholly contrary to the truth. Eager to find some silver lining to the cloud, the public fastened upon the glorious defence of the Third Army and contrasted it with Gough's apparent collapse.

I have no desire to minimise in any way the splendour of the achievement of Byng's men, but I trust I have made it clear that the burden which Gough's troops had to bear was incomparably the greater. In the first stage of the battle very nearly twice as many German divisions attacked Gough as fell upon Byng. Each of Gough's divisions had on the average to hold nearly 50 *per cent,* more front than had Byng, while the Third Army reserves were nearly twice as strong as those of the Fifth, yet at the end of the first day's battle Gough's left, where the gallant 9th Division beat off all attacks, had given less ground than some of Byng's divisions further north had been compelled to yield.

By the evening of March 21 our battle positions had not been penetrated except on the extreme right, where the Germans had crossed the dried-up bed of the Oise, but during the night and the next morning the enemy, helped by the fog, had discovered three weak points in our front, and, true to Ludendorff's principle, had pressed his advantage at these points till the line crumbled. These were days of gallant and desperate fighting against overwhelming odds, passing all preconceived standards of endurance and of self-sacrifice. The garrisons of many of our works held out long after the enemy, pouring through gaps in our line, had swept beyond them and completely cut them off.

As in the days of the crisis of the first Battle of Ypres, cooks, signallers, servants and odd-job men of all kinds rallied round the headquarters of battalions and fought on long after hope of support had gone. The Germans, surging past these devoted bands, which stood out here and there along the front like rocks surrounded by the incoming tide, pressed back Gough's right, and, as by the evening of the 22nd, he had thrown in all his available reserves, and only one French division had as yet arrived to help him, he felt that there was no alternative but to fall back to the Somme.

A bridgehead position had been prepared around Péronne on the east bank of the river, but there had been no time to complete the defences along the river itself. When the troops arrived in their new positions, to which they withdrew during the night, hard pressed by the enemy, they found only some rudiments of trenches with little or no wire in front of them. Many strange and baseless reports were circulated to account for this fact. It was said that Gough, being a cavalry general, had refused to allow his rear lines of defence to be wired, and had even ordered wire to be pulled up in order that the cavalry might have free scope. The fact is that the southern portion of Gough's front had only been taken over from the French about seven weeks before the German attack began.

During the early part of the winter the French had been able to hold this portion of the front very lightly, so that the troops they had there were not sufficiently numerous to maintain even the existing defences in good condition, and they had made no attempt to construct the new works necessary to withstand a great German attack. The country had been devastated by the battles of 1916, the roads were in bad condition, there was no light railway system, the broad gauge system was defective, and, as all the villages had been gutted, there was no shelter for the troops.

An immense amount of work had, therefore, to be done by the Fifth Army, the men labouring incessantly at the construction of defences in the battle zone and at improving the defective communications. The sole reason why the line of the Somme was not fortified was that there had been neither time nor labour available for the purpose. Gough had early realised that it was very probable that he would not have the time he needed to complete his rear lines of defence, and in February had asked our Intelligence Department to use every device at their disposal to cause the Germans to delay their attack.

Owing to the difficulty of carrying out a uniform retreat to the

Somme of the whole line in the dark a gap occurred in our front in the neighbourhood of Ham, and Germans succeeded in getting across the river at that place. Although very elaborate preparations had been made for blowing up the Somme bridges, and the men and explosives for this work were on the spot, yet the enemy's artillery, following up our retreat closely, in a number of cases exploded the charges prematurely, and in others cut the leads and so prevented the complete destruction of the bridges.

The Somme, like the Oise, was, in consequence of the abnormally dry winter, very low, and the enemy was able to cross at many places where in ordinary times the river would have been impassable. The result of this combination of untoward events was that by the night of March 23 the line of the Somme was already in the hands of the Germans on Gough's right, and the defence of the river further north was seriously compromised.

Meanwhile, the enemy had been pressing Gough's left, while it was falling back north of the Somme in conformity with the retreat of the centre of the Fifth Army behind the river, and the situation at the junction of the Third and Fifth Armies became critical. The Third Army, which, during the 23rd, had repulsed repeated attacks by the enemy in mass formation and had given very little ground, was consequently compelled to swing back its right across the Somme battlefields. During the 22nd the Germans extended their gains west of the Somme against Gough's right, and on his left had seized the heights north of the river and west of Péronne. Both flanks of the defenders of the river line at and south of Péronne were thus endangered, and there was no help for it but to fall back again.

The loss of the line of the Somme was a very serious matter, for the Germans now entered upon the zone in which were placed our depots, stores and hospitals. These had all to be abandoned or evacuated hastily, and consequently great quantities of war material of all kinds fell into the enemy's hands; much suffering was caused to the sick and wounded, of whom numbers had to be left untended and without shelter alongside the railway lines in the rear until the hospital trains could pick them up; the telegraph and telephone communications were disorganised, and the difficulties of organising defence increased as the danger grew. It was clear that the main object of the Germans was to reach Amiens and that the weight of their attack was falling upon the Fifth Army.

So, in order to allow Gough to devote his whole attention to the enemy advancing south of the river, Sir Douglas Haig placed that portion of the Fifth Army which was north of the Somme under Byng, and it then became a part of the Third Army. This new right of the Third Army was pressed back north of the Somme, and the Fifth Army south of the river, finding its flank exposed, had to continue its retreat. It was now the sixth day of the battle, March 26.

The danger of the Germans reaching Amiens and driving in a wedge between the British and French Armies was very nigh. Haig had ordered his last reserves to the point of danger, and it was doubtful whether Pétain would be able to send the French reserves to the battlefield in time. It was, as I have said, in this emergency that the conference at Doullens appointed Foch to the supreme command, and by so doing inspired the weary leaders and their men, battling against great odds, with fresh confidence.

Already, though they did not yet know it, the valour and endurance in adversity of our men was being rewarded, for the Germans, equally weary, could not sustain the momentum of their attack. Our airmen, who watched the long-drawn-out struggle from above, have described how, in its last stages, the infantry upon both sides were too exhausted to move, save at a slow walk, and would lie for hours opposite to each other without firing, having lost the energy to load and fire, save in a real emergency. Ludendorff had, as I have said, planned to get the last ounce out of his men, and in order to avoid loss of time in reliefs had left them to fight on until sheer exhaustion made them almost impotent.

He had hoped that before that stage of exhaustion was reached, he would have driven a wide breach in our line, but he had not reckoned with the doggedness of the British infantryman, whose spirit kept him fighting long after he ought to have collapsed. The line, though badly bent, was still a line, held by battalions reduced to the size of companies, brigades to the strength of weak battalions, but still held.

This was the state of affairs while Ludendorff was trying to get up fresh troops to the front and Foch was hurrying up the French reserves from the south to our aid, and it was then that an improvisation of Gough's gave just the time needed for our Allies to come up. He directed General Grant, his Chief Engineer, to assemble every man he could collect from his training schools, his engineers and the odds and ends of troops employed in special jobs behind the army, and form them into a reinforcing force. Later, as the chief engineer was required for his proper duties, the command of this miscellaneous body was given to General Carey, who happened to be free, and it became known to fame as Carey's Force.

It was joined by Canadian and American railway construction engineers, who were engaged in laying railway lines in the neighbourhood of Amiens. These men, though but few of them had had any real military training, volunteered to fight, as had the American railway engineers who had fought with Byng's men when the Germans made their counter-attack at Cambrai in November, 1917, and were the first American soldiers to take part in battle on the Western Front.

With this exception this little band of Carey's consisted almost wholly of men included in the fighting strength of the army, but, being hastily brought together, they lacked the equipment of an organised force. Nevertheless, this reinforcement, together with the skill and devotion of our cavalry, who, on our right, repeated in even more trying circumstances their achievements during the retreat from Mons, and with the aid of divisions brought up to Amiens from Gough's extreme right as they were relieved by the French, just enabled the battered remnant of the Fifth Army to bar the direct road to Amiens until the arrival of the Australians from the north and of the French troops from the south once more established a firm barrier against the tide of the German invasion. By the evening of March 28, the worst of the crisis was over, though the great battle was by no means ended.

On that day the Germans made a desperate effort to drive in at Arras, an effort designed to force us out of the Vimy Ridge, one of the main pivots of our defence. This attack, which involved the right of Horne's First Army, as well as the left and centre of Byng's Third Army, was delivered by the enemy in great strength, but it failed disastrously. When it ended, the Germans had gained a portion only of our outpost positions, and our battle positions had everywhere resisted their assaults. This time there was no fog to help the enemy, and Haig's system of defence was completely successful. It is not too much to say that this costly repulse doomed Ludendorff's campaign to failure.

We have the evidence of captured documents and of Ludendorff's statements in his *Reminiscences* that the chief object of this campaign was to separate the British from the French Army, the capture of Amiens being only a means towards that end. The danger of the Germans realising this plan would have been much greater than it actually was had they managed, as Ludendorff intended, to make a wide breach north of the Somme, for they would then have used that river between Péronne and Abbeville to hold off the French reinforcements coming up from the south, while they attempted to drive the British Army into the sea, and, of course, the farther north the breach the longer it would take the French troops to reach the danger point.

When one recalls how very near the Germans were to creating a real breach south of the Somme and how the French reserves came up only just in time to prevent such a calamity, there is little difficulty in imagining how much greater the peril would have been had the Third Army given way, and in appreciating the wisdom of Sir Douglas Haig's decision to keep the greater part of his very limited reserve north of the Somme. I believe it was the stout resistance of the Third Army upon March 23 and the retirement of the Fifth Army behind the Somme upon that day which induced Ludendorff to follow what he believed to be the line of least resistance, and to strike for Amiens by the southern bank of the Somme.

Then when he found that he could not overcome the resistance of the Fifth Army before the French came up, and realised that he would have to call a halt on the southern part of the battlefield to rest and relieve his exhausted men, he made the desperate attempt of March 28 to return to his first idea of creating such a breach north of the Somme as would enable him to roll up our line and force us back on the ports. From this second danger Byng's Third Army saved us. Checked on the northern battle-front, Ludendorff, on April 4, made one more attempt to reach Amiens by the southern route in a battle which lasted till the evening of the 5th; but Foch's vigorous methods had already brought up sufficient French troops, and again our cavalry covered themselves with glory, while four Australian brigades had strengthened our front south of the Somme, so that the great German effort to drive a wedge between the Allied Armies wore itself out.

Hardly had one crisis passed before another arose. On April 9 the Germans attacked and overwhelmed the Portuguese holding a portion of the Flanders front to the south of Armentières. Haig had greatly weakened his forces in the north in order to find troops to save Amiens, and the divisions sent to the Somme had to some extent been replaced in Flanders by exhausted divisions withdrawn from that battlefield and hastily reconstituted with reinforcements sent out from England. Thus, our men passed from one fiery trial to another.

This Flanders battle had been considered and rejected by Ludendorff when he formed his original plan, but, finding that his troops on the Amiens front were checked and that his Seventeenth Army, which had attacked Byng and Horne, had been so severely handled as to be incapable, for a time, of further effort, he determined to revert to it and to drive for the Channel ports.

By the evening of April 9, the Germans had forced their way across the River La we, midway between Armentières and Béthune, and had made such progress as to endanger our hold upon both towns. Béthune was saved by the splendid defence of the 55th West Lancashire Division of its front about Festubert and Givenchy. Sir Douglas Haig mentions as one of the many gallant deeds performed by this division the story of a machine-gun which was kept in action, although the Germans had entered the rear compartment of the "pill-box" from which it was firing, the gun team holding up the enemy by revolver fire from the inner compartment.

Not many months before this same division, under the same commander, Sir H. Jeudwine, had given way before the German counter-attack at Cambrai, when weary, weak in numbers, and holding a very extended front. It had then been subjected to a great deal of ill-founded criticism, but in this battle, it sent a proud answer to its critics and told them that the simple process of judging by results, which has so often been commended, is rarely applicable in war, and that the popular cry for victims when things are not going well is wrong in nine cases out of ten.

At the other end of the break the enemy made more progress, and despite the stout resistance of the 9th Division on the Messines Ridge, worked his way to the north and south of Armentières, at the same time deluging the town with gas shell to an extent which made life in it impossible. It was therefore abandoned on the 10th, while the next day Merville fell. The Germans now began a dangerous movement towards Hazebrouck, the central railway junction of Flanders, and on the 12th, it was as near capture as Amiens had been during the crisis of the March battle. So serious was the position that extensive preparations were made for flooding the approaches to Dunkerque and Calais and for sending back to England from those ports all personnel not immediately needed for their working; while, in order to shorten his fronts and to get reserves to meet this new German rush for Calais, Haig, with a sad heart, ordered a withdrawal from the Flanders ridges, which had been won at such cost in the previous autumn, to a line just covering Ypres.

But once again British troops, never so brilliant as in a defensive battle against great odds, surpassed all expectation. On the 13th the remnants of the 29th and 31st Divisions, strung out on a very wide front, contested every foot of ground with bullet and bayonet, and beat off a succession of fierce attacks from early morning until late afternoon, so gaining time for the 1st Australian Division, railed up from the Somme, to detrain at Hazebrouck, come forward and help to save that town.

The most pressing danger was then averted; but the Germans, though foiled in their attempt to open a direct way to Calais and Boulogne, still fought fiercely to extend their gains. On the 15th the arrival of reinforcements enabled them to capture Bailleul, and the strain upon the British Army had become all but insupportable. Two-thirds of the divisions engaged in the Flanders battle had been through the fiery trial of the Somme. As fast as they were withdrawn from the first battle their ranks were refilled with the drafts from home, which were composed mainly of boys of nineteen and under, and they were sent north. It was these splendid youths, many of whom went into the maelstrom of battle within a few days of landing in France, with little opportunity of getting to know their leaders or of accustoming themselves to strange and terrible conditions, who saved the Channel ports.

But Haig could not go on indefinitely reconstituting his shattered divisions and sending them back into battle, and he was very near the end of his resources. By the middle of April, however, French troops had come to our aid, and with their help repeated attacks by the Germans in the neighbourhood of Kemmel on the 16th and 17th were repulsed, and thereafter for a time the battle in Flanders died down.

The interest then shifted to the southern battlefield, where on April 24 the Germans made a last attempt to break through to Amiens, and for a time were in possession of Villers-Brettonneux. This was one of the few attacks made by the Germans in which they used tanks with success, and it was their tanks which cleared a way into the village for the German infantry. The situation was highly critical, for Rawlinson, who had assumed command on the Amiens front on March 28, was very weak, Haig having called upon him for every man he could spare to nourish the battle in Flanders, while if the Germans had managed to establish themselves a very short distance to the west of Villers-Brettonneux they would have been able to look down upon Amiens.

It was no time for hesitation, and a brilliant counter-attack made on the night of the 24th, before the Germans had time to establish themselves in their newly-won positions, saved us in yet another crisis. In this counter-attack, which was made by troops of the 4th and 5th Australian Divisions, by a mixed brigade made up from the 18th and 58th Divisions, and by part of the 8th Division, which had been holding the village and its neighbourhood, Villers-Brettonneux was recaptured and the gate to Amiens was securely locked.

Two days later the battle broke out again in Flanders, and on April 25 the enemy, reinforcing his troops on the Kemmel front with five fresh divisions, succeeded in breaking in on either side of Kemmel Hill, which was at the time held by the French, and in cutting off the garrison. This was a very serious blow, for in Kemmel Hill the enemy obtained a grand observatory, from the top of which he could overlook all our lines as far north as Ypres and could watch all the roads and railways leading thither from as far west as Poperinghe. Therefore, a further withdrawal of our front in the salient became necessary. In the result, however, the gain of Kemmel proved to be the enemy's undoing, for it encouraged him to make a great attack on April 29, which extended from near Bailleul to the north of Ypres.

The German infantry came on in massed formation with bayonets fixed, and were completely repulsed by our troops and by the French and Belgians on our flanks. On our front, between Kemmel and Ypres, the enemy's repeated and heavy assaults were all beaten back by the 21st, 49th and 25th Divisions, which, except at one point to the south of Ypres, yielded not a yard of ground. This failure was hardly less important in its effect on the campaign than that which the Germans had suffered on March 28, and, as will be seen, these two triumphs of our defence over the enemy's attack went far in preparation for the victories which came later in the year. On April 30 the battle came to a close with the recapture of the village of Locre, on the Bailleul-Ypres road, to the west of Kemmel, by our French Allies.

In rather less than six weeks the Germans had flung no fewer than one hundred and forty-one divisions against the combined British and French forces. Fifty-five infantry divisions and three cavalry divisions of Haig's army had stayed the attacks of one hundred and nine German divisions. The third German campaign of conquest in the West had been defeated by the grit and endurance of the British soldier, and by the timely appointment of Foch to the supreme command, but at a terrible cost. Our casualties amounted to more than 300,000 killed, wounded and missing—that is, very nearly double our losses in the eight and a half months of the Dardanelles campaign, and over 70,000 more than our losses in the three and a half months of the third Battle of Ypres.

In that battle we had captured 24,600 prisoners and 64 guns, and we had gained possession of the Flanders ridges. At the end of the battles of March and April we stood "with our backs to the wall," we had lost 70,000 prisoners, 1,000 guns, 4,000 machine-guns, 700 trench mortars, 200 tanks, and an immense quantity of stores. (The figures of losses of material are those given by the Ministry of Munitions, and represent the replacements necessary after the battles. The actual captures by the Germans were somewhat smaller.)

The worst result of the strain which had been thrown upon our army was that eight of our divisions had, in consequence of our heavy losses and of our lack of means to replace them promptly, to be reduced to skeletons, and were for a considerable period unable to fight even defensively in the line, while the Portuguese contingent had disappeared as a fighting force.

Such was the price which we had to pay for our failure to prepare adequately for a menace which had long been foreseen. Had the Government taken in time the measures which it had been urged to take, the reduction of two cavalry divisions and of more than one hundred infantry battalions might have been avoided, and both Gough and Byng might have had sufficient men to have enabled them to hold their battle positions against all attacks, while Haig's reserve might have been increased by at least two divisions. Our men had shown coolness, courage, determination and endurance in adversity which pass all understanding and are beyond all praise, but they should never and need never have been called upon for such sacrifices as they made without stint and without complaint.

CHAPTER 2

Foch *Versus* Ludendorff

Foch made his name before the war as a military thinker. First as a professor and then as chief of the French War College, he acquired a European reputation, and to have been a student under him was regarded as a special distinction by the officers of the French staff during the war. While at the War College he published two books which were regarded by the military world as the most inspiring and thoughtful studies of war which had appeared since Clausewitz produced his great work. It was these books which caused Lord Roberts to predict, some ten years before Germany threw down the gauntlet, that when the great European struggle, for which he was urging Great Britain to prepare, came, the world would hear of Foch, who was then unknown outside professional circles.

This reputation of Foch's had been built up by writing and by study. It was the reputation of a theorist, and since war is a very practical business, even the greatest of theorists is regarded more or less with suspicion until he has proved himself in practice. There were many in the French Army before the war who looked upon Foch as a bookman. It was the way in which he covered the withdrawal of the French Army from Lorraine, when Joffre's first offensive failed, and above all his brilliant blow delivered on September 9, 1914, near the marshes of St. Gond, in the first Battle of the Marne, which showed the world that Foch was as good at practice as at theory.

Great as were these early achievements, I doubt if anything shows Foch's mastery of his craft more clearly than his handling of the situation in the days which followed his appointment to the supreme command. The fate of the world hung in the balance, and there was no time for hesitation or delay. The new *generalissimo* had to form a headquarters rapidly, and to organise in the midst of a great battle the machinery necessary for the command of five million men extended over a front of four hundred and fifty miles, tasks which, in the circumstances, would have taxed the capacity of any ordinary man.

Not only did he do this, but he had not been in the saddle many hours before he made his personality felt. The success of Ludendorff's attempt to separate the British from the French Army and to capture the great railway junction of Amiens depended almost entirely upon the progress he made before the French reserves from the south reached the battlefield. The French staff had worked out the movements of troops towards Amiens with their usual care and precision. A systematic flow of divisions to the point of danger had been arranged for, but Foch wanted a flood, not a flow.

It has often been objected that the tendency of war schools is towards pedantry, that their students are inclined to be too much tied to the methods which they have learned during their course of study; and it might have been expected that Foch, who represented the essence of the teaching of the modern war colleges, would have been predisposed in favour of staff routine, but he fairly astounded the experts by his methods. It is the sign of the master that he makes system his servant, that he has the technique of his profession under his control, that he knows when to put rules aside and when to follow them. In that first week which followed the fateful meeting at Doullens of March 26, when he was given supreme control, Foch tore up all staff time-tables and by any and every means, orthodox and unorthodox, rushed troops to the point of danger.

They were brought up by train, by marches, in motor-lorries, in 'buses; with or without transport, with or without their proper complement of supplies and ammunition. The point was to get to the battlefield men who could fight; details of organisation could be straightened out afterwards. So, by inspiring those under him with his own fierce energy, Foch in the first ten days of his tenure of command brought to the battle nearly twice as many troops as had been estimated for by the French staff, and by so doing built up a barrier against which the waves of German troops beat in vain.

I saw Foch at the beginning of April, when he had been in control about a week, at his temporary headquarters in the town hall of Beauvais, and thus early he was satisfied that he had the situation in hand. Despite the immense burden and responsibility on his shoulders, he was perfectly confident and cheerful. He leaned back in his chair smoking his inevitable cigar and looking at the great map on the wall opposite on which each day's progress of the German offensive was marked in colour; he pointed out how that progress was steadily diminishing, how the marks on the map grew closer together, just as do the circles made by a stone thrown into a pond before the last ripple disappears. He said:

> I am still fighting, and I have first to stabilise the front of battle. Ludendorff will probably try again, but he won't get through. In a few days more I shall have his progress permanently blocked.

The day after I left Beauvais, on April 4, Ludendorff, sure enough, did make another great effort, but it ended in disaster for the Germans, and the front was stabilised.

I saw Foch again just a fortnight later, on April 16, at the height of the second crisis of the spring of 1918, when the Germans were on the outskirts of Hazebrouck, and appeared to be well on the road to Calais and Boulogne. Foch had then moved his headquarters to a small *château* behind Amiens, and the organisation of his staff was more or less complete. Despite this second shock and the exhaustion of the British Army, Foch had not lost one bit of his confidence. There were many criticisms in England at this time that he was leaving our army without support, and that the French should take a greater share in bearing the burden of meeting the great German offensive.

But Foch had himself measured accurately both the German strength and the endurance of the British Army, of which he had ample experience during the first Battle of Ypres, when he helped us to stop the first German rush to Calais. It is the experience of every commander on the defensive in battle to receive urgent appeals for reinforcements from his hard-pressed front. His quality as a general is tested by his ability to appreciate these appeals at their proper value, to know when and in what strength to send help from his precious reserves and when to disregard the appeal altogether. His chance of winning the battle depends upon his having reserves to use at the right time and place, and if they are weakened too soon all hope of victory is gone.

On April 16 the situation still looked doubtful on our front in Flanders; but Foch thought otherwise, he said:

> The battle in Flanders is practically over, Haig will not need any more troops from me.

Not even the loss of Kemmel a few days later ruffled him. He was right, and the battle in Flanders ended in a complete repulse of the second German effort to break through.

Foch used to impress upon his students the supreme importance in war of the will and spirit of the commander-in-chief. The commander, he said, is the sword of his army. The general who refuses to admit the possibility of defeat can compel victory; a general who thinks he may be beaten is halfway on the road to defeat. In those dark days of the spring of 1918 Foch did not fail to put these principles of his into practice, and it was his courage and resolution which laid the foundation of victory.

He was nobly supported by Sir Douglas Haig, whose calm, unruffled temperament enabled him to stand the appalling strain which began when his right crumbled on March 21 and continued until June, when the arrival of British reinforcements from the East and the steady growth of the American Army allowed him to breathe more freely. But for Foch an even more severe trial was coming. He believed that the most dangerous course which Ludendorff could take, and therefore the most probable one, was to continue the attempt to separate the British from the French Army, and he accordingly took measures to meet such an attack by the Germans.

There was at this time much talk of Foch's "army of manoeuvre," but it never existed, save in the imagination of those critics who had got hold of the term from a superficial study of Napoleon's strategy. Foch had all he could do to stop the holes which Ludendorff was making in the Allied front by sending divisions to reinforce the armies which were being pressed back. In order to have fresh divisions ready for this purpose he had to place in the line other divisions which had been sorely battered in battle and filled up with recruits whose training had been cut short. As soon as the battle in Flanders was ended Foch arranged with Haig to send down to the Chemin des Dames, on the Aisne front, five British divisions, of which four had fought the Germans both in the March battle on the Somme and in the April battle in Flanders, and the fifth had been heavily engaged in the former battle.

The Chemin des Dames ridge was looked upon as a position of great strength, and Foch did not think it likely that the Germans would attack it. He therefore withdrew from it a number of fresh French divisions, which he placed in reserve ready to meet the attack which he expected Ludendorff to renew upon Amiens, and replaced them with tired French and British divisions. While the Bavarian Crown Prince Rupprecht had been endeavouring to force his way to the Channel ports, the German Crown Prince had been resting his troops which had taken part in the Somme battle, and he had a great number of divisions in reserve down the valley of the Oise. These divisions were so placed that, while they threatened an attack upon Amiens, they could be moved just as quickly against the Chemin des Dames.

Ludendorff was, in fact, playing again the game he had played in March, and on May 27 he surprised the French and British troops on the Chemin des Dames by much the same methods as he had used against the British Third and Fifth Armies. Again, the boys, of whom the British divisions were in great part composed, covered themselves with glory on the right of the battle front, and saved Reims by their tenacity in ten days of battle which took the place of the rest they had been promised; but the Allied centre was overwhelmed, and the German Crown Prince drove straight through to the Marne, where his further progress was just checked in time by the arrival at Château-Thierry of American troops. This German drive brought the enemy within forty miles of Paris, and was a heavy blow both to Foch and to the French people. Simultaneously with the Crown Prince's attack, "Big Bertha" began bombarding Paris, and a number of air raids were made upon the French capital, from which an exodus began very similar to that which had taken place in 1914 before the first Battle of the Marne.

Foch was now in the most trying position in which a commander-in-chief can be placed in war. The enemy had deceived him and the capital of his country was in danger. Soldiers know that the general who makes no mistakes in war achieves nothing, and they understand how difficult it is for a commander who has been forced to stand on the defensive to divine what the enemy may do next; but the statesmen and general public of democratic countries very rarely appreciate the difficulties and limitations of defence, and the general who has failed to foresee and provide for an emergency is usually looked at askance by them.

Therefore, in any circumstances the position of a commander-in-chief whose troops have been worsted in battle is not enviable, but his troubles and responsibilities are increased tenfold when he is in command not only of troops of his own nation, but of the armies of Allies. One of the greatest tributes to Foch's strength of will and character is that in this time of trial he kept the confidence of the Allied Armies and of the Allied Governments, and both M. Clemenceau and Mr. Lloyd George deserve their full share of credit for the trust which they reposed in him despite the inauspicious overture to unity of command. The days were now fast approaching when this trust was to have its reward.

Ludendorff's March offensive had led to an appeal from the British Government to the United States of America to expedite the dispatch of troops to France. This appeal met with a prompt and warm response, and resulted in one of the most remarkable achievements of the whole war. Just as in the March crisis Foch had hastened the arrival of the French reserves, so by one means or another the transport of men across the Atlantic was increased until from the month of June onwards 300,000 American soldiers were brought over each month, a feat of transportation which is without parallel in the history of war.

This feat, which upset all Ludendorff's calculations as to the rate at which American troops could reach France, was made possible by the spirit and enthusiasm of the American people, by the supremacy of the British Navy, and by the self-denial of the British people, who, in order to save tonnage to bring American troops to France, willingly accepted restrictions upon imports into Great Britain which imposed upon them very real privations.

By the beginning of June these measures had begun to take effect, and the number of American divisions in France mounted very rapidly. At the same time a steady stream of seasoned British troops, withdrawn from other theatres of war, was pouring into France, and, owing to the respite which Ludendorff allowed the British Army while he was forcing his way toward the Marne, there was time for Sir Douglas Haig to assimilate and train the drafts sent out from England. This work of reconstructing the British Army was much helped by the arrival on the British front of several American divisions, of which some went into the line and thus enabled British divisions to be withdrawn for rest and training.

So, it came about that though by the middle of June the Germans were within forty miles of Paris and within forty miles of Calais and Boulogne, and Ludendorff had still strong reserves at his disposal, yet the danger of a crushing German victory was daily growing smaller. This was shown by the result of Ludendorff's fourth offensive, which took place in the second week of June, and was intended to improve the position created by the German Crown Prince's surprise at the Chemin des Dames. The drive to the Marne had left the Germans in possession of a triangular salient some twenty-six miles deep and about thirty-three miles wide at the base along the Aisne, the apex of the triangle being at Château-Thierry.

The triangle was somewhat confined for the assembly of large forces within it, and Ludendorff wanted more elbow room. Therefore, one of the Crown Prince's generals, von Hutier, attempted to widen the base of the triangle to the west of Soissons by an attack delivered between the Amiens and the Marne salients. The immediate objective of this attack was Compiègne, and had von Hutier succeeded in taking that town he would have linked up the two salients and have given Ludendorff a much more convenient front for an attack upon Paris. Foch, however, was ready, and foiled von Hutier by a counter-attack which was an earnest of what was to come later. The Germans did not reach Compiègne, their position for an attack upon Paris was not appreciably improved, and they got little return for very heavy losses.

After von Hutier's attack was brought to a stop Ludendorff set about preparing for his great effort. As to the result of this effort the Germans were more blatantly confident and boastful than they had been any time since their first victories of August, 1914. They said that the British Army had been exhausted by its defeats in the spring, and that we had no men with which to make good our losses. They said that it was utterly impossible that America should have in the time created armies fit to fight in battle, that the Allies were bluffing when they spoke about the large number of American troops in France. They said that the Allies had not at their disposal the shipping to make such movement of troops possible. The U-boats had seen to that.

★★★★★★★★★★★★

> Russia collapsed. There then arose the possibility which, before the autumn of 1917, no one had contemplated of seeking to bring about a decision of the war during 1918, by an attack on land, which would be certain to succeed if by that time the U-boat campaign had reduced tonnage to an extent which made the rapid transport of American troops impossible, or if our submarines were able to hit some of the enemy's transports. According to the reports made by the navy this was to be expected.—Ludendorff.

★★★★★★★★★★★★

Ludendorff informed his government on the eve of the battle that victory was certain, a fact not mentioned by Ludendorff in his *Reminiscences*, but disclosed by von Hintze, who was then Secretary for Foreign Affairs. As to the quality of the American troops, the German authorities issued this remarkable statement:

Demonstrations against the war are the order of the day in

New York. Of the enthusiasm announced in the Entente reports there is no trace amongst the Americans who have been called up for military service. Soldiers on embarkation almost make a despairing impression, and are kept together by a police force which has been specially created for the purpose.

This is but one of a large number of official and semi-official pronouncements distributed to the German press and amongst the German troops during the summer of 1918, and this policy of deception was, I believe, one of the contributory causes of the suddenness of the collapse when things began to go wrong. Soldiers and people then discovered that those in authority over them had either been lying to them or had been hopelessly wrong in their judgment, and they lost faith just at the time when faith was most needed. It is not at present easy to determine how far these misrepresentations were deliberate on the part of the German authorities and how far the responsibility lay with agents who sought for and sent in information which would be pleasing rather than the truth.

The German spy system has always been held up as a model of efficiency, and the popular belief was that the Germans knew everything which went on inside our lines or took place at our most secret councils. It is certainly true that the German spy system was very elaborate, and that it gave their authorities good information upon points of detail, but the test of any system of intelligence is the correctness or otherwise of the impression which it creates in the minds of the generals and statesmen who use it, and at every great crisis in this war the German intelligence system created a wrong impression.

In July, 1914, the Germans believed that Belgium would be terrorised into submission and that Great Britain, being fully occupied with Irish and labour troubles, would not fight. A month later, before the first Battle of the Marne, they held that the British Army had been annihilated and that the morale of the French troops was broken. The *Kaiser* had arranged the details of his entry into Paris, and had ordered a gala luncheon at the Hotel Majestic, near the Arc de Triomphe. In the spring of 1917, they believed that Great Britain was on the verge of starvation, and that six months of unrestricted U-boat warfare would bring us to our knees. (Ludendorff thought this would take a year, but believed it would be accomplished before America could intervene effectively.)

They were so completely out in their understanding of the psychology of the American people that they did not understand that an order to the United States not to send across the Atlantic more than one vessel a week, which was to be painted in a particular way and to follow a particular route to a particular British port, would infallibly arouse and unite all classes in an irresistible enthusiasm for the war. In September, 1917, Ludendorff, in a review of the position which he submitted to his government, implied that Great Britain, France and Italy were on the verge of exhaustion, and that their internal condition was more precarious than that of Germany, whose military position was far the stronger.

No account was taken in this document of the effect of America's economic and financial aid to the Entente. In July, 1918, before the second Battle of the Marne, the Germans were equally out in their count, and they christened beforehand the battle which they were to fight the "*Friedensturm*," the attack which would bring peace—of course a German peace. The Kaiser had a grand stand built for himself on a wooded height overlooking the Marne, and to this he mounted, on the morning of July 15 to see his troops advance to victory.

While the Germans were busy with their preparations for winning the war by one great final blow, Foch was also at work. He had divined Ludendorff's plan, and he was quite certain that the Germans meant to attack upon both sides of Reims—that is to say, that the German Crown Prince would renew his attempts to get to Paris. It happened, however, that the other Crown Prince, the Bavarian Rupprecht, had strong reserves in Flanders, and a short advance there would, as I have already pointed out, place the German guns within range of the Channel ports. Foch had been wrong in May, and he might be wrong again this time.

He was himself confident that he was right, but he had to convince the Allied statesmen that he was right, for he did not feel himself strong enough to deal with the German Crown Prince without drawing upon Haig for troops, and thus weakening the armies covering the Channel coast. He first sent southwards the eight French divisions which had been aiding us in Flanders, and asked Haig to move four British divisions to the neighbourhood of Amiens to relieve four more French divisions. This was a very serious reduction of Haig's strength; but Foch was not satisfied, and he asked that these four British divisions should be handed over to him for the counter-offensive which he was planning, and that yet other four British divisions should take their place about Amiens.

Haig being responsible to his Government for the safety of his army and the ports, felt that he must obtain their concurrence in this last step, though he was quite ready to take the responsibility upon himself of advising them to concur. It does honour to Foch, to Mr. Lloyd George, and to Sir Douglas Haig that in this critical time they all agreed. Both the British Government and the British Commander-in-Chief supported Foch, decided to back his judgment, and to accept the danger of weakening the British forces in the north, and he was thus enabled to mature his plans for the defeat of Ludendorff.

Many a general's plans in war have been upset because he was compelled by a nervous government to strengthen the defence of some point which they held to be vital to the national safety. The instances are few in which a government has shown itself ready to shoulder such responsibility as Mr. Lloyd George undertook on this occasion. Yet with the memory of what happened in April and May he had every excuse for hesitation. Fortunately, courage and a readiness to take risks for a great end are characteristics of the Prime Minister.

Foch's plans were based on a prolonged study of the conditions of trench warfare. The war on the Western Front has been repeatedly compared to a great siege. That comparison is accurate only up to a certain point. The conditions of trench warfare were, after due allowance is made for the changes due to modern improvements in arms, very like those which prevailed in some of the great sieges of the past.

There was the same deadly monotony of life in the trenches; there was a return to the weapons used in the past in the attack and defence of fortresses hand grenades, mortars and heavy artillery; there were the same hardships to be endured, due to the stationary life in holes dug in the ground, wet, cold and mud in winter, heat, dust and flies in summer; there were sallies by defenders and raids by the attackers, there were struggles for the outworks, and when the defenders tried to break out or the attackers to break in they both began by blasting a great breach in the defences with a concentrated bombardment of heavy artillery and followed this with an assault by the infantry.

There, however, the analogy ends. In the old days, once the assailants had broken through the defences into the town which they protected, their work was, with some rare exceptions, finished, and the place was at their mercy, but in the great war the worst of the struggle then began.

The defender, who was not cooped up in a town, but had ample space behind his lines and plenty of roads and railways at his disposal, was able to keep his reserves far back, where they could rest undisturbed by the enemy's artillery, and to bring them up fresh to the battlefield at a time when the attacking infantry was becoming wearied, when it had been thrown more or less into confusion by the stress of battle, when the difficulty of sending forward reinforcements and supplies of food and ammunition was for the assailant at its greatest. The essential difference between the siege warfare of old and the warfare as we have seen it during the great struggle in France and Belgium is that in the former a successful assault normally finished the business and brought victory; in the latter, the assault was but a prelude to a battle with the enemy's reserves.

From November, 1914, when trench lines were first established between the North Sea and the Swiss frontier, all the generals on the Western Front, British, French and German, were at work trying to solve the problem of how to break through. At first it was believed that this was mainly a question of having sufficient guns and sufficient ammunition of the right kind, of blasting a big enough hole in the defences. In 1915 Foch, with British help on his left flank, tried twice to capture the Vimy Ridge, and both times he failed with very heavy losses. In the same year Joffre tried, by a great assault delivered in Champagne, to burst through the German lines, and he, too, failed.

In the first half of 1916 the Germans, using much the same method of an artillery bombardment, followed by an infantry assault, tried to reach Verdun and were defeated. In the summer and autumn of that year Haig fought the first Battle of the Somme, which relieved Verdun and forced the Germans to retreat into the Hindenburg line, but ended there, like the other battles, in the deadlock of trench warfare. In 1917 General Nivelle succeeded General Joffre in the supreme command of the French Armies, and though Haig, in the Battle of Arras, carried out the part assigned to him by Nivelle, and the British Army bit deep into the German lines, capturing the Vimy Ridge, Nivelle's great attack on the Aisne front ended in a failure, which shook the confidence of the French Army.

Up to this time it had been argued that the success won had been sufficient to warrant the hope that with more and heavier guns, improved methods of gunnery and larger supplies of shell, the breach would be wider and deeper and that the assault must succeed, So the military policy in the Western theatre of war during 1915 and 1916 continued to be to increase the power and duration of the bombardment, and when a battle did not give the results expected it was always possible, as the munition factories of the Allies grew in size and numbers, to look forward to a still greater bombardment next time. But in 1917 the Allies suffered from no lack of equipment, and it was quite evident that lack of success was no longer due to lack of shell. The colossal bombardments which heralded these attacks literally tore off the surface of the ground. The guns had done their part, the breach was made, but the story was always the same.

The first bound forward of the attackers was almost invariably successful, and they easily overcame such of the enemy as remained alive in the bombarded area, with comparatively little loss to themselves. Then up came the enemy's reserves, and a slow hammer and tongs struggle developed, in which the attackers slowly gained ground at a very high price until gradually the attack lost its momentum and died away from exhaustion. Clearly the great bombardment was not the key to the problem, and it was necessary to look for some other solution.

During the autumn of 1916 and the summer of 1917, the French and British had fought a number of what in these days would be called small battles with complete success, the French around Verdun and on the Aisne front, the British on the Messines Ridge in Flanders. In these battles there was no attempt made to push the infantry far beyond the limits of the area which had been thoroughly pounded in the first bombardment, and in each of these, ground was gained and a considerable number of prisoners and guns captured very cheaply. This confirmed the experience gained in the opening phases of most of the great battles, namely, that it was comparatively easy for the guns to win the ground within their range and for the infantry then to advance and occupy it.

The Allies did not possess a sufficient number of guns to allow them to deliver a rapid succession of these punches against the different parts of the front, and it took a long time to shift a mass of artillery from one part of the line to another, but it was believed that a series of such blows delivered on the same front would end in the exhaustion of the German reserves and in a break through. This was called the attack with limited objective. The guns were to bombard an area of ground and the infantry to go forward and overcome the Germans, dazed and stunned by the bombardment; then the guns were to be moved forward on to the ground won, and the process was to be repeated until the infantry were able to break clean through.

On this principle the third Battle of Ypres was fought by the British Army in the late summer and autumn of 1917. That battle began on July 31, but, unfortunately, the month of August proved to be phenomenally wet and Ludendorff had devised a very successful answer to this form of attack. The mud of Flanders proved a terrible obstacle. It made the bringing forward of the guns and the masses of ammunition needed to feed them a work almost beyond human power, and the infantry had to endure indescribable hardship, with no cover from the enemy's fire save such as could be found in waterlogged shell-holes and trenches pounded by our artillery into a sticky mess.

At every step forward they sank to their knees or over into the gluey slime, which the soil of Flanders becomes when torn by shells and saturated with rain. Added to all this, the Germans neutralised the effect of the bombardment, upon which the plan of attack depended so largely for its success, by withdrawing all but a few men from the ground which would be most heavily shelled by us, and by meeting our weary infantry as they dragged themselves forward through the mud with counter-attacks by fresh troops. So, the fight up the ridges from Ypres to Passchendaele was a long, slow, costly business, and it came to an end before the problem of beating the enemy's reserves had been solved.

Then a new experiment was tried. Tanks had been first used by the British Army in the Battle of the Somme in small numbers. There are a great many people who believed, and still believe, that this was a great mistake; they hold that we should have waited until we had tanks in large numbers and then sprung a great surprise on the Germans. But it is an impossibility to simulate in practice the conditions of war, or to be certain how any new device will turn out until it has been tried in the field against the enemy. Further, the efficacy of any device to be used in war does not depend only, or even chiefly, upon its own perfections or imperfections; it depends mainly upon how it fits into the military machine. All the parts of an army, artillery, infantry, cavalry, tanks, machine-guns and aircraft have to learn to work together, to know what each can do and what are the needs of each, and this can only be learned by long practice together. The first experience of the tanks, in the autumn of 1916 and spring of 1917, was disappointing.

They were found to be too slow to keep pace even with the infantry, they broke down frequently, and there were many kinds of ground which they could not get over. In the Battle of Messines, the infantry found that the artillery had done all and more than all that was needed, and for the most part they did not wait for the tanks. In the third Battle of Ypres the mud proved altogether too much for the new weapon. So, for a time many of our generals and most of the infantry distrusted the tanks and regarded them as a failure. This did not damp the enthusiasm of the experts, who worked incessantly at improving the tanks, at devising new methods of employing them, and at showing the infantry how to work with them, and in November, 1917, the tanks got their first real chance. Haig decided to make a surprise attack on the very strongest part of the German front, the Hindenburg line west of Cambrai.

Hitherto, the time and labour required to collect a great mass of guns and the huge stores of shell for them had made it almost impossible to surprise the enemy, for this involved the extension of railway lines, the laying of tramways, the construction of roads, and a great increase in the normal traffic behind the lines. The German aeroplanes and spies always found out that something was up. Haig proposed to bring up a large number of tanks secretly at the last possible moment and to use them instead of guns to make the breach for his infantry.

The Germans had sent most of their reserves up to Flanders to meet our attacks at Passchendaele, and, relying on the strength of the Hindenburg line, had weakened the Cambrai front. The surprise was completely successful, and the tanks more than justified themselves by breaking clean through the most formidable defences which the Germans had been able to devise and by preparing the way for the advance of the infantry. Unfortunately, as I have already mentioned, the disaster to the Italian Army occurred at Caporetto, and Haig had to send five divisions southward to the help of our Allies, despite his urgent request to be allowed to keep at least two to support his attack at Cambrai. None of our five divisions fired a shot before the enemy were checked on the Piave, and we were furnished with a classical example of the advantages to a skilful enemy of interior lines of communication. This reduction in his strength so weakened Haig that he was unable to follow up his success, and when the German reserves arrived, they won back a good part of the ground we had gained.

This, then, was the position at the beginning of 1918, when Ludendorff was bringing his troops across from Russia and preparing for his great offensive. The attempt to break through by means of a great bombardment followed by an infantry assault had failed, so had the attempt to break through by means of a series of bombardments and assaults upon one part of the front; the attack with limited objective, the short, sharp punch in which the infantry moved forward and occupied the ground won in a single bombardment had proved a success, but the results gained by this method of attack had made little impression upon the whole long front; the use of tanks in numbers, in replacement of the prolonged bombardment, held out promise for the future.

Ludendorff was deeply impressed by our surprise attack at Cambrai, and believed he could break through if he brought off a surprise. He had very few tanks and no prospects of getting a large number, for the German munition factories could not at this period of the war find the necessary material; they had, in fact, more than they could do to keep the armies supplied with motor transport.

In 1918 the Germans had barely a score of tanks of their own manufacture, and these were of a type little, if at all, superior to our tanks of 1916. They had added to these by repairing some of the tanks which they had captured from us, but at no time did they possess any large number. It does not appear that Ludendorff was particularly impressed with the value of tanks before the events of the summer of 1918 taught him wisdom in this respect. He had, during the autumn of 1917, prepared an able memorandum on our methods in attack, in which he adverted on the dependence of our infantry upon what he termed material, its failures to seize opportunities when they presented themselves, and the delay caused by continually relieving infantry in the front line.

Much that he said was very true, particularly as regards our reliance upon bombardment as a means of gaining ground, but when he included tanks in his condemnation of "material" he forgot that he was writing of a new weapon capable of improvement. The development of aircraft during the course of the war should have taught him caution. It was not the tanks of Cambrai which made him think, but the effect produced by surprise. We lost a great number of tanks in that battle, because we had not yet learned how to use them, and did not appreciate their dependence upon the support of artillery, and Ludendorff, thinking of the success of the German counter-attack at Cambrai and of the derelict tanks lying within his lines, classed that battle as a "Battle of material."

So, he did not press his War Office to find means to provide him with tanks, and he set about getting his surprise by other methods. I have already described those methods and the measure of success which they achieved. He certainly, in his attacks in the first half of 1918, gained more ground, took more prisoners and guns and inflicted heavier losses than any other general had succeeded in doing on the Western Front. He was very nearly successful in his first drive for Amiens in March. He failed, as all other generals had failed, because his progress was stopped by the defender's reserves. Just at the time when the German troops were wearied, when it was becoming impossible to sustain the momentum of the attack by sending forward fresh troops and supplies from the rear, Foch brought the French troops from the south upon the scene.

Then Ludendorff made the mistake of trying for just a little more. His first effort had worn itself out by March 29, with the failure of the great attack upon the Arras front, but six days later, on April 4, after an interval not long enough for the systematic preparation of a fresh battle, but long enough for the Allies to strengthen their forces and improve their defences, he made another attempt to break through which was shattered and only served to deplete his strength. He repeated this mistake in Flanders at the end of April, when he thought he had found another soft spot. At this time, it was a question whether he would be able to keep forces enough in hand for a last smashing blow before the arrival of American troops finally turned the scale in favour of the Allies, and he fell into the same error as every other German general on the Western Front, the error of underrating his enemy and believing that the next blow must be the smashing blow.

When his first attack in Flanders had been checked he tried again on April 29 and suffered a severe defeat. The effect of his failures of March 28, April 5, and April 29 was that he required time to make good his losses, rest his troops, train them and replenish his stores of munitions. When the Crown Prince's attacks in May and June were stopped by the action of the American troops at Château-Thierry and by Foch's counter-attacks, Ludendorff needed a full month to prepare for his last effort, and during that month the Allied reserves, far from being used up, were growing daily stronger. The German had failed to solve the problem. The reserves stood between him and victory.

A short time before the Germans started their last offensive Battle of the war a meeting of the Supreme War Council took place at Versailles. The Allied statesmen were naturally very anxious about the situation. The Germans were still within forty miles of Paris and within the same distance of the Channel ports, and they had sprung three great surprises upon us in two months. The British generals had not thought it possible that the Germans would get almost to the outskirts of Amiens, would capture Kemmel Hill and menace Hazebrouck; Foch had not foreseen that the German Crown Prince would reach the Marne. It was true that the balance of strength had been steadily shifting in our favour.

The British Army had made a marvellous recovery from its reverses in the spring, and with the arrival of seasoned troops from Palestine, who had not suffered the heavy losses endured by all our troops on the Western Front and, therefore, had a far higher proportion of men in the prime of life, and of experienced officers and non-commissioned officers, was in as good shape as ever. Haig's strength, which had fallen to forty-nine effective divisions in May, had risen in July to fifty-three divisions, and, thanks to the development of our munition factories, not only had our heavy losses in guns and war material been promptly replaced, but we were stronger in artillery, machineguns, tanks and aeroplanes than we had been in March.

When Pershing heard at the end of March that the conference of Doullens had appointed Foch to the supreme command he had four combatant divisions to offer the new *generalissimo*, but of these only one, the 1st American Division, was considered sufficiently trained to take its place in the line. Early in July there were twenty-five American divisions in France, and twelve of them had completed their training and were ready to take part in battle; such had been the effect of the speeding up of the transport of American troops across the Atlantic.

While the forces under Foch's control had been growing, Ludendorff's had begun to dwindle. The Germans had reached their greatest strength early in May, when they had two hundred and seven divisions on the Western Front, but they had not found it possible to replace at once all the losses incurred in the battles of May and June. Altogether the position was much more favourable than it had been six weeks before, yet the fighting strength of the Germans was still greater than that of the Allies. On the eve of the second Battle of the Marne they had a superiority of over a quarter of a million rifles; in guns they were about equal to the Allied artillery; it was only in machine-guns, tanks and aircraft that they were inferior.

With the flow of American troops to France assured, Foch was certain of having an ample reserve in due time, and Ludendorff had no means of increasing his; but at the moment the number of American troops trained to take part in battle was not sufficient to give the Allies a definite numerical superiority at the front. So, the statesmen were still anxious, feeling that they could not afford a fourth surprise by the Germans.

Foch was always and rightly reticent as to his plans. He would not do more than express his confidence in general terms. The essential difference between his mind and the minds of the German generals was that he regarded war as an art, not as a science. "There is nothing absolute in war," is one of his favourite axioms. He believed it to be beyond the power of the human mind to foresee all the factors that would influence the actions of the opposing general, all the changes and chances on the front which would influence the actions of opposing troops and often decide the issue of battles.

Therefore, he acted on certain broad principles which, he was persuaded, governed the application of his art, just as there are principles which govern the arts of painting, music and architecture; but he could no more tell beforehand what form each of his strokes would take than a painter can tell you beforehand with what stroke of his brush he will get his effects. The artist's strokes depend upon the inspiration and the circumstances of the moment, but they are not haphazard strokes. They are all made in accordance with the principles of art and on a general plan. The Germans, on the other hand, believed more in the plan than in the inspiration. They were very good planners.

Von Moltke's first plan for the invasion of France was excellent; so, in its details, was Ludendorff's plan for his offensive in March, 1918. Both failed in the execution of their plans because they allowed scientific planning to take precedence of the principles of the art. So, Foch did not tell the Allied statesmen assembled at Versailles, in these trying days when the Germans were engaged in tuning up their war machines for their last great blow, very much of his plans. One of them asked him point blank: "But, General, if the Germans do make their great attack, what is your plan?" and Foch answered by striking out three rapid blows, with his right, with his left and again with his right, following these by launching out a vigorous kick. There was the principle of the art dramatically described.

Foch had been thinking deeply over the problems of the war which I have described in the first part of this chapter—how to break through, how to defeat the enemy's reserves, how to apply the old principles of war to the new conditions of trench warfare, which made a war of movement and manoeuvre as it had been conceived in the past impossible. He had had his bitter experiences like other generals. His attacks on the Vimy Ridge had failed, and he had acquired a reputation in certain quarters of being reckless, regardless of the lives of his men. Statesmen, anxiously watching the appalling casualty lists and the dwindling man-power of the nation, were suspicious of a general with such a reputation.

It is not generally known that for a time Foch was under a cloud. After a nasty motor accident which befell him in the summer of 1916, he was given the duty of studying the possibility of a German invasion through Switzerland, a job which, for a time, practically put him on the shelf, and after he had finished that he was literally placed on the shelf for a few weeks, early in 1917, when he was actually put on half pay. From this he was recalled, largely, I believe, through the influence of M. Clemenceau, who had not then become Prime Minister of France, to be Chief of Staff in Paris. While in Paris he had time for thinking.

The main facts before him were the failure of the great assault upon one part of the front, the terrible cost in life of the slow hammer and tongs struggle in which it always ended, and the success of the limited punches. Therefore, as a principle, he determined not to be drawn into a protracted struggle, not to attempt the great break through until the enemy's reserves were exhausted, and he proposed to exhaust these reserves by a series of limited punches. Hence the three short, sharp blows, followed by the big kick. Not that he had in July, 1918, worked out in detail the great plan by which the war was won. He could not have told the statesmen in Versailles whether he would be ready for the big kick in the autumn of 1918 or whether he would have to wait for it until the following year.

He has said himself that all that he had in his mind when he delivered his first punch on July 18 in the second Battle of the Marne was to relieve Paris and that the purpose of the second punch, made by Haig on August 8, was to relieve Amiens. It was only when the succession of victories won by the British Army between August 8 and September 9 began to produce the effect at which Foch was aiming, the exhaustion of the German reserves, an effect made certain by Pershing's victory of September 12 at St. Mihiel, that he decided on the great battle which began on September 26 and decided the result of the war.

All other generals on the Western Front had tried the big kick too soon; most of them had begun with it and had not thought it necessary or possible to prepare for the maximum effort of which they were capable by preliminary fighting. In distant Mesopotamia Maude at the end of 1916 had, by a carefully planned series of limited attacks, worn down the resistance of the Turks and had then forced his way across the Tigris and routed their army; but those operations were, as compared with the vast front in France, on a small scale, and the enemy was very inferior in skill and equipment to the Germans, so the application of Maude's methods to the problems of the Western Front did not leap to the eye.

In 1917 Haig was, as I have said, near reaching the solution at Cambrai, but the Caporetto disaster supervened, and Cambrai became a secondary enterprise instead of the climax of a great campaign. In the spring of 1918 Ludendorff had, as I have pointed out, made a great advance in battle tactics, but he committed the mistake of aiming from the first at a breakthrough, and he allowed himself in each battle to be drawn too far by his early success, so that he was too late and too weak when he was ready for the *Friedensturm*. Foch had always taught before the war that the decisive act of the battle in the war of manoeuvre must be prepared systematically by a number of preliminary combats, and that the opening for the knockout blow had to be created. That was a military doctrine which was universally accepted. He discovered how to apply to the new conditions of trench warfare these old principles of war, and therein lies his title to greatness.

Fortune favours the brave and the thoughtful, and Foch was fortunate in that the fierce struggles which had preceded the turn in the tide of war had been very far from fruitless. The great offensive campaigns of the Allies and their resolute courage in defence had sapped the military strength of Germany, and in July, 1918, the cream of her army had perished. Foch had to put the finishing touches to a process which had been long at work. The advent of the American Armies gave him the men, the vast output of the Allied munition factories the material, in particular the great improvements which had been made in the tanks since their first appearance in battle and the quantities of them available gave him just the means he needed for carrying through his scheme. Cambrai had proved that tanks could replace the long bombardment and obviate all the slow preparation which it involved.

Even Cambrai had not, however, established that confidence between the infantry and the tanks which was essential to success, nor had the co-operation between tanks and artillery been completely worked out. Cambrai had shown that tanks are particularly vulnerable to artillery fire, and the Germans were known to have placed a number of guns in forward positions along their front for the special purpose of dealing with our tanks. At Cambrai one resolute German artillery officer, working his gun to the last from behind a park wall, had knocked out a number of our tanks as they came in view, much as a sportsman bowls over rabbits bolting from ferrets in a warren. Early in July a comparatively small operation carried out by Rawlinson's Fourth Army settled all these problems.

Haig was even then planning a battle to free Amiens, but the clearing of the Villers-Brettonneux plateau and the capture of Hamel was a necessary preliminary to the larger adventure. Rawlinson entrusted this task to the Australian Corps, who were given sixty of the newest type of tanks to help them. The choice was happy, for the Australians had had an unfortunate experience with tanks at Bullecourt in 1917 and were distrustful of them. The work of infantry and tanks in combination was carefully practised beforehand, and on July 4, when the attack took place, it was carried through "according to plan." The tanks, working behind a powerful artillery barrage, which protected them from the enemy's guns, overcame the German machine-guns and drove their infantry into their dug-outs, where they fell an easy prey to our infantry. Thereafter, the Australians could not speak too highly of the tanks, and mutual confidence was established.

This little engagement, which ended in the capture of all our objectives and of one thousand five hundred prisoners, was also noteworthy for the fact that four companies of the 33rd American Division took part in it. These men had been training in the line with the Australians and had eagerly prepared to join in the fight when at the last moment orders came up that they were not to participate, as their training for battle was not completed. Nevertheless, they went over the top with the Australians, who are reported to have said of them that the Americans were good lads but too rough!

With this fortunate experiment faith in the tanks spread. The commanders already believed in them, and now that belief in their power to "make good" spread to the ranks. Nor was this the only good which the action of Hamel brought us. Our reverses in the spring had naturally affected the morale of the army. The men had never wavered in their determination to hold on, to "stick it out," but their confidence in their superiority over the enemy and in their power to drive him back had been shaken when they saw him gaining more ground and making larger captures than either we or the French had ever succeeded in doing. It was as essential to restore that confidence before we could hope to attack successfully on a great scale as it was to establish confidence between tanks and infantry.

Rawlinson, in a series of minor operations, of which Hamel was the latest and the most successful, shook the enemy's confidence and built up that of his own men, and the brilliant work of the tanks added the last touch, so that when the crisis came both men and material were ready. Tanks made surprise, that greatest weapon of generalship, much easier than it had been, they saved life and economised troops, and, therefore, that quick succession of punches for which Foch was seeking his opportunity became possible. The artist had his materials to hand. Honour to him that he knew how to use them.

CHAPTER 3

The Preparation for Armageddon

Ludendorff's *Friedensturm* was to be developed from the salient with its head at Château-Thierry on the Marne, which the German Crown Prince had made in his May attack. The Germans had spent the time since that attack was stopped in training their men for just such another assault, and proposed again to pour in a mass of troops wherever they could make a hole in the Allied defences. But railways are necessary to keep a mass of troops supplied with their needs in battle, and it happened that the only railways which could be used to supply the German troops in the Château-Thierry salient passed through the town of Soissons, which lay in the north-west corner of the salient not far from the German front line.

For his advance upon Paris Ludendorff wanted railways on the eastern side of the salient as well. Therefore, the first part of his plan involved the capture of Reims, so that he might repair and use the railways running through that city. He intended to capture Reims by a big attack delivered on the Champagne front to the east of the town, combined with another attack to the south-west of Reims. These attacks were designed to unite on the River Marne near Epernay and thus cut off Reims and all the troops defending it. Simultaneously, a third attack was to be made southwards across the Marne between Château-Thierry and Dormans.

When these attacks had all developed satisfactorily the German troops on the western face of the salient between Soissons and Château-Thierry were to come in and co-operate in the advance upon Paris, and for this purpose their troops were, at the beginning of July, reorganised under a general and staff recently brought across from the Russian front. This was a big scheme, but there is evidence that it was intended to be still bigger and that Ludendorff proposed, when his movement against Paris astride the Marne was in full swing, to develop yet another attack upon Paris from the north by issuing from the Amiens salient, which he had created in March, and that farther north still Rupprecht was preparing for an advance in Flanders.

Probably owing to the carelessness engendered by over-confidence the Germans took fewer pains to conceal their intentions before this battle than they had done earlier in the year, and Foch was ready for Ludendorff's first moves, which opened on July 15. (Ludendorff says that before the battle the coming attack near Reims was talked of throughout Germany.) The great attack to the east of Reims fell upon the army of General Gouraud, who adopted and improved upon the same defensive tactics as we had intended to use against the Germans in the March battles, but had been prevented by the fog from applying successfully with the single exception of the battle on the Arras front on March 28. Gouraud, applying these tactics with better fortune and great skill, foiled the enemy's plans.

He had the good luck to capture a party of Germans on the eve of the attack, and from these prisoners he ascertained the exact time at which the bombardment would open and the enemy's infantry advance. He left in his front trenches only a few troops to watch for and break up the German assault, and withdrew his main line of resistance behind the area swept by the full storm of the hostile bombardment, while his own guns, which had been reinforced, poured a tornado of shell upon the German infantry as it moved forward, with the result that it was a disordered mass of field-greys which flung itself against the French battle positions, and except at two points on either flank of the attack these withstood the shock. The small breaches which the Germans succeeded in making were quickly closed, and the attack ended for them in a disastrous defeat.

This brilliant defence by Gouraud, in the centre of whose army stood part of the 42nd American Division, laid the foundation for our subsequent victories and of itself was sufficient to cause the failure of Ludendorff's plan, for one arm of the pincers with which he had intended to nip out Reims had failed to act, and twenty-five picked German divisions specially rested and trained for the enterprise had been shattered. Throughout the three and a half years of trench warfare on the Western Front no attack made on such a scale had met with so little success in its opening phase.

It had come to be regarded as inevitable that the defender should lose ground, prisoners and guns. Gouraud lost very little more ground than that which he had deliberately abandoned to the enemy, few prisoners and no guns. While these events were taking place to the east of Reims the Germans, in their remaining two attacks south-west of the city and across the Marne between Château-Thierry and Dormans, did make some progress, and before Foch struck back, he wished to see that front steadied. It was steadied mainly by the firm courage of the American troops who formed part of General Degoutte's army, and particularly of the 3rd and 28th American Divisions, which held the sector east of Château-Thierry, and by the stout resistance of Berthelot's army on the heights south of Reims.

On the 17th it looked to be possible for a time that the Germans would force their way up the Marne valley to Epernay, but the gap which they had made was not wide enough, and they were in the position of a man who has got his head through a fence but finds the hole too small for his body.

Then, on the fourth day of the battle, July 18, Foch sprang the first surprise, for which he had been quietly preparing, upon the Germans. While the enemy were still trying to make progress from the southern and eastern faces of the Marne salient, General Mangin attacked the western face between Soissons and Château-Thierry. It required great courage and determination to make that attack as it was made. The Germans had still a superiority of more than 250,000 infantry on the Western Front, and Foch, as well as Mr. Lloyd George and Sir Douglas Haig, had to take risks. When the first plans for that counter-stroke were made by the French generals on the spot they considered that the most which they could do was to attack on a front of some twelve miles. Foch came down and insisted that the front of attack should be more than doubled.

"We haven't the men!" said the French generals.

"I know that," replied Foch; "still you must attack the whole of the German flank." The spirit which turned the first Battle of the Marne into a decisive victory for the Allies was to win in the second Battle of the Marne another triumph.

The popular faith in Foch's army of manoeuvre led to the belief that the *generalissimo* had brought up large reinforcements of fresh troops at the right moment and had overwhelmed the Germans with superior numbers. This was very far from being the case, and Foch had, in fact, at his disposal few troops who could by any stretch of imagination be called fresh. The French divisions were tired by the long defensive struggle which followed on the Crown Prince's May attack. The 1st American Division was on its way to a well-deserved rest after a long spell in the line on the Montdidier front, the 2nd American Division had only been relieved in the first week of July after its bitter struggle in Belleu Wood. Of all the Allied troops on the western side of the German salient only the 26th American Division, which had taken the place of the 2nd north of the Marne, was unwearied by its previous efforts. But Pershing was as convinced as was Foch himself of the importance of a counter-attack against the German flank and insisted that his 1st and 2nd Divisions could and would fight, and they were brought up to strengthen Mangin's battle.

The 1st American Division only reached its positions on the evening of the 17th, while part of the infantry of the 2nd Division did not come up until the attack was actually in progress. The late arrival of this reinforcement helped to keep the Germans in the dark as to what was afoot, and Mangin was able to use the great forests of Villers-Cotterets, which lay behind his post, to screen his preparations. His method was adapted from those employed by Haig at Cambrai in the previous November. He opened with a very short but intense bombardment which lasted just long enough to drive the Germans to their dug-outs and to cut their telephone communication. Then a mass of tanks followed the barrage through the German defences, to be followed in turn by a rush of French and American infantry. The Germans were taken completely by surprise. (Ludendorff mentions that two deserters came over to the Germans on the 11th and said that a great tank attack was in preparation in the Villers-Cotteret forest. As the days passed and nothing happened, the Germans appear to have believed that this was a false alarm.)

They had been thinking only of their advance to Paris, and had neglected their trenches, with the result that there were none of the formidable rear lines of defence which they had been wont to throw up rapidly and skilfully with the aid of the forced labour of the French peasants and of prisoners of war. (Ludendorff makes the influenza epidemic largely responsible for this neglect.) Mangin's chief object was to get to a position from which he could prevent the Germans from using the railways passing through Soissons. His main effort had been made between the Aisne and the Ourcq, the front of battle being extended south of that river by a French division and the 26th American Division.

By the evening of July 19 Mangin's guns dominated both the railway junction and also the main road connecting Soissons and Château-Thierry. Ludendorff had failed to get Reims, and now had lost the use of the one artery of supply which enabled him to maintain the great mass of troops he had crowded into the Marne salient. His troops across the river, struggling hard to maintain what they had won, were at once in difficulties, and there was nothing left but to withdraw them. That withdrawal was not easy, for a Franco-American counter-attack had given the Allies possession of heights on the south bank of the river from which many of the bridges thrown by the Germans could be shelled, while the enemy's infantry was continually harassed by attacks from the air.

Now, as I have explained, the principle upon which Foch had determined to act was to deliver a series of punches, each with a definite but limited object. His idea was to press the enemy so long as he gave way before the punch, but to avoid a slow, protracted struggle when the German resistance began to harden. So, Mangin, having achieved his purpose of taking the railways through Soissons, stopped, rested and relieved his troops, and it fell to Degoutte to attack next in a north-easterly direction from the Château-Thierry front against the Germans yielding on the Marne.

The fresh vigour of the Americans—28th, 3rd and 26th Divisions, with the 4th and 32nd in support—swept the enemy back from the Marne to the Ourcq, behind which river they attempted to stand between Oulchy-le-Château and Fère-en-Tardenois. Simultaneously, two of the four British divisions sent down from the north by Haig, the 51st and 62nd, reinforced the French and Italian forces on the eastern side of the salient, and there, too, but more slowly, the Germans were compelled to give ground. Meantime, the two remaining British divisions, the 15th and the 34th, joined Mangin, who, on July 23, was ready for another blow. (The 51st was the Highland Territorial division, the 62nd the West Yorkshire Territorials, the 15th a Scottish division of the "second thousand" the 34th had been reformed of battalions from Palestine.) This was delivered between the Ourcq and Soissons, and threatened the flank of the Germans opposed to Degoutte on the Ourcq.

Degoutte's army had been reinforced by the transfer to it of the 42nd American Division from Gouraud, which relieved the 26th, and by the appearance in the front line of the 32nd American Division, which relieved the 3rd, and under this combined pressure from the west and the south the German defence between the Ourcq and the Aisne gradually broke down.

On July 26 the 15th Scottish Division captured Buzancy, east of the main Soissons-Château-Thierry road, and Degoutte was able to enter Fère-en-Tardenois. Then followed two days of fierce German counter-attacks delivered by reinforcements sent southwards by Rupprecht. These attacks were a last attempt by the Germans to hold the north side of the Ourcq valley, and they were broken by the 32nd and 42nd American Divisions. On July 31 the last crisis of the battle was over and the whole valley of the Ourcq had been won by Degoutte.

Ludendorff now found that he was left with no leisure to restore his lines of supply, that the salient was daily getting narrower, and that congestion and confusion within it left him no alternative but to come out of it altogether. Accordingly, he retreated behind the Vesle and Aisne, pressed on all sides by the Allied forces, which had been strengthened by the 77th American Division. The Germans got across the rivers in the first days of August. Paris was relieved of the menace which had hung over her for six weeks, and a second time the Marne had proved fatal to German hopes.

It is one of the remarkable coincidences of the war that twice, confident of victory, the Germans should have crossed the Marne, neglecting to protect their right flank, and that twice a blow against that neglected flank should have brought their offensives to ruin. It is little less remarkable that in the first Battle of the Marne the first five divisions of the British Army, crossing the river near Château-Thierry, in their first offensive campaign after the retreat from Mons, should have advanced north-eastwards through Oulchy-le-Château and Fère-en-Tardenois to the Vesle and the Aisne, and that the first American divisions to take part in an offensive battle should have traversed exactly the same ground.

The Germans behind the Vesle and the Aisne were posted in strong positions; by withdrawing from the salient they had extricated themselves from the difficulties in which Mangin's blow at Soissons had placed them and were ready to put up a strong resistance. Foch thereupon tossed the ball to Sir Douglas Haig, who, on August 8, attacked the enemy on the Amiens front. In the Battle of Amiens the 3rd British Corps, with which was a regiment of the 33rd American Division, the Australian and the Canadian Corps, belonging to the Fourth British Army under Sir Henry Rawlinson, attacked the western face of the great salient, which the Germans had driven into our front in March, on a front of about eleven miles, while the First French Army, commanded by General Debeney and placed by Foch under Haig's orders, prolonged the front of battle by about four miles to the south.

The plan of attack, like Mangin's, was based on the experience gained at Hamel and on what we had learned from Ludendorff's methods in the Battle of March 21. I have described how, on that day, the Germans opened a sudden and intense bombardment from a mass of guns brought up secretly at the last moment, and how they profited from the heavy fog which enveloped the battlefield. In the early years of the war fog or bad weather of any kind had been regarded as a fatal obstacle to successful attack, because it blinded the gunners and prevented them from creating the breach for the infantry assault. Time and again in the early days of trench warfare, when the Germans were firing five shells to our one, a day of fog had been hailed by our infantry with joy as a day of rest and of relief from shell-fire.

Time and again attacks planned by us and by our French Allies were postponed because the weather conditions made it difficult, or even impossible, for the artillery to ascertain by preliminary trial the exact adjustment of their guns needed for the bombardment of the targets allotted to them. This process of registration of targets had been regarded as an indispensable preliminary of battle, and when a great mass of guns was to be employed it was a slow and elaborate business. Time and again it had given us warning of the enemy's intention to attack and had warned the enemy that we were preparing to attack him; it was one of the factors which had made it all but impossible to achieve surprise.

But by 1918 the development of scientific gunnery had made it possible to ascertain for the gunners beforehand the exact adjustment required to enable them to reach any given target under any reasonable conditions of weather. So, the slow process of registration became unnecessary. It was possible to open a great bombardment without previously alarming the enemy, and, best of all, the attackers became far more independent of the weather than they had ever been. Fog became an aid instead of an impediment to attack, because, under its protection, guns, tanks and infantry could be massed unseen. So, for this battle of August 8 two thousand guns were collected on Rawlinson's front of attack, many of them being brought into action at the last moment, and hardly any had opened fire from their new positions before they all crashed out together.

A friendly mist covered the final assembly of the assaulting troops and of the tanks, and these burst through the enemy's lines almost simultaneously with the opening of the bombardment which rolled on ahead of them in the form of a crushing barrage. In no battle of the war was the power of the tank better displayed. The tank of the summer of 1918 was, in speed, ability to overcome obstacles and turn quickly in any direction, a vastly improved machine from that of the Somme Battle of 1916. About two hundred of these were employed in the first line, with as many more in support, and they not only during the battle drove avenues for the advance of the infantry through the German defences, overcame their nests of machine-guns and spread demoralisation in the German ranks, but, by thus relieving the artillery of many of the complicated tasks which had formerly fallen to them in helping the infantry forward, they also helped the process of simplifying and speeding up the preparations for battle.

Haig's first orders to Rawlinson to prepare for battle went out on July 13, a little over three weeks before the attack, while the preliminaries for the great attacks, which in former years had begun with days of shelling, had taken months. It had in these circumstances been impossible to keep secret from the army what was intended. Talk of the "next push" went on in every mess, and as sick, wounded and men on leave came home items of information were pieced together. So, London usually had beforehand a very fair idea of what was afoot, and we may be reasonably certain that what was known in England was also known at the enemy's headquarters.

But the speed with which the Battle of Amiens was prepared made it much easier to preserve secrecy, and the army had very little notion of what Haig and Rawlinson were planning. The men of the Canadian Corps who were brought down from Arras at the last moment had no idea where they were going. Their hospitals had been sent north into Flanders, and the most circumstantial reports were in circulation that the Canadians were going to join Plumer for a great attack on the Ypres front. Canadian battalions were put into the line on the Kemmel front, where they were identified by the enemy. Even King Albert was deceived, and inquired indignantly why he had not been told of this offensive which was about to take place on his right. There were no rumours to attract the enemy's attention towards Amiens and many to draw it elsewhere.

The result was that Rawlinson sprang an even more complete surprise upon the enemy than had Byng at Cambrai. The tanks, lumbering forward through the mist, were through the German defences and amongst the troops in the fields and billets behind before they were aware that any attack had taken place. The headquarters of divisions, and even in one case of a corps, were surprised, and the tanks did invaluable service in cutting the German telegraph and telephone communications. One of our whippets, on the first morning, got through to a depth of more than six miles behind the front and, though quite alone, succeeded in causing rare havoc to the German wires before it was surrounded and its occupants were forced to surrender. The cavalry, following hard after the tanks, made many captures and completed the demoralisation of the enemy.

Owing to the disorganisation of their means of communication and the difficulty which the German generals had in ascertaining what was happening and in sending out their orders, control for a time broke down, and this, in conjunction with the alarm spread by our tanks, seriously affected the morale of the German troops. Ludendorff says that "August 8 was the black day in the history of the German Army," and Colonel Bauer, the head of Ludendorff's artillery section at headquarters, in his account of the negotiations between his chief and the German Government, speaks of "the events of the inglorious eighth of August." The work begun at Hamel was completed, and the morale ascendancy established by tanks, artillery and infantry working in combination affected both private and general in the German Army. By August 10 the Australians and Canadians had, with the help of the Cavalry Corps, broken through the German lines to a depth of twelve miles.

North of the Somme the 3rd Corps had had a harder struggle, for the enemy there was on the alert, the surprise was not complete and the nature of the ground made it impossible to use tanks; but none the less the greater part of the ridge dividing the Ancre south of Albert from the Somme was gained. Twenty German divisions were defeated by thirteen British infantry divisions, three British cavalry divisions, and an American infantry regiment, and nearly twenty-two thousand prisoners and four hundred guns were captured. The immediate effect of the advance of the Australians and Canadians south of the Somme was very similar to that of Mangin's blow at Soissons. The Germans were deprived of the use of the railways passing through Chaulnes, which had supplied their troops, between the Somme and the Oise, and had to carry through another withdrawal.

Debeney, who was not aided by tanks to the same extent as we were, at first made slower progress than did the Canadians on his left, but as the difficulties of the Germans increased, owing to the threat of the Canadian attack to their communications, not only was Debeney able to press forward towards Roye, but Humbert, on his right, joined in and drove the enemy back from the Lassigny plateau, which had been won by von Hutier in June, so that by the middle of August the Germans between the Somme and the Oise were almost everywhere back in the lines which they had held in the summer of 1916. Then, in accordance with the theory of limited punches, the attack was stayed. The Amiens salient had disappeared, as had the Marne salient, and the main lines of railway through Amiens, which the enemy had dominated since the end of March and which were the main channels of communication between the French and British Armies, were cleared.

No sooner was Humbert established on the Lassigny plateau, and the battle front on the Amiens salient for the time being at a standstill, than Mangin, on Humbert's right, opened an attack between the Oise and the Aisne at Soissons. Mangin began on the 18th with a local operation which sent the Germans back into their battle positions, but did not alarm von Boehn sufficiently to cause him to send up reserves, of which he had none too many. Von Boehn had just assumed command of the armies which had hitherto constituted the German Crown Prince's right, in order that that young gentleman might be better able to devote his attention to the reorganisation of his centre after the buffeting it had received in the second Battle of the Marne.

Von Boehn's front extended from Soissons to Albert, and he was anxiously watching Haig. He did not, therefore, wish to send off troops prematurely to his left, and Mangin caught him napping. On the 19th Mangin extended his front of attack, and by the 20th had gained possession of the whole of the heights between the Oise and the Aisne, having captured 8,000 prisoners and 200 guns.

Foch's system of manoeuvre was now in action, and it is worthwhile again pausing for a moment to compare his quick rapier thrusts with Ludendorff's heavier and slower sword play. It will be remembered that Ludendorff's attacks on the British front, begun on March 21, had ended on April 29 with the repulse between Bailleul and Ypres. Then ensued a pause of twenty-seven days, for the third Battle of the Aisne did not begin until May 27. This ended on June 2, and was followed after a week's interval by von Hutier's attempt to reach Compiègne, which was stopped on June 13. It was not until July 15, thirty-two days later, that the Crown Prince was ready to begin the second Battle of the Marne, and each of these respites which Ludendorff had allowed the Allies made his next task the more difficult.

Now see how Foch, who had not the superiority in numbers which Ludendorff had had in the spring, gave his adversary no time

British tank moving forward at the Battle of Amiens

to recover. He makes his counter-attack on July 18, and the second Battle of the Marne ends with the Germans behind the Aisne and the Vesle on August 6. On August 8 Haig opens the Battle of Amiens, and on the 12th, it ends with the Germans in their lines about Chaulnes. Meanwhile, on the 9th, Humbert has already begun the Battle of Lassigny, which comes to an end on the 16th, and from the 17th to the 20th Mangin is driving the Germans from the Aisne heights. As soon as he stops, Byng, on August 21, begins the Battle of Bapaume; but ere that Foch's strategy had effected a vital change in the enemy's plans.

Haig's victory of Amiens gave rise to anxious debates at German Headquarters. The blow had been utterly unexpected, and the revelation that the British Army had so quickly recovered its fighting power came as a great shock. Ludendorff was so overwhelmed that he tendered his resignation, which was refused. He has stated that Haig's victory had convinced him that there was no longer any hope of German victory, and he at once advised his government to seek the best terms which they could obtain from their enemies. (Ludendorff.) On August 14 a conference was held at Great Headquarters at which both the Chancellor and the Foreign Minister were present, and over which the emperor presided. Ludendorff then expounded his views on the military situation, and declared that, while the army could still for a time present a strong front, the military situation could never be better than it then was.

He urged that the best course for Germany was to propose terms while she still occupied large stretches of the territory of her enemies and while the process of driving the German troops out of them was likely to prove long and costly. Such a change of front, coming so soon after the promises of victory which on Ludendorff's authority had been held out to Germany, filled the German statesmen with dismay. It was held that to undeceive the people so bluntly and brutally was politically impossible, and the negotiations which resulted in Prince Max of Baden becoming Chancellor were set on foot.

While the emperor and his advisers were thus seeking for a way out of their difficulties Ludendorff changed his military policy. His purpose was now to stand on the defensive, to avoid exposing his troops to any more such defeats as he had recently suffered, and to present a barrier to the Allies which they would hesitate to attack. He had had again to draw heavily upon Rupprecht's reserves to stop the hole caused by the collapse of his defence in the Amiens salient, and it had become imperative that he should economise troops somehow.

He therefore decided on a general shortening of his front.

He began to draw out of the salient he had made in Flanders in April, and attempted to follow this by a repetition of the manoeuvre which had been so successful at the beginning of 1917. Then he had upset General Nivelle's plan by a withdrawal into the Hindenburg line, and now he proposed to retire slowly over the same ground to the shelter of the same vast system of defences, in which he hoped to stand until a peace not unfavourable to Germany had been concluded. As in 1917, he wished this retirement to be deliberate and to cause us the maximum of delay and inconvenience. It would have suited him admirably to have completed the movement about the time when the weather broke in the late autumn.

We would then have been left without shelter in the desert of the old Somme battlefields, while his troops were established in the elaborate dug-outs of the Hindenburg system or billeted in the intact towns and villages to the east of it. Fortunately, Haig divined this scheme. At this time the Hindenburg line ran much nearer to our front between Albert and Arras than it did in the Somme valley, and Haig proposed to upset Ludendorff's plan of retreat, to force him out of the Somme uplands and turn the line of the river from Péronne southwards, by striking from the Albert-Arras front through Bapaume towards the nearest portion of Ludendorff's goal.

On the eve of the Battle of Bapaume, which, as I have said, began on August 21, Haig issued an order to his troops which, while hinting at the probability of a German withdrawal, called their attention to the great change which had been wrought by the victories of the Marne and of Amiens, and asked for their greatest efforts in pressing back the enemy wherever he gave way. The brunt of this new battle fell upon Byng's Third Army, which had the task of pressing in north of the Ancre towards Bapaume, while Rawlinson's Fourth Army cooperated on its right by advancing astride the Somme on Péronne. By the evening of the 21st the success of Haig's plan was practically assured by Byng t who gained the line of the Albert Arras railway.

The consequence was that, when on the 23rd a general attack on the whole front of the Third and Fourth Armies followed, the German defence north of the Somme gave way, and the Thiépval Ridge, Pozières, Courcelette, Martinpuich and Miraumont fell in rapid succession to Byng's men. The effect of this upon our men was electric. In 1916 the capture of each of these places had cost us a long, slow, bloody struggle, and the prime manhood of our new armies lay buried thick around them. They are names as sacred to the National Army of Great Britain as Minden, Salamanca, Waterloo and the Alma are to the old Regular Army. They had been yielded in March in sorrow and pain after a noble defence against odds. Now, in a few hours and at comparatively small cost, the same regiments which had perforce retreated from them with heavy hearts had once more thrown the enemy back from this sacred soil. No one who has not tasted the bitterness of retreat can appreciate the full thrill of an advance over ground made familiar by victory and defeat.

Times had indeed changed from the days of the first Battle of the Somme. The army was from long experience suspicious of announcements from Headquarters which foretold the collapse of the enemy. Too often these had come to men who had seen them falsified by a stubborn and skilful foe, but now Haig was clearly right. The day had come to strike swiftly and boldly, and with new confidence in themselves and in their chief our men pressed forward across the horrid desolation created by Hun savagery and by the still more terrible ebb and flow of war.

The Germans strove hard to gain time to carry through the ordered retreat which they had planned, their machine-gunners in particular fighting with that devotion which marked them throughout the war; but we had now found the answer to the German machine-gun, and one hundred tanks had been sent by Haig into the battle to help the infantry forward. By August 26 Byng's progress in the north had, as Haig had expected, begun to cause the Germans great anxiety for the safety of their troops between the Somme and the Oise, and these too retreated, followed by Rawlinson's Fourth Army and the French Armies under Debeney and Humbert. By the night of the 29th Rawlinson's men had reached the left bank of the Somme opposite Péronne, Debeney had hustled the Germans through Nesle, and Humbert had occupied Noyon.

On this same day the Germans evacuated Bapaume, which Byng was encircling from the north and south, and were driven completely from the Somme plateau. The battle was brought to a noble close by one of the most brilliant feats of arms of the whole war. While Byng had been closing in on Bapaume the Australian Corps had been steadily pushing the Germans back up the Somme towards Péronne, and in the early hours of August 31 the 5th Australian Brigade, having crossed the river on improvised bridges and worked their way towards Mont St. Quentin, surprised the German defenders of that hill, which dominates Péronne, and carried it by assault.

As the result of this achievement the Australians were able to enter Péronne the following day, and the German defences along the Somme as far south as Ham were turned. In the Battle of Bapaume thirty-five German divisions had been driven in ten days across the scene of the struggle which in 1916 had lasted from July 1 until November 17, and they had lost 34,000 prisoners and 270 guns. Ludendorff's retreat, far from enabling him to economise troops, was exhausting his dwindling resources as rapidly as a battle accepted voluntarily.

While the Battle of Bapaume was in progress Haig had been quietly transferring the Canadian Corps from the Amiens battlefield back to Arras, whence it had come, and on August 26 the 2nd and 3rd Canadian Divisions, with the 51st British Division, which had been moved north from the Marne, attacked east of Arras and captured the important hill of Monchy le Preux. Horne's First Army, to which these divisions belonged, followed up this success by driving the enemy back into the northern extension of the Hindenburg line, known as the Drocourt-Quéant switch. This Drocourt line had been completed by the enemy after the Battle of Arras, in April, 1917, and for eighteen months he had been hard at work improving it until it had become almost as formidable as the main Hindenburg line, with which it connected at Quéant.

It was assaulted in the morning of September 2 by the 1st and 4th Canadian Divisions and the 4th, 52nd, 57th and 63rd British Divisions, assisted by some forty tanks. These six divisions not only broke clear through the network of German defences and gained possession of the whole system in less than seven hours, but in doing so they routed nine German divisions, who had all the advantage of defensive works which they knew thoroughly and believed to be impregnable. This great feat had, as Haig had hoped it would, far-reaching results. With their right flank threatened, the Germans south of Quéant had to hurry back to the shelter of the Hindenburg line, and by September 9 they were back in the outpost positions in front of their main defensive system. On September 6 the French occupied Ham, on the Somme, and Chauny, on the Oise, and a few days later were within sight of La Fère.

Haig's manoeuvre had the simultaneous effect of hastening the German withdrawal in Flanders, and by September 6 we had reoccupied Bailleul and Merville and were back in Neuve Chapelle, while the 27th American Division had passed beyond Kemmel Hill. Thus, in one month all the ground won by Ludendorff in his first two attacks of March and April had, with the exception of a portion on the Ypres front, been regained, and the British Army had amply avenged the reverses of the spring.

The two German attempts to derange the plans of the Allies by a retreat into the Hindenburg line had had very different results. In 1917 we did not discover what they were at until their preparations had been completed. Their retreat then lasted almost exactly three months, and during those three months we fought the Battle of Arras, in which the Canadians stormed the Vimy Ridge. That was the most conspicuous success we had gained up to that time on the Western Front, and, including our captures in that victory, we, in those three months, secured about 21,000 prisoners and 220 guns, an achievement of which we were at the time rightly very proud.

In 1918, when Ludendorff again tried to escape from his embarrassments by a similar retreat, we drove the Germans back over almost exactly the same distance between August 21 and September 9—that is, in twenty days—and in that time, we captured 53,000 prisoners and 470 guns. Ludendorff could no longer retreat according to plan.

While Haig was hunting the Germans back into the Hindenburg line Pershing was engaged in collecting his scattered divisions, in forming them into the First American Army, of which he assumed personal command, and in establishing an American sector of the front. This by the end of August extended round the St. Mihiel salient northwards to a point opposite Verdun. The St. Mihiel salient was a relic of the first German offensive of 1914. In an attempt to break through to the south of Verdun the enemy had in September of that year gained possession of a portion of the heights of the Meuse, including the fort of the Roman Camp and the little town of St. Mihiel on the river below it.

The heights of the Meuse were part of the defensive system of the eastern frontier of France, and along them had been constructed a chain of forts connecting the fortresses of Verdun and Toul, of which the fort of the Roman Camp was one. Though on the map the St. Mihiel salient looked to be a narrow wedge which could be swept by shell fire from both flanks, in reality the wooded heights afforded the enemy splendid shelter and gave him commanding positions of exceptional strength which dominated all the approaches. In 1915 Joffre had tried again and again to drive the Germans out, and both Les Eparges, on the northwest corner of the salient, and Apremont, on its southern face, became names of ill-omen in the French Army. Thereafter the French left the salient alone, and it became a quiet sector of the front.

In September, 1918, the St. Mihiel salient was held by nine German and Austrian divisions, of whom six were second-class troops. Ludendorff had decided to withdraw to the base of the salient in order to economise troops, and some of the German heavy artillery had been removed before the Americans attacked. Probably the enemy relied upon the strength of his position and upon the ease with which he could observe all preparations for attack to enable him to make a leisurely retirement at the proper moment. If this is so, he was surprised by the method and swiftness of the American advance, which began on September 12. The main attack was made by the 1st Corps of four divisions and the 4th Corps of three divisions against the southern face of the salient, and was directed northwards so as to cut in east of the heights of the Meuse.

Simultaneously the 5th American Corps attacked with two divisions on the north-western front of the salient and drove in eastwards towards the southern attack. One French division attacked on the left of the 5th Corps, and two more connected the 5th Corps round the nose of the salient at St. Mihiel with the main attack. The battle opened with a four hours' bombardment, and then, at five in the morning, the American infantry advanced behind their barrage. Either because the morale of the German troops was not good or because they knew that it had been planned to come out of the salient, the resistance was on the whole feeble, and in thirty hours the two American attacking forces had joined hands and the salient had been wiped out with astonishingly little loss.

The whole operation was carried through according to programme. It was not necessary to employ any of the American reserve divisions, of which six were in readiness, and, as will be seen, they were at once available to begin preparations for another and more formidable task. The battle resulted in the capture by the First American Army of 16,000 prisoners and 443 guns.

The St. Mihiel salient had long broken up the stretch of front between the Moselle and Verdun, so that any considerable offensive movement by the French into Lorraine had been impossible. The front was equally unpromising from the German point of view for an attack directed against Nancy. The result of this was that this portion of the long line had, after the failure of Joffre's attempts in 1915 to reduce the salient, become dormant and had been very lightly held by both sides. But now that the salient was gone and the front had been straightened out, the Germans found their great fortress of Metz menaced with attack, and also the French iron fields of Briey, to the north of Metz, which they had captured in the early days of the war, and were of even more importance to them than the fortress.

American Headquarters allowed it to be whispered in confidence that Pershing's real objective was these iron fields, and doubtless some of these whispers found their way into the German lines. In any event Ludendorff, almost to the very end, showed his nervousness as to an American attack on the east bank of the Meuse, and, hard up as he was for reserves, he kept troops to watch for an attack which did not begin to develop until the German plenipotentiaries were on their way to sign the Armistice.

This victory of Pershing's completed the series of preliminary punches, and Foch was now ready for the knock-out blow. His immediate object had been to free Paris and Amiens and to clear the strategic railways which he needed for the free movement of his troops; his ultimate object had been to prepare for a decisive victory by exhausting the German reserves. We have seen how he achieved the first; let us now see how he stood as to the second.

At the end of May, just before the Crown Prince William's attack on the Chemin des Dames, the German forces in the West had reached their greatest strength. They then had 207 divisions on the Western Front, and of these about 66 divisions fit to take part in battle were in reserve. In the third week of September, after Pershing's victory at St. Mihiel, the number of German divisions had fallen to 185, for in order to make good his heavy losses Ludendorff, whose income in man power from Germany was quite insufficient to meet expenditure, had been compelled to draw upon his capital, and to break up 22 of his divisions in an endeavour to keep the remainder up to strength.

Two more divisions were on their way across from Russia and six others were placed under orders to move, but of these, three had to be diverted to help Mackensen in the Balkans out of difficulties in which he was placed by the collapse of Bulgaria, and none of the remainder reached the front in France before the great battle was joined, and they were, moreover, of poor quality, for all their best men had been taken from them to meet the never-ending call for drafts for the Western Front. Even these drastic measures proved insufficient, and none of Ludendorff's divisions had its full establishment of men, so he had

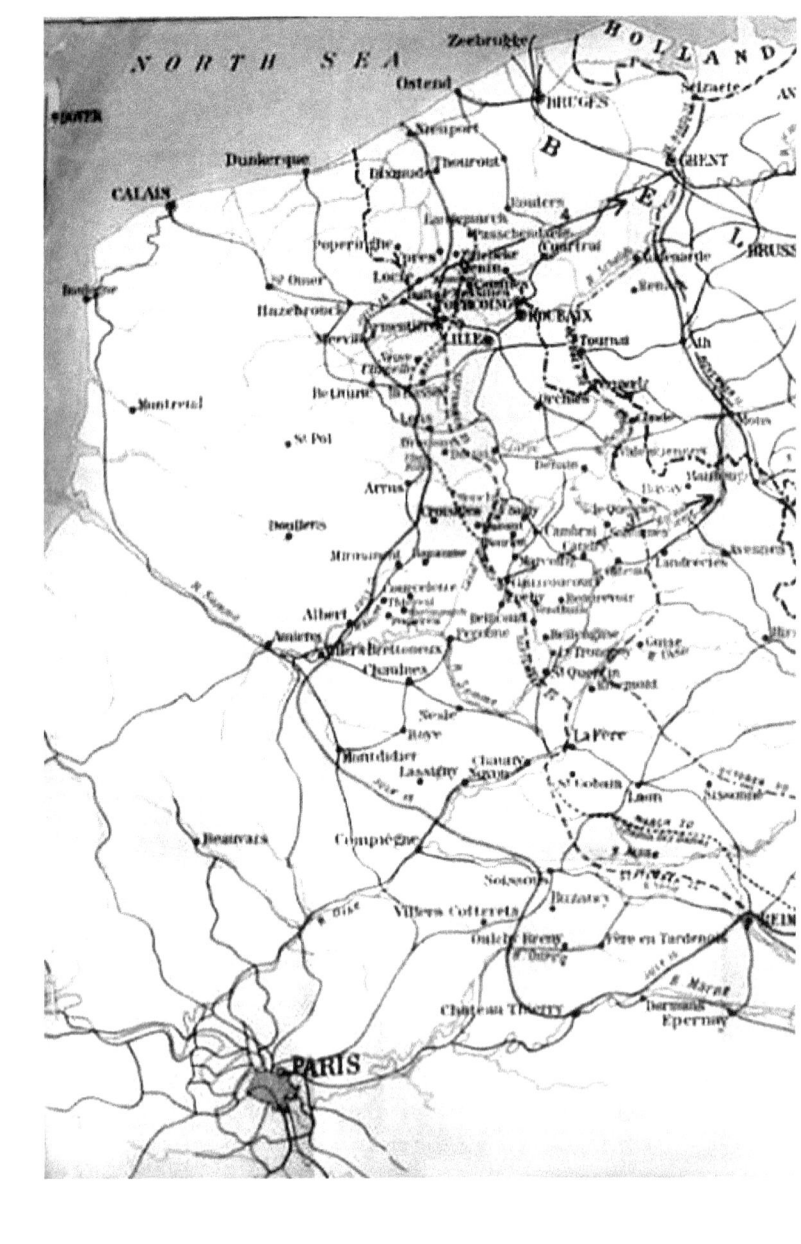

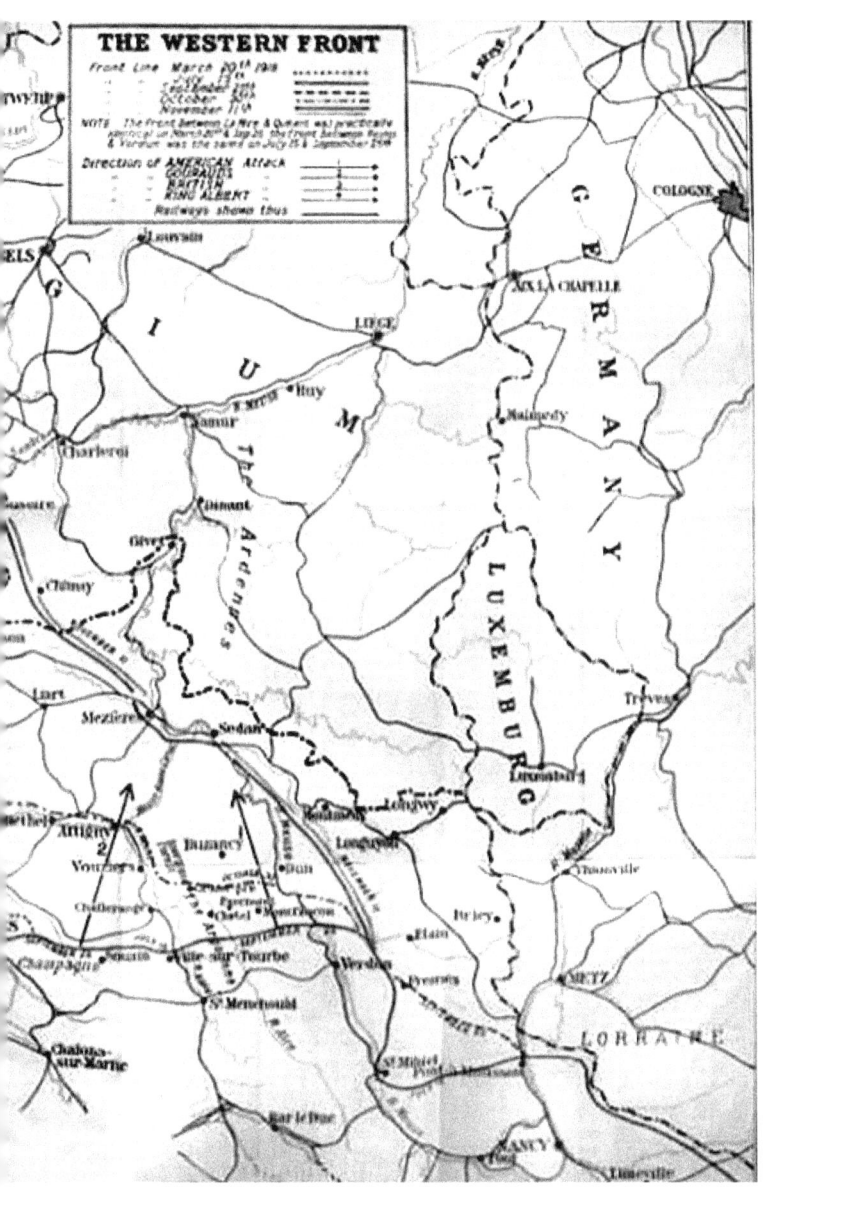

to swallow his pride and appeal to despised Austria for aid, with the result that six Austrian divisions arrived on the Western Front, and of these two had been defeated at St. Mihiel. The reserve of 61 rested and fit divisions in May had fallen to 21 in September, and there were available to swell it only the five divisions coming from Russia.

As I have already pointed out, this weakening of the German Armies had not been due solely to Foch's skill. In part it was the consequence of Ludendorff's mistake in his spring campaign of compromising between the policy of a succession of attacks intended to prepare for a great final effort and the policy of attempting to break through in one great battle. He failed in the first by continuing his assaults beyond the period when he was inflicting more loss than he suffered, and he failed in the second because he would not or could not continue them to the point where decisive success was obtainable, and in acting as he did, he sapped his strength.

Still more was the exhaustion of Germany's man power the fruit of the Allied efforts during the previous years. It is easy in the light of after knowledge to criticise the Allied generals and to say that their methods were wasteful of life. Certainly, if they had known in 1915 what they knew in 1918 their procedure would have been different and the war would have been over sooner; but that criticism is best answered by the fact that the man who is today universally recognised as the outstanding figure of the war was himself engaged in doing that to which the critics object.

It is commonly asserted that the Allies should have remained on the defensive in the West in 1915. That argument overlooks the fact that it was always present in Joffre's mind that the Germans might at any time elect to do the very thing which they came so near achieving in March, 1918. I believe it to have been one of the greatest of the many German blunders that they did not attack in force in the West in 1915, before our new armies were ready and our munition factories had become really productive. In 1916 Verdun was saved because we were able to extend our front to the Somme and free a great number of French troops; an attack made before we were in a position to bring such help to our Allies might have had very different results.

The one means of averting that danger was to take every opportunity of making the Western Front more secure by pushing back the German lines and of exhausting the military power of Germany. Here lies the root of the long barren controversy which raged between the "Easterners" and "Westerners" throughout the greater part of the war.

It was necessary to be safe in the East in order to be strong in the West, but it was at no time possible before the summer of 1918 to make the West safe by success in the East, because the Allies had not the force necessary to protect their vitals in the West against possible danger and at the same time carry through a decisive campaign in more distant fields.

Therefore, the policy of seizing every favourable opportunity of exhausting Germany's military power by attack in the West was the right policy if the methods followed were not always the best. It was that policy which emptied the depots in Germany, and though it came near to emptying both our own and the French depots, it had its reward in 1918, for without it neither could Foch's skill in two short months have materially reduced the enemy's strength nor could American aid have enabled us to win when we did win.

While the German strength had been going steadily down, the Allied strength had been going steadily up. Between the middle of July and the beginning of August nine American divisions took part in the second Battle of the Marne, and there were then three more on the British front, which had practically completed their training for battle. Pershing at the Battle of St. Mihiel had fourteen divisions in action or in reserve, while at that time there were two on the British front and nine more almost ready—twenty-five American divisions in all—upon which Foch could reckon at once, and more to come, each of these divisions being about twice the strength of a British, French or German division.

The British Army, which in July could only bring into the field fifty-three divisions, in September had, thanks to the arrival of reinforcements from other theatres of war, grown to fifty-nine divisions, two of which were, however, still in process of reorganisation. Thus, while the fighting strength of the Germans and Austrians in the West had fallen by sixteen divisions since Foch had delivered his first punch, that of the Allies had increased by the equivalent of about thirty-two, counting one American division as equal to two German divisions.

Since July 18 the Allies had captured more than 2,000 German guns and large stocks of shell, while the blockade, on which we had founded so many premature hopes, was at last beginning to have results directly bearing on the military situation, and made it increasingly difficult for the Germans to replace their lost and damaged war material. For example, the mechanism of the German guns necessitated the use of brass cartridge cases, but by this time the supply of brass and

Columns of German prisoners taken by the St. Mihiel salient.

copper had run very low, and the most elaborate and tyrannical system of perquisition could extract no more from the occupied territories, so that inferior substitutes had to be used. The power and efficiency of the German artillery was diminishing as fast as the strength of their battalions, while the Allied guns had gone up from about 18,000 in May to 21,000 in September, and they had almost unlimited supplies of munitions.

But it was not in numbers and material alone that the Allies had gained. The German soldiers who had been sent over from Russia had come into touch with Bolshevist theory and practice. They had seen soldiers' committees in control, and officers degraded and insulted, and it began to occur to them that the iron discipline under which they had been brought up had not behind it the power which they had imagined was there. They infected their comrades with a distrust and suspicion of authority which spread rapidly as defeat followed on defeat and the promise of a speedy and victorious peace became a mockery.

On the other side of the wire the success of Foch's strategy had filled France with joyful relief and inspired the Allied troops with confidence. The work begun at Doullens on March 26 was completed, and for the first time in the war a real sense of corporate unity pervaded the ranks. The British Army, having made one of the most marvellous recoveries in the history of war, was sure of its superiority, individual and collective, over the enemy. The grim, determined, stolid endurance of the spring had been changed by the series of victories which began with the Battle of Amiens into eager, irresistible enthusiasm.

The second Battle of the Marne had taught the Allied leaders that the untried American troops could fight and win with far less training than they had calculated to be necessary; the victory of St. Mihiel had shown that an American Army could take the field as an entity. Every one of the data upon which Ludendorff had based the plan for the *Friedensturm* had been proved to be false. The spirit of France was as high as ever; the British Army, far from being exhausted, had struck hard and often and with conspicuous success; the Americans were not only present in numbers, but had taught the Germans to fear their dash, skill and valour.

Chapter 4

Armageddon

Foch, having prepared the way for his decisive thrust by his series of preliminary punches, was about to launch the Allied Armies against the most formidable of all the German defences. The name "Hindenburg Line" originated with the British soldiers, who so entitled the great system of German works which had been discovered towards the end of 1916 behind the Somme battlefield.

At the end of August, 1916, when Hindenburg and Ludendorff first arrived at Great Headquarters, the German military situation was by no means rosy. Russia was still formidable, the Austrian Army required a great deal of support, Roumania was about to enter the field, the Verdun offensive had proved to be a disastrous failure, the British Army had grown to formidable dimensions, and the Franco-British attacks on the Somme were pressing the Germans hard and eating up their reserves. Ludendorff wished first to finish off Russia and Roumania, and in order to do this he had to make the situation in the West safe and to be able to economise troops there. The only way in which he could do this effectively was by shortening his front.

He could not give up any ground in Belgium without endangering his hold upon Ostend and Zeebrugge, which were invaluable as bases from which submarines and destroyers could attack the British communications across the Channel, while the country about Bruges and Ghent gave him an excellent jumping-off place for aeroplane raids upon London and the south-east of England. He did not wish to abandon Lille, because great pains had been taken to fortify the place, which had become the northern pivot of the German defensive system, while the great manufacturing district surrounding the town was of the utmost value. Nor did he wish to come away from the Vimy Ridge, for it covered a great part of the Lens coalfields, and in the hands of the Allies would be a strong barrier against a German offensive when he was ready to attack in the West.

West of Laon the St. Gobain massif formed a pivot for his centre, which it was important to hold. Between Reims and Verdun, a withdrawal would not shorten his front, and would bring his enemy dangerously near the railway which connected Metz with Sedan and Mézières, part of his main lateral line of communications. In the east he could not give ground without exposing Metz to bombardment and Alsace and Lorraine to invasion. Between the Vimy Ridge and the St. Gobain massif, however, his front formed a great arc, into which the French and British had bitten deep during the Battle of the Somme. By coming out of this arc he would shorten his front, get his troops out of an embarrassing position, and would be yielding French territory which was of no special value to him. Accordingly, he determined to construct a chord for the arc, and to draw back to the chord in his own time. So, the Hindenburg line was begun.

The original section of the Hindenburg line started just east of Arras, where it connected with the defences of the Vimy Ridge and ran south-eastwards to the Canal du Nord, eight miles west of Cambrai; thence it followed an almost north and south line past the western outskirts of St. Quentin, through La Fère, to the St. Gobain massif. It was this portion of the line which leaped into fame when Ludendorff carried out his withdrawal in the early months of 1917. He had realised that he would be attacked again on the Western Front in the spring of that year, and that his armies between the Oise and the Scarpe were, as the result of the Battle of the Somme, in no condition to meet attack. He tells us that there was no alternative to withdrawal. (Ludendorff.) Having completed his defences, he slowly brought back the bulk of his troops and material, leaving only rear-guards in his front line.

He then proceeded to lay waste systematically the country he intended to abandon. Every article of value was removed from the French towns and villages, all the able-bodied inhabitants were deported, and most of those who were too young, too old or too feeble to be of service were collected in two or three centres to be rescued by the Allies when they advanced. The trees were cut down, not even the orchards being spared, the villages were set on fire, the towns were gutted, explosives being used for the more solid buildings which fire could not damage sufficiently, the wells were fouled, every road and railway bridge was destroyed, the railway embankments were blown in, the rails were torn up, and mines were exploded under every cross-roads, making craters which effectively barred wheeled traffic.

As a last refinement a series of devilishly cunning booby traps was devised, consisting of wires connected to German helmets, pianos, door-handles, the steps of dug-outs or of houses, which when touched exploded charges and cost us the lives of many of our men. The systematic and skilful savagery of the modern German created a devastation which shamed the best efforts of his untutored forbears. This was all part of Ludendorff's scheme of defence. He knew that the time and labour required to restore the communications, to repair the bridges, and provide water and shelter for their troops would derange the plans of the Allied generals, and as a purely military measure the scheme was an unqualified success.

Nivelle had intended that one of his attacks should be made against the southern part of the front from which the Germans had retired, and he had no time to prepare properly for another to take its place, with the result that his attempt on St. Quentin was repulsed, while Ludendorff, by shortening his front, obtained the reserves necessary to meet and check the main French attack on the Aisne. Only the British part of Nivelle's campaign met with any considerable measure of success, and in the Battle of Arras a part of the Arras arm of the Hindenburg line was rolled up.

Before the Battle of Arras started the Germans had begun to prepare for the possibility of the capture of the Vimy Ridge by digging a northern extension of the Hindenburg line, which ran from Quéant, ten miles west of Cambrai, and then northwards through Drocourt and east of Lens to the southern defences of Lille. This was the line known to the British Army as "the Drocourt-Quéant switch," and broken by them on September 2, 1918. It was the beginning of a vast extension of the Hindenburg system carried out throughout 1917, during the whole of which year the Germans were on the defensive. Lille and Metz became the main pivots of this extended system. The term "line" as applied to it is a misnomer, for nowhere did it consist of a single line of trenches.

It was composed of a whole series of trench lines enclosing a heavily fortified area many miles in depth. The Germans, to mark their sense of its importance, named its various sections after the heroes of German mythology. (See map following). The Drocourt switch they called the "Wotan position"; the section covering Cambrai and St. Quentin, the "Siegfried position"; that south of St. Quentin and west of Laon, the "Alberich position"; behind the Champagne front came

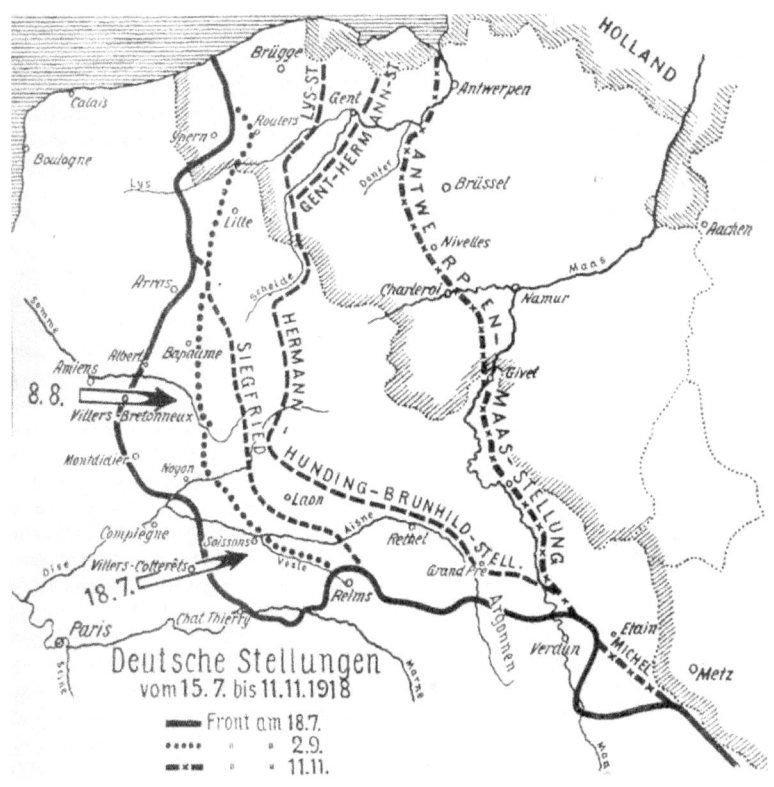

THE GERMAN DEFENSIVE SYSTEM

the "Brunehild position"; and the southernmost positions, which ran east of the Argonne to the Meuse and thence to Metz, were called the "Kriemhilde and Michel positions."

Thus a great barrier was built up from north to south covering Douai, Cambrai and St. Quentin and protecting the railway connecting Metz with Sedan and Mézières. Of the various sections of this barrier, the Siegfried system in front of Cambrai and St. Quentin, which was begun first, was the most elaborate; the Kriemhilde section had not the same depth, partly because the ground on the Meuse-Argonne front was naturally very defensible, and the approaches to the Kriemhilde line were more difficult than those leading to other sections, and partly because the original German trenches between the Meuse and the Argonne were never penetrated by Allied troops from the first days of trench warfare until they were stormed by the First American Army on September 26, 1918.

The principles on which these lines were elaborated were worked out by the Germans as the result of a close study of their experiences in the first Battle of the Somme. If that battle cost us dear, it and the Battle of Verdun destroyed the flower of the Germany Army, and it became evident to the German leaders that a few more such struggles would exhaust their military strength. By the summer of 1916 the work of Mr. Lloyd George at the British Ministry of Munitions and of M. Albert Thomas at the French Ministry had begun to take effect. For the first time in the war the Allies on the Western Front were superior to the Germans in gun power and in the number of shells at the service of the guns.

The bombardment preliminary to the infantry attack by the British in the Somme battle lasted seven days, and was heard in the suburbs of London, 150 miles away. The Germans realised that at this period of the war bombardment had become the principal means of attack by the Allies, and that their strongest trenches would crumble to pieces if exposed to the full blast of the tornado of shell which could be hurled against them.

Until "sound ranging" was highly developed, which did not take place till later, the accuracy of artillery fire depended upon observation. The guns required eyes, particularly the medium and heavy guns, which fire from a long distance behind the front lines. Even the best observation from aeroplanes will not replace in a great artillery attack the eyes of an observer on the ground connected by telephone with the guns. The Germans therefore designed the Hindenburg lines so that observation of them from the ground should be as difficult as possible. Whenever it could be done, they were constructed along the back slopes of ridges, not along the top or on the front slopes, where they would be easily seen. In order to keep the observers and the guns at a distance, and to disorganise the attacking infantry, strong outpost positions were built often as much as three or four miles in front of the main positions.

The troops in these outpost positions were intended to fall back before a heavy attack, after delaying it as much as possible by machine-gun and rifle fire, and with this method of defence it would not be necessary to keep large numbers of troops in the very front lines, which would be exposed to the worst of the bombardment. This was, in fact, an early version of the system of defence which Gouraud applied so brilliantly when he defeated the great German attack of July 15, 1918.

★★★★★★★★★★

This was the system of defence when strong lines were in existence as battle positions. When the battle positions were pierced, it was usually necessary to dispute every yard of ground. The outpost system was abandoned by the Germans in the later stages of the third Battle of Ypres and in September, 1918, and by us on the front of the Fifth Army after the German attack of March 31.

★★★★★★★★★★

In the Siegfried section the system was given great depth, so that if the attackers succeeded in storming the first lines it would be necessary for them to pause until the guns had been brought forward and the stocks of shell brought up for a renewed bombardment of the rear lines. Between Cambrai and St. Quentin, the Siegfried system, from the outpost positions near Epehy to the rearmost line near Beaurevoir, was as much as ten miles deep. The most elaborate wire entanglements were provided in front of each line of trenches. They were often arranged in geometrical patterns, so that the angles could be swept by machine-gun fire, and there were, in places, as many as eight or nine belts of barbed wire in front of the trenches.

Standing, after the great battle had been won and the Siegfried system had been pierced, on the ridges east of the St. Quentin Canal, in the heart of the system, one looked over miles of dense entanglements running in every direction, and was filled with amazement that it should have been possible for flesh and blood to storm a way through such obstacles. Heavily concreted shelters for the infantry and machine-gunners were provided in the fire trenches, while farther back great underground barracks were constructed at a depth to make them proof against the heaviest bombardment.

When we first broke into the Hindenburg line with Byng's tank attack of November, 1917, we found that the Germans had hollowed out the ground under many of the villages, piling the chalk into the buildings so that it would not attract attention and would add to the immunity of the dugout from bombardment. These dug-outs were fitted up on a lavish scale so as to provide for the comforts of the occupants. They were often boarded in and fitted with electric light, while water and sleeping bunks were provided, and they were furnished with numerous stairways, so that the men in them could come out quickly when the bombardment was over.

Through the middle of the Siegfried system ran two canals, the Canal du Nord and the St. Quentin Canal, which near Cambrai becomes the navigable Scheldt. Both of these canals, which run in places through deep cuttings, were used by the enemy, who dug deep into the banks to provide shelter for his men. Between Bellicourt and Vendhuile the St. Quentin Canal ran underground for a distance of 6,000 yards, and this tunnel, when blocked up, provided the Germans with a ready-made underground barrack, which was fitted out for occupation, and connected by numerous shafts with the trenches above. Along the top of the canal, which constituted a very serious natural obstacle, numbers of concreted machine-gun emplacements were built, so that the whole length of the canal where it ran above ground could be swept by cross fire.

Such were the defences upon which the Germans, not without justification, pinned their faith. In keeping with the names bestowed upon them, legends had grown up in Germany as to their extent and strength, and they had therefore acquired great political as well as military importance. While they were intact the German people felt that loss of territory or reverses in the field were not matters of great concern, for at the worst there lay behind these bastions, rich provinces of France and the greater part of Belgium, which could be exchanged for favourable terms of peace. The German leaders could still tell us to look at the map. When they were broken the effect both upon leaders and upon people was as overwhelming as it was unexpected.

The Allied defences have often been contrasted unfavourably with these elaborate and intricate German trench systems, but the conditions on the two sides were very different. In the first place, from the

Riqueval Bridge, 1918, Hindenburg Line offensive

beginning of 1915 until the end of 1917 the Allies were, with the exceptions of the German gas attack at Ypres and the Battle of Verdun, almost always attacking, devoting all their energies to the attempt to break through the trench barrier, and the vast preparations required for the battles which were fought during that period left little labour over for the elaboration of defences. In the second place, the Germans were much more favourably placed than the Allies as regards labour.

They had Russian prisoners of war in great numbers, and the fact that the Hague Convention forbade the employment of prisoners of war upon military work counted as nothing with them. They were also able to employ forced labour from the populations of Belgium and the occupied districts of Northern France, and with these two sources of supply they could carry out the most extensive works without calling upon the army for more men than were necessary for planning and supervision. The construction of these great defensive systems therefore did not involve the withdrawal of any soldiers from the fighting front, and did not interfere with the rest and training of the troops in war.

The Allies, on the other hand, could only provide labour for the construction of rear lines of defence at the expense of their armies, or of the factories in the homeland which provided for the great and ever-growing demands of the armies and fleets, and had to meet the urgent call for more and more ships.

It is quite true that in the first years of the war the German infantryman dug better and worked harder at his trenches than did the British infantryman or his French comrade, but this industry would not have sufficed for the construction of the Hindenburg system, and as time went on and the quality and discipline of the German troops declined the new German trenches, on ground won in attack, which had necessarily to be constructed by the soldiers, grew less and less formidable. Mangin, in his attack of July 18 in the second Battle of the Marne, found little behind the enemy's front line, and Rawlinson had the same experience in the Battle of Amiens of August 8. Time and labour made the Hindenburg systems possible.

Those systems had, as I have said, been designed to meet a great bombardment, but by the time Foch was ready to assault them the conditions had altered fundamentally. Bombardment had ceased to be the only or even the chief means at the service of the Allies for opening the road for the infantry attack. The perfected tank was able to break through any belts of barbed wire, however dense, and force its way across any trenches, given reasonably favourable conditions of ground.

I do not maintain that tanks alone would have enabled us to break through the Siegfried system, for the two canals formed an obstacle which the tanks could not cross, and the gaps in and between the canals were not sufficiently wide to allow of a really effective breach being made where they occurred. In the Battle of Amiens, the lessons of Hamel had been applied on a great scale, and with complete success. The triumph of the tanks in that battle had been greatly due to the suddenness and to the power of the bombardment which fell upon the German artillery. Both methods of attack had to be combined, and were combined with rare skill. But it is certain that neither Foch's skilful preparation for the great battle, nor the valour of the infantry, would have brought us victory if we had had to rely upon bombardment alone in order to batter down the German defences.

The acres of wire entanglement which surrounded the trenches of the Siegfried system would not have been cut without that prolonged artillery preparation which had failed in the past to solve the problem of attack in trench warfare. With the warning which this preparation would have given them the Germans would have been able to shelter their machine-guns and infantry in the vast dug-outs which they had prepared, and have brought them out after the barrage had gone forward. Even when we had tanks, they sometimes succeeded in doing this, as the Americans fighting with us on September 29 found to their cost. The tanks were needed not only to clear a way for the infantry through the wire but to crush the enemy's machine-gun nests and keep his men in their underground shelters.

Failing this the exhaustion of the enemy's reserves would not have sufficed to give us victory in the great battle, for the German troops holding the line would have been able to break up our attacks without support from behind. The tanks had proved their efficacy in the preparation for Armageddon; now they were to take their part in the culmination towards which Foch had been working, and few things helped us more in the decisive struggle than the morale ascendancy which the success of the tanks in the preliminary battles had given us over the Germans.

Captured German orders and other documents bear testimony to the dread with which the enemy regarded tanks at this time. Ludendorff had completely changed his views regarding them, and in a circular dealing with the methods of meeting tank attack, he wrote:

Our earlier successes against tanks led to a certain contempt for this weapon of warfare. We must now reckon with more dangerous tanks.

A German Army order issued after the Battle of Amiens said:

The enemy now relies chiefly upon tanks for the success of his attacks. This weapon can only be overcome by the strictest attention to the prescribed counter-measures. I hold all commanders down to company-commanders personally responsible that there is no relaxation at any time in their counter-measures. Specially selected lookout men are to be always in position day and night to give warning of the approach of tanks. Messages regarding the attack by tanks are to be given absolute priority, and are to be sent immediately to the artillery, which is specially detailed to fire upon tanks. All infantry officers must know the exact position of this artillery in their section. An officer is to be appointed in each trench to have charge of the light signals for giving warning in case of tank attack.

This is the type of order which is the refuge of authority when caught napping. The German leaders had delayed too long to study the possibilities of tanks and the most effective means of meeting them. The "counter-measures" presented in this order might have availed against tanks alone; they were useless against tanks, artillery and infantry working in combination. They were, in fact, worse than useless, they were harmful, for they served to demonstrate to the German soldier, who was already in mortal fear of tanks and prepared to make their appearance an excuse for surrender, that his chiefs were as frightened of them as he was, and that they had no effective reply ready.

There are few things more depressing to the men in the ranks, or more calculated to shake their confidence in their leaders, than the knowledge that the enemy possesses a powerful weapon with which they are not provided. We had bitter experience of this in the winter of 1914-1915, when we had to hold the line without the aid of trench mortars, with a totally inadequate supply of hand grenades, and with little support from heavy artillery, with all of which the Germans were well provided. They had no more expected or desired the deadlock of trench warfare than we had, but they had prepared for the siege of fortresses, and had the appliances for siege warfare ready, and we had not.

Our men then bore the strain of meeting superior equipment with superhuman endurance, and in 1918 the German troops failed to stand a like test. Their own tanks were few in number and of inferior design, and their knowledge of our superiority in that weapon had shaken their confidence in the defences before they were attacked. Sooner or later in war an antidote is found to every device of attack or of defence, and the combination of gun and tank proved to be the antidote to the Hindenburg line, while the Germans were not allowed the time to find an antidote to the tank.

The anti-tank gun, on which they had relied after their first experience of the effect of artillery fire upon tanks, had been successfully countered by our barrage. They then invented an anti-tank rifle, firing a heavy armour-piercing bullet, but it had not much success, and towards the end they were producing an anti-tank machine-gun, which might have been more successful, but was in the field too late to receive a fair trial. It would be idle to suppose that no reply to the tank would have been forthcoming had the war gone on longer. All that is certain is that British ingenuity found the answer to the problem presented by German field fortifications before German ingenuity discovered how to overcome the tank.

The general plan for the great battle which was to decide the issue of the war was determined by Foch in consultation with the Allied commanders-in-chief before Pershing won the victory of St. Mihiel. That victory served to confirm the *generalissimo* in his intentions. As a result of the second Battle of the Marne, and of the retreat of the Germans into the Hindenburg line before the British blows, the German front ran roughly from north to south from the North Sea coast near Nieuport, just east of Ypres, by Armentières, west of Douai, Cambrai and St. Quentin to the River Oise near La Fère.

Starting from the Oise it made a big bulge westwards round the St. Gobain Forest along the Oise and the Vesle to Reims, where it again straightened out and ran eastwards through the Champagne heathlands across the Argonne Forest .to the Meuse, north-east of Verdun. Behind this front at a distance of about forty-five miles from the British lines opposite Cambrai, and of about twenty miles from the Meuse-Argonne front, ran the main line of railway connecting Metz, Sedan, Mézières, Maubeuge, Mons, and Brussels. This railway line formed the spinal cord of the German defensive system, was Ludendorff's main means of moving his reserves and military stores rapidly from flank to flank, and was his last good line of lateral communication west of the Ardennes.

Foch proposed to strike at this spinal cord from either side of the great bulge in the enemy's line. (The direction of these various attacks is shown on the map following.) The First American Army was to advance between the Meuse and the Argonne upon Sedan, while Gouraud drove in between the Argonne and Reims towards Mézières. This constituted the right wing of the Allied battle front.

The intention was that Gouraud and the Americans should pinch out the Argonne Forest by advancing on either side of it, for the French had learned by bitter experience what a terrible obstacle the forest presented when defended by the skilled and determined German machine-gunners, who in a country where it was almost impossible to get at them with tanks or with artillery, were in their element.

Actually, this intention was not realised, and the prolonged stubborn fighting of the American troops through the forest has concentrated attention in the United States upon the struggle in the forest, to such an extent that the battle has come to be popularly known as the Battle of the Argonne, but the main American forces were always to the east of the Argonne, and the axis of Pershing's attack ran through Montfaucon to Sedan. The attack to the north of the bulge was to be made by the First French Army and the First, Third and Fourth British Armies between the Scarpe and the Oise, and was to be directed through St. Quentin and Cambrai towards Maubeuge.

It was known that Ludendorff, in his anxiety to protect Cambrai and to secure his precious Hindenburg line, had been weakening his forces in Flanders, and Foch proposed to take advantage of this by making a third attack into Belgium with the Belgian Army, reinforced by a portion of Degoutte's army, which had been sent northwards from the Aisne, and the Second British Army. This attack, if successful, would clear the Belgian coast and threaten the enemy's communication with Germany north of the Ardennes. Foch believed that the two main attacks on either side of the bulge would force the Germans to withdraw from it, and the French Armies around the bulge were, while the three attacks were in progress, to keep the enemy in the bulge occupied, and prevent them from retiring at their leisure. The Fifth British Army, which had been reconstituted under the command of General Birdwood, was to carry out a similar role on the Lille front between the main British attack on Cambrai and the Flanders attack.

Such was the plan, vast, simple and bold. Now that all is over, and the plan has been brilliantly and completely successful, the courage and determination of the men who formed it and carried it through is apt to be overlooked, more especially as the continuous and rapid succession of victories, which began with the famous counter stroke of July 18, produced in the public mind an exaggerated impression of weakness and even of collapse in the enemy. It seemed as if Foch had brought back the trumpets of Joshua, and that German defences fell before him wherever and whenever he chose to advance. Yet in the third week of September the German resistance was far from broken. If the enemy's infantry had lost much of the dash and initiative which distinguished it in 1916, and the subordinate leaders had not the skill of their predecessors who had fallen in battle, his artillery, though weakening, was still powerful and well directed, and his machine-guns were manned by picked men of high courage, and had, from long experience, become more formidable than ever.

The strongest of the German trench lines still lay in front of the Allies, lines which the enemy believed to be impregnable. Many of the American divisions which were to take part in the battle had had little or no war experience, and the last stages of their training had been hurried through. The American commanders and staffs had had no opportunity of handling such masses of troops as were to be employed, and though St. Mihiel had proved to be a very complete success, it had disclosed defects in the American organisation and staff. It was thought, particularly in the British War Cabinet, that it would be wiser to defer forcing a decision until the American troops had learned more and the American army had increased in size, that the attempt to break through should be postponed until the spring of 1919.

Those who held this view were not without hope that the anticipations which they had long cherished would be realised, and that Germany would collapse when her props were knocked away. One of these props, Bulgaria, was on the point of surrender, and the news both from Austria and from Turkey was encouraging. It might never be necessary to assault the impenetrable barrier in the West.

Though Foch was in supreme control, his special function was to co-ordinate the strategy of the Allied Armies, and the commanders-in-chief of those armies remained responsible to their governments for the lives and wellbeing of their men. It was a question of fighting a battle on a scale which had never yet been attempted, a battle in which millions of soldiers would take part, and hundreds of thousands of lives were at stake. Had Haig and Pershing hesitated, and the arguments in favour of hesitation were many, the great plan could not have been consummated. Haig was, however, confident in himself and in his men. Believing absolutely in their superiority over the Germans, and that no defences could hold them back, he was ready to take on his shoulders the heavy responsibility of deciding to push on at once.

The British Government, while unwilling to veto the plan, felt so doubtful of its success that they were not prepared to support it. Mr. Lloyd George, in daily contact with our difficulties in raising men for the prosecution of the war in all its varied aspects, dreaded the casualty lists of another Somme or Passchendaele, and his sympathies with the theory of victory by the way round were this time more powerful than his courage and his readiness to take risks. Even Foch felt that he could not take the responsibility of ordering the army of another nation to advance against the serried lines of the Siegfried system. So, Haig was left to bear the burden alone. He tells us in his dispatch of January 7, 1919, how he took it up. After describing the broad lines of Foch's plans and of the attacks to be carried out by the Allied Armies, he goes on:

> The results to be obtained from these different attacks depended in a peculiarly large degree upon the British attack in the centre. It was here that the enemy's defences were most highly organised. If these were broken, the threat directed at his vital systems of lateral communication would of necessity react upon his defence elsewhere.
>
> On the other hand, the long period of sustained offensive action through which the British Armies had already passed had made large demands both upon the troops themselves and upon my available reserves. Throughout our attacks from August 8 onwards, our losses in proportion to the results achieved and the numbers of prisoners taken had been consistently and remarkably small. In the aggregate, however, they were considerable, and in the face of them an attack upon so formidably organised, a position as that which now confronted us could not be lightly undertaken. Moreover, the political effects of an unsuccessful attack upon a position so well known as the Hindenburg line would be large, and would go far to revive the declining morale not only of the German Army but of the German people.
>
> These different conditions were present to my mind. The probable results of a costly failure, or, indeed, of anything short of a decided success, in any attempt upon the main defences of the Hindenburg line were obvious; but I was convinced that the British attack was the essential part of the general scheme, and

that the moment was favourable.

Accordingly, I decided to proceed with the attack, and all preparatory measures, including the preliminary operations already recounted, were carried out as rapidly and as thoroughly as possible. (Supplement to the *London Gazette*, 7 January, 1919, para. 32.)

In making this decision Haig staked his future; not that such a consideration weighed with him for a moment; but he must have known that failure, with a doubting Government behind him, could have for him but one result. At the time the fact that the War Cabinet sent no congratulations to the army on the victories of Bapaume, of the second Battle of the Scarpe, of Epehy, or of Cambrai, victories which gave us nearly 100,000 prisoners, caused much comment. The reason of this neglect was that the War Cabinet to the last doubted of victory and did not wish to appear to exult until all danger of a setback was over. So not until Foch assured Mr. Lloyd George on October 7 that Haig's hammer blows had done their work was any message sent.

Pershing was equally sure that the proved valour, the vigour and enterprise of the American soldier would more than compensate for any lack of experience and training. These were fateful decisions, for if we had not attacked the war could not have been ended before the spring of 1919. The firmness and courage of these two men gave us victory in 1918.

The victory of Bapaume, and the piercing of the Drocourt line in the Battle of the Scarpe, had forced the enemy on the front covering Cambrai to take refuge behind the Canal du Nord, but southwest of Cambrai, and west of St. Quentin as far as the Oise, he still held strong advanced positions some three miles in front of the main Hindenburg system.

These positions included the outpost defences of that system and some of the British works which had been prepared to meet the March attack. It was necessary, therefore, before the Hindenburg line could be attacked, to clear the Germans out of these works, and this Haig did between September 12 and 18, while Pershing was busy at St. Mihiel. During this period fifteen divisions of the British Third and Fourth Armies fought the Battle of Epehy, and drove twenty German divisions back into the main Hindenburg line, capturing 11,750 prisoners and 100 guns. Simultaneously Debeney's First French Army performed the same function between St. Quentin and La Fère.

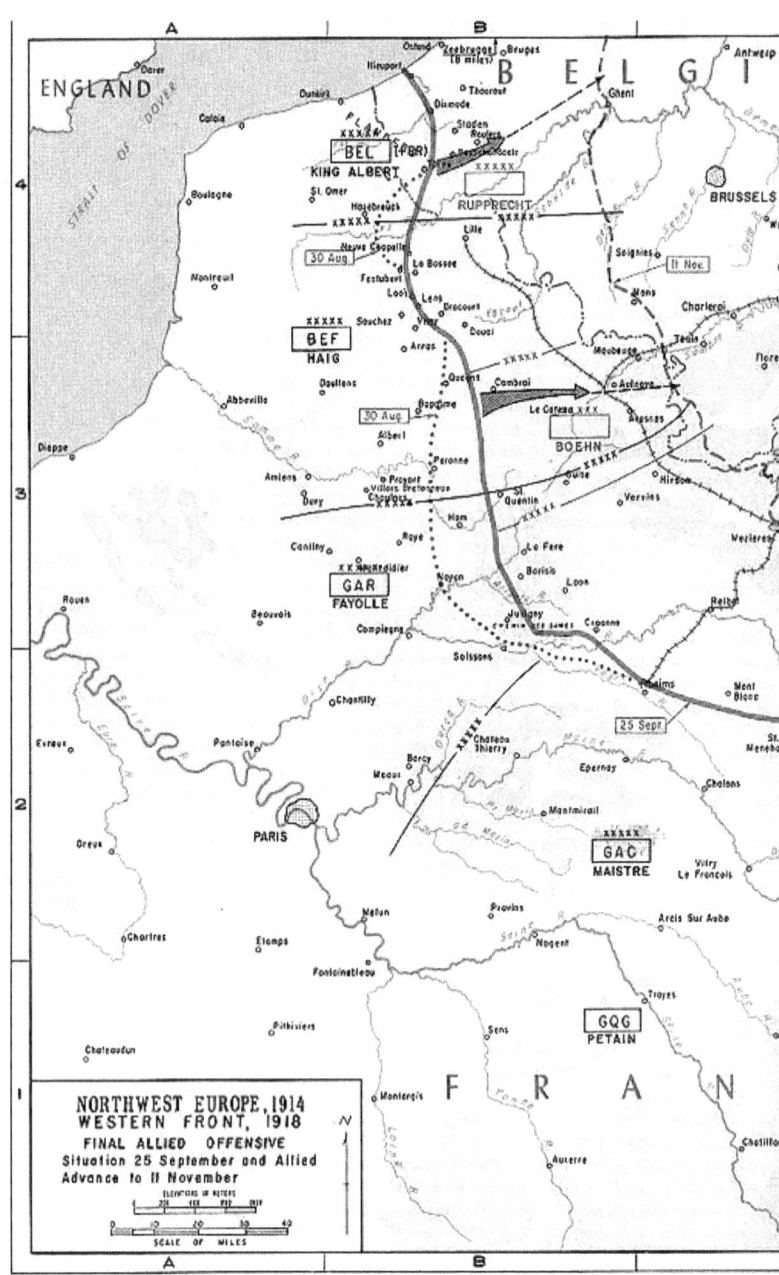

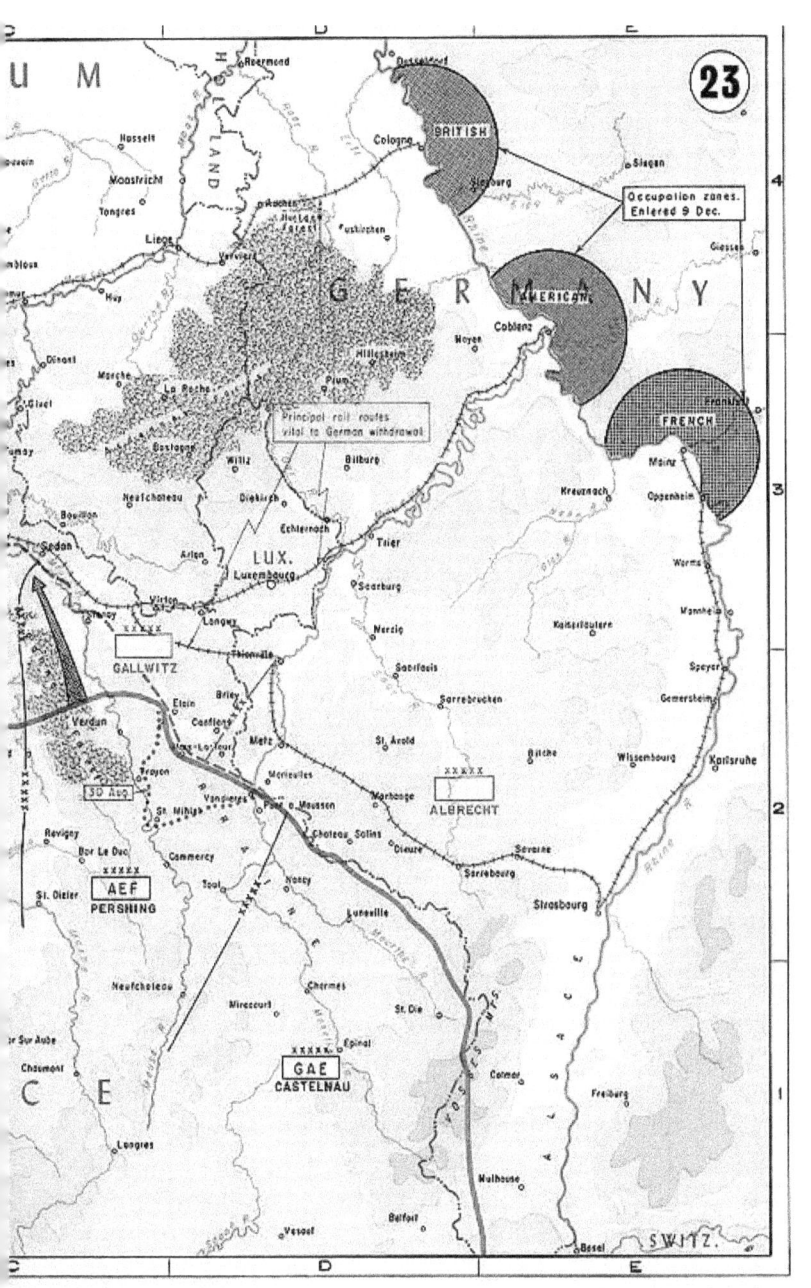

While these events were taking place on the Cambrai-St. Quentin front Pershing was quietly transferring troops from the St. Mihiel salient to Verdun. This movement had begun as soon as it was seen that the American divisions in the front line would succeed in the task of obliterating the salient, and that the reserve divisions would not be needed. It was carried through with the utmost secrecy, the American troops on the new front created by the Battle of St. Mihiel doing everything that was possible to produce the impression that the advance would be continued towards Metz and Briey. Between the Meuse and the western edge of the Argonne, which had been inactive for more than a year, French troops continued to hold the trenches while the First American Army assembled behind them, and they were not relieved until the night of September 25-26.

There is little doubt that the Germans were surprised when the great battle opened with an American attack between the Meuse and the Argonne, for they had not reinforced their front, which was held by four divisions, who were overwhelmed by the nine American divisions which advanced against them. By the evening of the 27th the Americans had taken the first line defences on the whole front of their attack, and in the centre had pressed forward to a depth of some seven miles, to the southern slopes of Montfaucon. This hill dominates the surrounding country, and for that reason the Crown Prince William had had built for himself on it a palatial dug-out from which he directed the operations in his unsuccessful attempt to capture Verdun.

A gallant attempt to storm the hill and the village on its summit made with the aid of tanks in the evening failed, but both were carried in a second attack the next day. By the evening of September 29, the Americans were in possession of the first and second German systems of defence between the Meuse and the Argonne, and had in places penetrated the third system. Ten thousand prisoners fell to Pershing in this first advance.

Ludendorff now became suddenly aware that he was menaced by a deadly blow at his lateral communications. He could write off St. Mihiel as a regrettable incident; he was, in fact, preparing to come out of the salient when he was attacked. The majority of the troops defending it had been of inferior quality, and the Germans could always throw the blame for their failure upon the Austrians who fought with them. But the capture of Montfaucon was quite a different matter. The Americans were on territory which had not been trodden by Allied troops since the early days of 1914, having broken through defences which had been prepared and held by the Germans since the first days of trench warfare, trenches established on ground as difficult to attack as that on any part of the whole long front. There was no question of yielding voluntarily a foot of that ground, which was especially precious to the Germans as their lines through it ran nearer than elsewhere to the Metz-Maubeuge railway. The American advance, therefore, confronted Ludendorff with a crisis which had to be dealt with at any cost.

While the battle had opened thus auspiciously on the Verdun front, Gouraud had attacked simultaneously in Champagne on a front of eighteen miles from the west of the Argonne towards Reims. The Champagne hills had been the scene of Joffre's first efforts to wear down the enemy by the "nibbling" process, and of his attempt to force a way through the trench barrier in one great rush in September, 1915. The left of Gouraud's battle front included part of the ground on which he had defeated the German attack of July 15, when bombardment and counter-bombardment had torn the surface of the heathlands and left an area of desolation and destruction, which, if less deep than that of the Somme battlefields, could only be compared in its intensity with that on the Ypres front.

Forward movement across country so pitted with mine craters and shell holes was very laborious, and the Germans held all the heights commanding the lines of the French advance. Gouraud's progress on the first day was therefore slower than Pershing's, and by the evening of the 27th his infantry had only got forward some three miles. It took him three days of hard fighting to force his way clear of the old battlefields, but by September 30 he had won through, and thenceforward his difficulties diminished just when those of Pershing began to increase. On October 1 he was on the outskirts of Challerange, some nine miles from his starting point, having captured 13,000 prisoners and more than 300 guns, and having made Ludendorff realise that he constituted a danger not less imminent than that of the American advance. There for the present I must leave the right wing of Foch's battle to turn to the British front.

The British attacks were timed to begin in the early morning of September 27, and on the evening before a great bombardment opened on a thirty-mile front, from a point about two miles northwest of St. Quentin, as far as the Sensée River north-west of Cambrai. Then in the grey light of early dawn the 4th, 6th, 17th and Canadian Corps, thirteen divisions in all, of Byng's Third Army and Horne's

First Army advanced on the Cambrai front, stormed the immensely strong Canal du Nord, swept beyond Bourlon Wood and Fontaine-Notre Dame, the extreme limits of our advance in the first Battle of Cambrai of November, 1917, and captured Sailly, more than six miles from their starting point, taking over 10,000 prisoners and 200 guns. By this blow Cambrai was threatened from the north, whereas in the previous battle we had attempted to approach the town from the south-east, where the St. Quentin Canal was a formidable obstacle to our troops, and we had in one bound got sufficiently near to the railway lines, which converged on Cambrai and made it one of the most important junctions in the hands of the Germans, to be able to deny their use to the enemy.

I have already mentioned that Ludendorff had, in his anxiety to protect Cambrai, been withdrawing troops from Flanders. Doubtless he remembered our experiences in the third Battle of Ypres, and recalled the fact that the Flanders mud had there done more to check our progress than had the German troops. The season was already far advanced and there had been a good deal of rain. The state of his reserves was such that in order to meet the American advance west of the Meuse, and the British advance on Cambrai, both of them blows aimed at his vitals, he had to take chances somewhere, and he decided to take them on the Flanders front.

He left less than five divisions to hold the seventeen miles of front, from near Vormezeele, four and a half miles south of Ypres, to Dixmude, and on September 28 this thin line was attacked and overwhelmed by the Belgian Army, supported by some French divisions, and by six divisions of Plumer's Second Army, the whole under the command of King Albert. The success won by the gallant Belgian king, who had seen his army cooped in for four years behind the floods of the Yser, and had only left it at rare intervals, living with his queen in a little villa within range of the German guns and in a district incessantly attacked by the enemy's bombing aeroplanes, was startlingly complete and exceeded the wildest expectations.

The Flanders ridges, up which we had hewn our way at heavy cost in three and a half months of fighting in the autumn of 1917, were won in less than forty-eight hours. The French and Belgians, following up this success vigorously on the left of the battle, swept forward beyond Passchendaele, and by the evening of October 1 had penetrated almost to the outskirts of Roulers, while Plumer, throwing in three more divisions, drove across the Messines Ridge, cleared the Lys valley from Armentières to Comines, and advanced to within two miles of Menin. Thus Lille, like Cambrai, was menaced from the north.

While King Albert was putting the finishing touches to his victory the crisis of the great battle had been reached and passed. The bombardment which had begun on the evening of September 26 on the front of the British Fourth, Third and First Armies, had been continued on the front of the Fourth Army throughout the 27th and 28th, while the other two armies were fighting their way towards Cambrai. During the final stage of that bombardment nearly 1,000,000 shells, weighing some 25,000 tons, were poured into the German lines. This wholesale expenditure of ammunition took place during about one-tenth of the period of the whole battle, and on considerably less than one-tenth of the fronts attacked.

During the war of 1870-71 the total number of rounds fired by the German artillery in the field amounted to 360,000, as compared with 4,362,500 tons of shell fired by the British artillery alone on the Western Front, and yet, so tremendous had the effect of the German guns appeared to be in those days, that Napoleon III. told his enemies after his surrender at Sedan that he felt himself beaten by their artillery. Science and industry have in less than fifty years developed man's power of destruction to an extent which makes comparison with the past futile.

With this artillery attack we reverted to former methods, and the reason for doing so was, that immediately behind that part of the German front to be attacked by the Fourth Army, ran the St. Quentin Canal, which merges near Cambrai in the navigable Scheldt, is capable of taking the largest barges and is unfordable. With such an obstacle in their path tanks could not be used to prepare the way for the infantry, except against such portions of the German line as lay west of the canal, and against the two stretches where the canal ran under ground, one of about four and a half miles between Bellicourt and Vendhuile, the other of about 1,000 yards long just north of St. Quentin known as the Le Tronquoy Tunnel.

Further, there was no longer any question of obtaining surprise, the Germans were well aware that we intended to attack, and therefore one of the great objections to a prolonged bombardment disappeared. So, the guns again came into their own. It was long since the Germans had been subjected to such a dose of shelling, and many of their troops having come from the Eastern Front, or being fresh drafts from Germany, had never experienced a really intense and prolonged bombardment. The morale effect of this cannonade was therefore very great. It drove the enemy into his deep dug-outs and tunnels, and prevented his carrying parties from bringing up food and ammunition. At 5.30 a.m. on September 29 Rawlinson's Fourth Army attacked the heart of the Hindenburg line, on a front of twelve miles, with the 9th British Corps and the 2nd American Corps with the Australian Corps in support behind it. Debeney's First French Army extended the battle front to the south, while two corps of the Third British Army prolonged it to the north as far as the loop in the St. Quentin Canal at Marcoing. This was the decisive day of the great battle and was marked by many glorious feats of arms.

The 9th Corps attacked the St. Quentin Canal at and north of Bellenglise, the 46th Division, North Midland Territorials, leading, the men advancing equipped with lifebelts, requisitioned from the Channel steamboats, and carrying mats and rafts. Here and there they managed to cross by foot bridges, which the enemy had been unable to destroy, but the majority dropped down the sheer sides of the canal, swam across, clambered out and stormed the German trenches on the top of the eastern bank. Then swinging southward, they surprised the enemy before he had realised the new direction of the attack, and on this one day the division captured over 4,000 prisoners and 70 guns.

The 2nd American Corps attacked the Bellicourt Tunnel front, which the Germans, knowing that it was exposed to tank attack, had fortified with especial care. The 30th American Division stormed through the intricate web of barbed wire and the network of trenches which surrounded Bellicourt, and breaking clean through this section of the main Hindenburg line, carried the village, only to be attacked in the rear by the German machine-gunners who had come out of their subterranean shelters in the tunnel. The Australians coming up in support had to tackle these pests without the aid of artillery or tanks, for both the barrage and the tanks had gone forward with the Americans, but they overcame them, and another breach in the Hindenburg line was effected.

The 27th American Division attacking on the left of the 30th, had an especially difficult task, for the westerly bend in the canal at Vendhuile made it impossible for the British troops farther north to keep pace with the advance of the 27th, and its left flank was exposed to cross fire of artillery and machine-guns from the ridge north-east of Vendhuile on the eastern bank of the canal. Two regiments of the division, the 106th and 107th, had therefore to fight desperately hard to safeguard the left of the division, while the right and centre pushed on to the village of Bony. Later the British 12th and 18th Divisions forced their way across the canal to the north of the tunnel, and relieved the pressure on the left flank of the 27th American Division which had beaten off repeated and fierce German counter-attacks.

On September 30 and on the following days the yielding enemy was driven back on the whole front of the Fourth, Third and First Armies. On the right of the Fourth Army the 1st British Division had, by the 30th, gained possession of the Le Tronquoy Tunnel, and crossed the canal to the north of St. Quentin, a feat as splendid as that of the 46th Division on the previous day. Its immediate consequence was that the Germans retired from St. Quentin, which fell into the hands of the French on October 1. The Australians, passing through the Americans, sent the right centre of our battle front forward to within touch of the last line of the Hindenburg system which ran through Beaurevoir. The New Zealanders and the 3rd British Divisions crossed the canal to the south of Cambrai, while the Canadians all but encircled the town to the north. By October 3 the Fourth Army had broken through the Beaurevoir line, and by the 5th the whole line of the canal, and the Hindenburg defences along it, were in our hands.

The victory was complete and decisive, and in winning it the three British Armies had captured 36,500 prisoners and 380 guns. Thirty British and two American divisions with a British cavalry division had defeated thirty-nine German divisions, holding the strongest defences ever devised by the wit of man. At last, after four years of dogged effort the great trench barriers had been pierced, for between the British Army and its objective, Maubeuge, there lay but one German line, which the enemy, believing the Hindenburg system to be proof against all assaults, had not troubled to complete. This line lay some fourteen miles back, and its artificial defences consisted of nothing more formidable than a thin fence of barbed wire, with the sites of the trenches to be dug behind it marked out upon the ground.

The victors of Cambrai looked out over rolling, wooded, and well-watered country with something of the joy and wonder which filled the soldiers of Zenophon when at the end of their great march they first saw the sea. The leafy trees, the harvested fields, the green meadow lands and the valleys were to an army which had lived and fought for four years surrounded by hideous devastation, with the stink of the blood-soaked, battle-torn ground ever in their nostrils, more convincing evidence of achievement than tens of thousands of prisoners and hundreds of guns.

The effect of the three great blows on the Meuse-Champagne front, on the St. Quentin-Cambrai front, and in Flanders was, as Foch had hoped it would be, to cause the Germans to yield in the intervals between those attacks. By the end of September, the enemy had begun to withdraw between Lens and Armentières before the left of our First Army and our Fifth Army, and there were signs of retirement from the St. Gobain bulge. He was at once pressed by the French and British forces on those fronts, and the battle thereupon enveloped the whole 250 miles from Dixmude to the Meuse. Foch's great conception had been realised; he had delivered his big kick and the whole German front was crumbling under it.

For a time, on the British front at least, the German morale broke down, prisoners were taken from the German infantry in great numbers and without much resistance, and there were signs of confusion and disorder in the enemy ranks, though the German artillery retained much of its efficiency and the machine-gunners continued to fight with their old devotion and skill.

More important still the resolution of the German High Command was badly shaken. There were no men in Germany to replace the tremendous losses in the field, and many of Ludendorff's divisions were reduced to mere skeletons. He had piled up behind his front, for his great offensive, enormous stocks of shell, and of military stores, and had had neither the time nor the transport to remove them. The Allies had captured thousands of guns. The output of the German munitions factories was quite incapable of making good these losses, and he had ample evidence that the Allied factories had not yet reached the zenith of their production. In September Haig had more guns, more machine-guns, more ammunition and more aeroplanes than he had ever possessed, while the growth of the American army was daily bringing more and more guns into line.

With dwindling resources, Ludendorff saw himself faced by three great dangers; in the east the Americans, more numerous and efficient than he had believed they could possibly be, were threatening his communications between Metz and Mézières; in the centre the British Army had beaten the best of his troops in their strongest defences, and he had no more Hindenburg lines to stay its progress; in Flanders the Belgians, whom he had classed as capable only of defence, had won their way into, the open and were fighting with unexpected dash. Lastly, Bulgaria had collapsed, Mackensen was in dire straits and was clamouring for reinforcements to enable him to escape from the Balkans.

Under the pressure of these calamities Ludendorff threw up the sponge on the evening of September 28. The next day he and Hindenburg met the Kaiser and the Foreign Secretary, who had come to headquarters, and insisted on an immediate request for an armistice. In the afternoon the Kaiser, without consulting his military advisers and much to Ludendorff's disgust, issued his pronouncement on the introduction of Parliamentary Government and von Hertling ceased to be Chancellor. Ludendorff then sent one of his staff, Major Freiherr von der Bussche, to Berlin to explain to the Vice-Chancellor von Payer, who was in charge of the Administration while Prince Max of Baden was endeavouring to form a government, that an immediate offer of peace must be made. (Ludendorff's account of these proceedings is contained in his *Reminiscences*. He suppresses many of the documents I have quoted.)

Von Payer pressed for delay, pointing out that there was no Government in power to negotiate, but Hindenburg, who had accompanied the *Kaiser* to Berlin, immediately replied:

Main Headquarters, Oct. 1, 1918. 1.30 p.m.
To Major Frhr. von der Bussche, for Vice-Chancellor von Payer. Provided that a guarantee can be given between 7 and 8 o'clock this evening that Prince Max of Baden is forming the Government, then I agree to postponement until tomorrow morning. Should there, however, be any doubt about the formation of the Government, then I must insist that the declaration be made known to the foreign powers tonight.

(Signed) Von Hindenburg.
Made known to His Excellency von Payer on October 1, 2 p.m.
(Signed) Frhr. von Der Bussche.

This note was naturally assumed in Berlin to be a cry of despair, and when we consider the events which led up to it this seems to be the only possible interpretation. It is now maintained in defence of Hindenburg and Ludendorff that the object of this startling message, to which Ludendorff makes no reference in his *Reminiscences*, was to hasten the formation of the new Government, but the formation of a Government could not by any stretch of imagination be supposed to influence the military situation on the front, and there was no reason, if that situation had not been held at German Army Headquarters to be desperate, why Prince Max should not have been given as much time as he needed to form his Administration.

Ever since Haig's victory of August 8 Ludendorff had been pressing his government to open negotiations, because he was then convinced that Germany's military position must go from bad to worse. It seems more than probable that, when the Hindenburg line was broken, he wanted an immediate armistice, because he feared that a general collapse was imminent and that he might, if he could not obtain a cessation of hostilities, be forced before long to accept an unconditional surrender. It is absurd to suppose that he, with his great military experience, could have imagined that the Allied and Associated Powers would agree to any terms of armistice, after they had just won the greatest victory in the whole course of the war, unless those terms made it impossible for Germany to resume the struggle in any form.

An offer to conclude peace made immediately after the strongest German defences had been pierced is obviously very different from such an offer put forward when the Hindenburg line was still intact, and could in the circumstances be nothing less than an open acknowledgment of defeat. It is, therefore, only reasonable to suppose that Hindenburg and Ludendorff believed that their armies had been decisively beaten and that there was no better alternative to such an acknowledgment. The defence that they were influenced by the political rather than by the military situation has been put forward in Germany in support of the fiction that the German Army was unbeaten, and that it was the politicians and the German public who lost their heads and surrendered when it was still possible for the German Army to wring favourable terms from us.

This defence is shown to be untenable by a statement, made on October 2, on the military situation to the party leaders of the Reichstag by Major Freiherr von der Bussche, who, as Ludendorff admits, had been carefully coached by him and presented his views correctly. The statement ran:

> In a few days the situation has fundamentally changed. The collapse of the Bulgarian front has entirely upset our disposition of troops. Our communications with Constantinople were threatened, as well as the shipping route indispensable for the transport of our supplies on the Danube. We were compelled, if we were not to leave the *Entente* a free hand in the Balkans, to send German and Austro-Hungarian divisions ear-marked for the

Western Front to those regions, abandoning the Black Sea and Roumania. We were obliged to make an immediate decision. The entrainment of our troops had already begun. We have every justification for hoping that the situation in the Balkans may be re-established, at all events sufficiently to guard our own interests. Unfortunately, as I shall explain, this cannot be done without great detriment to the situation as a whole.

Almost simultaneously with the offensive in Macedonia, violent enemy attacks have been made in the West. They have not found us unprepared. All possible measures have been taken to hold them up. Divisions from the East were on the way to relieve the sorely tried divisions in the West. Unfortunately, a portion of these troops had to be diverted to the Balkans. The last men capable of bearing arms had been withdrawn from the East. We calmly awaited the decisive battle. The *Entente* knew how to conceal from us where the attacks would take place. From the sea to Switzerland preparations for the attack were in progress. The most extensive was against Lorraine and the Sundgau, and we were forced to distribute our reserves and to keep the whole front in a state of readiness for the attack. Considerable forces had to be stationed, especially in Lorraine and in the Sundgau, for the defence of German territory.

After carrying out the necessary movements, we were absolutely convinced that we should emerge victorious from the coming battles, and that we should be able to break the opposition of our enemies by the enormous losses which we anticipated they would suffer. Consequently, by putting in reserves at the right time, we have been able to hold up the enemy at all those places where, by means of tanks, by surprise attacks or superiority in numbers, he has penetrated our lines. The fighting of the last six days may be termed successful for us, in spite of the loss of prisoners and material.

In comparison with our successes in the spring offensive the enemy has made little progress. In the majority of cases his continuous onslaughts have been countered with unusual obstinacy on the part of our troops. According to our own reports the enemy has suffered the heaviest losses.

The majority of our troops have fought splendidly and made superhuman efforts. Their old brave spirit has not died out. The numerical superiority of the enemy has not been able to terrorise our men. Officers and men vie with each other in deeds of valour.

In spite of these facts, the High Command has been compelled to come to the enormously difficult decision that in all human probability there is no longer any prospect of forcing the enemy to sue for peace. Two factors have had a decisive influence on our decision, namely, tanks and our reserves. The enemy has made use of tanks in unexpectedly large numbers. In cases where they have suddenly emerged in huge masses from smoke clouds, our men were completely unnerved. Tanks broke through our foremost lines, making a way for their infantry, reaching our rear, and causing local panics, which entirely upset our battle control. When we were able to locate them our anti-tank guns and our artillery speedily put an end to them.

But the mischief had already been done, and solely owing to the success of the tanks we have suffered enormous losses in prisoners, and this has unexpectedly reduced our strength and caused a more speedy wastage of our reserves than we had anticipated. We were not in a position to make use of similar masses of German tanks. Our manufacturers, under the existing pressure, were absolutely unable to supply them in large numbers, without causing other more important things to be neglected. The question of reserves has, however, been the decisive factor. The army entered the fray with depleted numbers. In spite of using every possible device, the strength of our battalions sank from about 800 in April, to 540 by the end of September. And these numbers were only secured by the disbanding of 22 infantry divisions (66 infantry regiments). The Bulgarian defeat has eaten up 7 more divisions. There is no prospect whatever of raising the strength. The current reserves, consisting of men who are convalescent, combed out men, etc., will not even cover the losses of a quiet winter campaign. The inclusion of the 1900 class will only increase the strength of the battalions by 100, and that is the last of our reserves. The losses of the battle which is now in progress are, as I have stated, unexpectedly large, especially as regards officers. That is a decisive factor.

If the troops are to stem the onslaught or to attack, they require more than ever the example of their officers. The latter must, and have, sacrificed themselves unreservedly. The regimental commanders and leaders fought in the front lines together with their men. I will give one example only. In two days of fighting one division lost all its officers, dead or wounded, and three regimental commanders were killed. The small number of reserve officers has sunk to nothing. The same applies to the N.C.O.'s. The enemy, owing to the help he has received from America, is in a position to make good his losses. The American troops, as such, are not of special value, or in any way superior to our men. In those cases, in which, owing to numbers alone, they gained an initial success, they were finally held at bay by our troops. They were, however, able to take over large portions of the front, thereby permitting the English and French to liberate some of their experienced divisions and in this way form an almost inexhaustible supply of reserves.

Up till now our reserves have been adequate to fill the gaps and drafts have duly arrived. The hardest attacks were repulsed. The fighting was described to be of unparalleled severity. Then our reserves began to fail. If the enemy continues the attack, the situation may demand a withdrawal from extensive sectors of the front. We can continue this kind of warfare for a measurable space of time, we can cause the enemy heavy losses, devastating the country in our retreat, but we cannot win the war.

This decision and these events caused the idea to ripen in the minds of the field-marshal and Ludendorff to propose to the *Kaiser* the breaking-off of hostilities, so as to spare the German people and their Allies further sacrifice. Just as our great offensive of July 15 was abandoned, when the sacrifice entailed no longer warranted its continuation, so the decision now had to be taken that it was hopeless to proceed with the war. There is still time. The German Army is still strong enough to hold the enemy for months, to achieve local successes and to expose the enemy to fresh sacrifices. But every day brings the enemy nearer his goal, and will make him less inclined to conclude a peace with us which will be satisfactory on our side.

Therefore, no time must be lost. Every day the situation may become worse, and give the enemy the opportunity of recognising our momentary weakness, which might have the most evil consequences for peace prospects as well as for the military situation. Neither the army nor the Homeland should do anything which would make our weakness apparent; on the other hand, the army and the Homeland must stand together more closely than before. Simultaneously with the peace offer a united front must be shown at home, so that the enemy recognise our unbending will to continue the war, if the enemy will not make peace with us, or only a humiliating one. If this should be, then the endurance of the army will depend on a firm attitude at home, and on the power of the Homeland to inspire the army."

This is a very human statement. It contains the excuses and explanations of men who find themselves beaten and are endeavouring to shuffle out of their responsibility. Much is laid to the account of Bulgaria, who by collapsing unwarrantably has upset the best laid plans of the German Great Headquarters. Ludendorff's advocate says truly that the last man capable of bearing arms had been withdrawn from the East. For some time before the end of September the German divisions on the Russian front had been combed out and the fittest men had been sent westwards to help make good the losses in France. It is obvious that the German battalions in the Western Front would not have been permitted to fall almost to half their proper strength, and that twenty-two divisions would not have been disbanded had there been men in the East available for service in the West.

The situation on the Bulgarian front began to be critical on September 19, and by no possibility could troops starting westwards after that date have been in time to save the Hindenburg line. Therefore, the statement that "the collapse of the Bulgarian front has entirely upset our disposition of troops" is a gross exaggeration intended to throw dust in the eyes of the Reichstag leaders and save the face of the General Staff. The defeat of Bulgaria was certain to bring down Austria sooner or later and made the position of Germany hopeless, but the General Staff knew quite well that it would be many months before the Allies would be able to attack the southern frontiers of Germany, and that, vast as was the political effect of these events, they had no immediate influence upon the military situation in France.

Bulgaria had asked for an armistice on September 25, for she was very anxious to get it concluded before Mackensen, who was hurrying troops towards Sofia, could intervene. The armistice was signed on September 29, and the fact that Bulgaria had asked for terms and had sent plenipotentiaries to meet Franchet d'Espérey was notified to the world in our Wireless Press Summary of September 28. These facts must therefore have been known to German Great Headquarters on

October 2, but not a word is said of them to the Reichstag leaders, who are led to believe that "the situation in the Balkans may be re-established."

After this exordium on Bulgaria's delinquencies comes the true reason for the demand for the immediate opening of peace negotiations. The German Armies in the West are in imminent peril, and if hostilities are not stopped promptly, they may be unable to escape an overwhelming disaster. That is in plain English what the statement means. The German troops have been fighting splendidly, and the General Staff had made every possible preparation to meet the expected attack, but our superiority in tanks and the exhaustion of the German reserves have made the position hopeless.

I had written all that I have said in the earlier part of this chapter on the effect of our tanks before this document came into my hands, and it is interesting to see how completely it confirms all the information on this point which we had obtained before the armistice. Not less interesting is the tribute paid to Foch's strategy. Great Headquarters were in fear of attack along the whole front from the sea to Switzerland, and the remarkable statement is made that the most extensive preparations for attack were against Lorraine and the Sundgau, that is the frontier district of Alsace, east of Belfort. This is evidence of the effect of Pershing's victory of St. Mihiel and of the activities of the Second Army in simulating an offensive towards Briey and Metz.

It is difficult to make this anxiety square with the disparaging remarks about the American troops, for the German General Staff must have known that the majority of the troops on the Lorraine front were American. This is probably another attempt to save the face of the General Staff, who had declared roundly that the Americans would not be able to train troops to fight in any numbers during 1918. As we know, preparations for an offensive into Lorraine were not completed until sometime later, and at this time there were no preparations at all for an invasion of Alsace.

Therefore, this statement is an admission that Foch had very completely hoodwinked Ludendorff. Most interesting of all is the evidence of the efficacy of Foch's method of exhausting the German reserves before fighting his great battle. The picture drawn of the state of the German Army is impressive, and tallies exactly with information received from other sources.

Truly the question of reserves was the "decisive factor." The German reserves were exhausted and therefore there was nothing to be done but to make peace as quickly as possible. As the staff officer naively remarks, the decision had to be taken that it was hopeless to proceed with the war for the same reasons as led to the abandonment of the great offensive of July 15. The offensive of July 15 was abandoned because the Germans were soundly beaten in the second Battle of the Marne. On October 2 the Great Headquarters were compelled to advise that the struggle should be abandoned because the German Armies had been beaten.

Hindenburg, on the morning of October 3, confirmed the statement made the previous day by his representative in the following memorandum:

Berlin, Oct. 3.

To The Imperial Chancellor.

The High Command insists on the immediate issue of a peace offer to our enemies in accordance with the decision of Monday, September 29, 1918. In consequence of the collapse of the Macedonian front, and the inevitable resultant weakening of our reserves in the West, and also the impossibility of making good the heavy losses which have occurred during the battles of the last few days, there is no prospect, humanly speaking, of forcing our enemies to sue for peace. The enemy, on the other hand, is continuing to throw fresh reserves into the battle.

The German Army still stands firm and is defending itself against all attacks. The situation, however, is growing more critical daily, and may force the High Command to momentous decisions. In these circumstances it is imperative to stop the fighting in order to spare the German people and their Allies unnecessary sacrifices. Every day of delay costs thousands of brave soldiers their lives.

(Signed)   Von Hindenburg.

The appeal to the Homeland to stand firm, with which the gloomy review of the situation made to the leaders of political parties ends, is curious as coming from men who were pressing with all their energy for an immediate opening of negotiations to men who were anxious to delay so fatal a step until they were better assured that it was unavoidable. Von Payer in particular seems to have taken a much calmer view of the situation than did the soldiers, and before acceding to counsels of despair he wanted to know more. On October 3 he therefore sent Hindenburg the following memorandum:

Berlin, October 3, 1918.

Before coming to any decision as to a peace move, I would request Your Excellency to answer the following questions:—

(1) How long can the army hold the enemy the other side of the German frontier?

(2) Must the Chief Army Command expect a collapse, and if so, when?

(3) Is the military situation so critical that action should immediately be taken to bring about an armistice?

(4) In the event of your reply to question 3 being in the affirmative, is the Chief Army Command aware that a peace move, under pressure of the critical military situation, may lead to the loss of German territory, namely, Alsace-Lorraine and the purely Polish districts of the Eastern provinces?

(5) Does the Chief Army Command agree to the dispatch of the enclosed draft note?

I should be grateful to Your Excellency for an immediate answer.

  (Signed)   Payee, Representative Imperial Chancellor.

The draft note referred to is presumably the first request for an armistice sent to President Wilson. Prince Max had arrived in Berlin, and he was no more eager than his vice-chancellor to hoist the flag of surrender, but the soldiers were insistent. The same day (October 3) Hindenburg gave the following answer to von Payer's questions:

October 3.

(1) The question cannot be answered in exactly the form in which it is put. The holding of the front depends on many factors, amongst others on the resources and ability of the enemy to continue his attacks, and on the duration of our power of resistance.

At present the German Army is standing firm. It will withdraw from sectors if forced, clinging toughly to enemy soil. The duration of such withdrawals cannot be determined beforehand. But it is to be hoped that they may protect German soil until next spring.

(2) Answer to question 1 applies to this question. I do not believe that there will be any general collapse. As long as valuable reserves are at hand the yielding of the front consequent on enemy break-throughs need not have such a result.

(3) This question is answered by my communication of October 3 to the Imperial Chancellor.

(4) Unless things should change, the Chief Army Command will take into consideration the surrender of small French-speaking portions of Alsace-Lorraine. For it there is no question of the cession of German territory in the East.

(5) Draft note was advised, but not enclosed.

These answers and the memorandum to which they refer are very cautious, but leave no room for doubt as to the opinion at Headquarters. The holding of the front is *possible*; the army *may* be able to resist until the spring; the wholesale surrender of Alsace-Lorraine need not be considered *unless things* change, but it is impossible to guarantee any of these things. The situation is highly critical and at any moment it may be necessary to take momentous decisions, that is to say, disaster may overtake the German Armies. Therefore, it is imperative that negotiations should be opened at once.

On October 4 Prince Max of Baden became Imperial Chancellor, and the next day the first request for an armistice was dispatched to President Wilson. The greatest battle in the world's history had been fought and won. There was to be bitter fighting before the end came, for Ludendorff made an attempt to rally which met with some measure of success, and the discipline of the German Armies, which in the first days of October appeared to be cracking, again for a time asserted its influence. None the less, it was the great battle begun on September 26 which decided the issue of the war. This battle was so vast that no single name has ever been suggested for it. (While this book was in the Press, 1919, M. Louis Madelin, in the August number of the *Revue de Deux Mondes*," has called the great struggle "the Battle of France." This name just fails to be apposite, for an important part of the battle was fought in Belgium.)

During its course we British fought the second Battle of Cambrai, the Battle of St. Quentin, and took a part in the Battle of Flanders, the Americans fought the Battle of the Meuse-Argonne, the French the Battle of Champagne, while the Belgians with French help fought the Battle of Flanders. These great struggles, however, made up a whole, conceived and directed by one man. Foch's long-thought-out plans and careful preparations had their reward. He was ably supported by Haig, Pershing, Pétain and King Albert, and each of the Allied Armies on the Western Front had played its glorious part in Armageddon.

Foch had worked patiently and skilfully up to a great climax, and when the climax was reached the whole of the huge machinery under his control had been set in motion and every one of its parts had answered to his controlling hand.

CHAPTER 5

Ludendorff Tries to Rally

On none of the three fronts of attack which made up Foch's great battle was it easy to gather the fruits of victory. In Flanders King Albert and Plumer, having crossed the ridges, had behind them ground over which the tide of war had ebbed and flowed for more than four years, and now that it had been finally turned back it had left a morass of stinking mud which had obliterated every road and track. Behind the main British battle lay the deepest zone of devastation on the whole long front.

From Vimy Ridge to the eastern outskirts of Amiens, and thence through St. Quentin northwards by Cambrai to Douai, in an area of over one thousand square miles, there was hardly a house to be found intact, no village which had not been gutted; the surface of the ground was torn and blasted by shell fire, the vegetation withered by poison gas, the roads had been destroyed, the railways torn up, and all the bridges over the many rivers and canals blown down. Behind Gouraud in Champagne lay a somewhat narrower but equally horrible belt of desolation. In rear of the Americans were the battlefields of Verdun.

Therefore, on all the fronts the repair of the communications behind the armies was a stupendous undertaking, which not all the skill and tireless energy of the engineers and working parties could complete quickly. Without food, ammunition and military stores the victorious troops could not get forward, even against a badly shaken enemy, and these could not be brought up to them until the roads and railways had been to some extent restored. So everywhere progress was for a time slow. The Belgians were within two miles of Roulers by October 1, but it was not until October 14 that King Albert, having bridged the muddy gulf behind him, was able to advance and enter the town.

Cambrai had been enveloped north and south by British troops on September 30, but the Germans were not completely cleared out of the town until October 9. Debeney, with the First French Army, had entered St. Quentin on October 1, but by the 10th he was only eight miles east of the place. Only on the front between Cambrai and St. Quentin was any rapid progress made. Gouraud had by September 29 advanced about six miles through the German lines, but by October 9 his men were only one and a half miles farther forward.

Neither Gouraud's advance to the west of the forest nor that of the Americans to the east of it had been sufficiently deep to force the Germans out of the Argonne. Now that forest runs roughly from north-east to south-west along a series of rough ridges which separate the valleys of the upper Aisne and of the Aire. These forest-clad ridges gave the Germans splendid vantage ground from which to harass with artillery and machine-gun fire the Allied troops on either side of the Argonne, and if these troops were to get on there was nothing for it but to clear the forest.

By September 28 the American left had penetrated some three miles into the Argonne, but on that date the centre was nearly five miles ahead on the outskirts of Exermont, and was being worried by the German guns firing from the Argonne heights into their flanks and rear. To clear these heights and enable the centre to advance, the American left had to force its way forward through nine miles of the most difficult country on the whole Western Front. Under modern shell-fire woods become an almost impenetrable tangle of fallen timber, which affords ideal nests for the enemy's machine-guns. This tangle was made still more difficult by cunningly-placed wire entanglements and stretches of rabbit netting.

The forest is cut up by deep ravines with almost precipitous sides, which made it very hard for the infantry to keep touch, while tanks could be of no help to them, and even the most experienced artillery would have been put to it to give them support. It was a question of hard slogging infantry fighting, and the American infantryman did slog hard, and after eleven days of continuous, grim, dogged effort, by October 10 he had won his way through.

Simultaneously with the advance in the Argonne, which fell to the left of the 1st American Corps, the right of that corps and the 5th and 3rd Corps worked their way forward to the latitude of the northern edge of the forest, while east of the Meuse sufficient progress was made, in conjunction with French troops, to safeguard the flank of the troops west of the river. In all this fighting the casualties of the American First Army were very heavy and the hardships imposed on the troops severe. It is difficult to see how this could have been avoided in the circumstances in which the battle was fought. There was undoubtedly lack of co-operation between the infantry and the artillery and between the aircraft and both. It is equally true that the eagerness of the American infantry to get forward landed them in awkward salients, in which they suffered very severely, and that attempts to rush machine-gun nests by direct attack had to be paid for at a heavy price.

In fact, the experiences of the American Army in this their first great continuous offensive battle were in some respects similar to our own experiences in the first Battle of the Somme. No one will maintain that the quality of the infantry of the British Army, which in the summer of 1918 drove the Germans across the Somme battlefields into and through the Hindenburg line, can be compared with the quality of the infantry (who, two years before, won their way up the Somme heights. Then the pick of the manhood of the British Empire fought and fell, while in 1918 the ranks contained a high proportion of middle-aged men and boys. Yet in 1916 we gained comparatively little at a great price, and in 1918 we won much with far less sacrifice of life. The deterioration in the quality of the German troops in those two years does not wholly account for the change.

The essential difference in the two battles is that the first was won by sheer inexperienced valour, the second by valour combined with skill. We have learned in this war that it is possible to train the -individual soldier and get him to meet the terrible conditions of the modern battlefield in far less time than had been supposed to be necessary. The clerk from the counting-house, the ploughman from the fields, and the hand from the factory have all shown that with a few months' instruction they can acquit themselves, under conditions such as man has never been called upon before to face, better than the best of the soldiers of old, provided they are sent to take their places in an organisation which has been perfected and of which all the parts are working smoothly together.

Contrary to general expectation, the great war has shown that civilisation and education by developing intelligence have improved the fighting powers of the race, that the trained will can triumph over the weaknesses of the flesh. But the war has also shown conclusively that the experience of the past still holds good in that the training of the individual is a very small step toward the making of an army. It is even a shorter step today than it was in the past, for the organisation of the modern army is infinitely more complex than was that of the armies of old.

In 1918 all the parts of the British Army had learned, both by long and bitter experience and as the result of Sir Douglas Haig's careful and systematic teaching, to work together for a common end. Commanders of all grades had learned their jobs, the staffs knew their business, infantry, cavalry, artillery, engineers, trench mortars, machine gunners, tanks and aircraft knew each what the other could do and what the other needed. Sir Douglas Haig had, from the time when he assumed command of our armies in France, established a system of instruction which was continually developed and improved until in 1918 it was the most complete organisation of its kind which has ever assisted an army in the field.

Unfortunately, from the middle of 1916—when the first Battle of the Somme began—until the German attack in Flanders ended on April 29, 1918, the army had not the opportunity to make full use of the means of training at its disposal.

The first Battle of the Somme merged in the Battle of the Ancre, which ended in the German retreat to the Hindenburg line. Then came in succession the Battle of Arras, the Battle of Messines Ridge, and the third Battle of Ypres, while the winter of 1917-18 had to be devoted to preparation, with depleted ranks, for the expected German offensive.

The respite which the Germans allowed us between the end of April and the beginning of August, 1918, afforded us the longest period of good weather for training and instruction which we had enjoyed since the Battle of the Somme, and it proved invaluable. The result of that period of reconstruction, when the full benefits of Haig's instructional arrangements were felt, showed themselves in the Battle of Amiens and in the victories which followed it.

Sir Douglas Haig has often been accused of having maintained an extravagant organisation behind his front at the cost of the fighting ranks. He was looking forward confidently to the day when he would get his enemy on the move, and when that day came, he was ready. It was the perfection of the organisation of the services behind the British lines, a perfection which was the outcome of long experience, and the scale on which these services were equipped, as much as the increased skill of the fighting ranks, which enabled the British Army to fight continuously and victoriously for three months and keep up that succession of hammer blows to which Foch has paid a generous tribute.

The American Army had had little of the war training which had taught the British Army its lesson. Many of the divisions which fought in the Meuse-Argonne battle went into action then for the first time. That being so, it was inevitable that there should be defects in co-operation and that a high price should be paid for victory. I have already described the difficulties of the ground over which the American troops fought. The difficulties which confronted the services of supply were not less formidable. On the stretch of eighteen miles between the Meuse and western edge of the Argonne—a front of battle occupied by nine American divisions in the first line, equivalent to eighteen British or French divisions—there were only two main roads running in the direction of the advance, one of them on the extreme right flank, along the valley of the Meuse, exposed to artillery fire from the heights in the hands of the Germans on the east bank of the river, the other on the left flank along the eastern edge of the Argonne, exposed to artillery fire from the forest.

There was one more road, which ran through Montfaucon, parallel to the American line of advance, but it was a very poor one, and the bottom soon fell out of it under the combination of wet weather and a never-ending stream of traffic. Between these on the front of the main American advance there were only narrow cross-roads connecting the villages, and these roads had been shelled to pieces. The hilly and wooded nature of the country made the task of constructing new roads, of repairing the existing ones, and of laying railways very laborious, and consequently in the early stages of the battle the transport had to be crowded on to the very few roads which were fit for traffic.

On September 28 the main American advance east of the Argonne had penetrated through the German lines to a depth of seven miles. Eleven days later it was barely two miles farther forward. This slow progress was by no means only due to the necessity of clearing the Argonne, for the centre and right of the First American Army was not troubled by flanking fire from the forest. The difficulties of getting forward food and ammunition and of sending up timely reinforcements and of relieving tired troops caused even more delay. Just as happened in our early battles, so in this, the first great American effort in the war, some divisions had to give ground because they could not be supported in time.

The roads behind the army, too few and too poor to take the immense amount of transport which was seeking to find its way forward, became hopelessly congested, and in some cases masses of vehicles were so jammed that they could not be moved either forward or backward for long periods. The consequence of this was that it was not possible to get a regular supply of food up to the troops in front, and cases occurred in which the men did not receive their usual rations for four days.

There has been a great deal of talk of the breakdown of the American administrative services, and unquestionably things did go wrong; but the critics who lay stress on the defects of organisation which showed themselves are apt to overlook the conditions under which battle was joined. It was a question of attempting to force a decision by a great combined attack on the main German defensive positions at the end of September or of deferring a decisive attack until the following spring. It is probably true that no French or British staff would, after long experience of previous failure, have advised an attack on the Meuse-Argonne front until elaborate improvements and extensions of the roads and railways behind the front of attack had been carried out, and until equally elaborate preparations for prolonging those roads and railways into the territory captured from the Germans had been completed.

It is probably equally true that French and British soldiers, after the bitter lessons of the past, would not have attacked with any confidence unless they had ocular evidence that everything had been done beforehand to help them forward. There are times and occasions in war when the valour of ignorance has its advantages. With greater experience the American infantry would have learned to overcome the German machine-guns with less loss of life, and the services of supply would have worked more smoothly. Had the American Army waited to gain that experience, the war would certainly have been prolonged by at least six months, and the cost in life would certainly have been far greater than it was.

Pershing must have taken all these factors into consideration when he threw in his vote for fighting the great battle which began on September 26. He decided that the vigour and valour of his troops would more than counter-balance their lack of battle experience, and he was justified in the result. From September 26 until the Kriemhilde system was finally broken, by making the fullest use of his man power, for 630,000 American troops were engaged in this battle, he continuously menaced the Metz-Mézières railway, and forced Ludendorff to employ more than forty divisions in an ineffectual effort to stem his advance. The American attack, therefore, formed an essential part of Foch's plan, and had it not been successful it is almost certain that the Germans would have been able to withdraw in fairly good order to the Meuse, and that we should not have forced them to sign an armistice on November 11; but before it was successful there were many delays. The first rush forward of September 26 changed to slow progress and a long struggle as much against the difficulties of Nature as against the resistance of the enemy.

During the first week in October, then, the Allies were, for the reason which I have explained, delayed on all the main fronts of attack to a greater or less degree. This gave the Germans time to pull themselves together to some extent, and Ludendorff began to see a possibility of re-forming his armies on a new line. There was a good deal of exaggeration at various periods of the war on our side as to the prowess of the Germans as diggers, and they were reported to have defensive lines constructed right back to the Rhine. These existed only in the excited imaginations of those who at one time were disposed to believe that in matters military the Germans were demigods, but it was true that when the Siegfried position was broken through Ludendorff still had defences to which to withdraw. His military policy at this time is indicated in Hindenburg's note of October 3 to the vice-chancellor.

The army was to fall back as deliberately as possible, when retreat was necessary, to successive positions, and he hoped to be able to keep the Allied Armies out of Germany at least until the spring. This programme entailed a slow retirement to the Meuse, and a prolonged stand on that river when it was reached. His left flank, opposite the Americans, was the nearest part of his lines to the Meuse, and his right, in Belgium, farthest from that river. Therefore, the two first steps necessary for a readjustment of his front were to delay the Americans and to begin withdrawing his right from Flanders.

It was equally important that the British advance through Cambrai towards Maubeuge should be checked, for the British were considerably nearer to the Meuse at Namur than were the German troops about Ostend and Roulers. Lastly, it was necessary to withdraw from the bulge in the German line west of Laon, for the position there became daily more precarious once the Siegfried line was broken.

In looking over his map (the positions as described in the earlier map), Ludendorff saw that by beginning to retire at once in Flanders he might hope to establish his troops behind the Ghent Canal and the

River Scheldt as far south as Valenciennes. With his northern flank on the Dutch frontier east of Zeebrugge, and a formidable water obstacle in front of his positions to protect them against the dreaded tank, there was a chance of gaining the time necessary to organise an orderly and gradual withdrawal from Belgium, provided Haig and Debeney could be checked sufficiently long between Valenciennes and the Oise.

This was the weakest link in his new chain. The beginnings of a defensive position had been prepared connecting the Scheldt south of Valenciennes with the Oise west of Guise. This line, to which the Germans had given the name of the Hermann position, was very far from complete, because it had always been supposed that it would take us so long to work our way through the Siegfried system, if we ever seemed likely to penetrate it, that there would be plenty of time to complete the Hermann position. However, the greater part of the Hermann position followed the course of the River Selle, and had great natural strength, which it was hoped would compensate for the lack of artificial protection.

South of the Oise Ludendorff was better prepared to meet and stay the progress of his enemies. East of the St. Gobain massif and of Laon he had the Hundung position, which extended as far south as the Aisne and connected with the Brunhilde position. Both these positions were well fortified, particularly the latter, which stood in the way of Gouraud's advance. The German trenches ran along the north bank of the Aisne, through Rethel, towards the Argonne, and the river lay immediately in front of them, while the north bank here dominates the south bank. It was, therefore, a very formidable obstacle to attack directly, and might be counted upon to delay Gouraud for a considerable time.

East of the Argonne as far as the Meuse ran the Kriemhilde position, which had a depth of some two miles, and had not yet been reached by the Americans. East of the Meuse and across the base of the St. Mihiel salient there was the Michel position, which was well entrenched. Behind the Brunhilde and the Kriemhilde positions there were the Hagen and Freya positions, which, like the Hermann position, had only been sketched out.

On the existence of these various defensive lines, natural or artificial, Ludendorff's plans for rallying his forces and keeping the Allies out of Germany until the spring of 1919 were based. He proposed to carry through an immediate and extensive retreat in Belgium, French Flanders and Artois, to abandon the Belgian coast, Bruges, Courtrai,

Lille and Douai, and to establish his front behind the Scheldt through Ghent and Valenciennes. On the front of Haig's main attack, he set about retiring to the Hermann position along the Selle, and hoped to compensate for its weakness by massing along it the troops he had economised by shortening his front in the north. He began a withdrawal of his centre from the St. Gobain massif and from Laon into the Hundung line, and prepared for a similar withdrawal in front of Gouraud into the Brunhilde lines. East of the Argonne his programme was to make the most of the natural difficulties of the country to delay the progress of the Americans towards the Kriemhilde position as long as possible.

If the last phases of the war in the West are to be followed, it is important to understand this scheme of Ludendorff's and to appreciate both where and when he meant to stand and fight and where and when he meant to retreat. After the Hindenburg line was broken the front was in a continual state of flux; news arrived almost daily of fresh progress by the Allied forces, and it was difficult to discriminate between victories won by hard fighting and the consequences of those victories.

There was hard fighting before the enemy was completely smashed, for Ludendorff's plan was attended with a certain measure of success. By October 14, when King Albert was ready to attack again in Flanders, the arrangements for the German retreat were well advanced, and it was on the whole well conducted, though the enemy's rearguards had to struggle to gain time, and in spite of their resistance he had to abandon numbers of guns and great quantities of stores of all kinds. Roulers fell to French troops on the 15th, Thourout was occupied by the Belgians on the 16th, and the next day they entered Ostend. Plumer, meanwhile, had entered Menin and Courtrai and crossed the Lys, On October 18 the Fifth British Army, farther south, had found Lille evacuated by the enemy, and four days later the whole of the Belgian coast was in our hands, and the Germans had reached the line of the Scheldt from Valenciennes to Ghent.

There have been many curious examples during the war of the difference between the mentality of the Germans and of other European peoples, but I doubt if there has been anything stranger than their conduct during their retreat through Flanders and Belgium. At the last moment before they retired, they brought into many of the principal towns, wagon-loads of the flags of the Allies, which included one peculiarly German invention—a composite banner made up of the colours of their chief enemies, and hawked these round for sale to the inhabitants in order that they might decorate their houses fitly for the welcome to the incoming troops. It is out of the question that this traffic in their shame can have taken place without the assistance of the German authorities, who were not too proud to allow money to be made out of their defeat, but pretended shortly afterwards that they were too proud to acknowledge themselves beaten.

The retreat of the German centre from the St. Gobain massif, Laon, the Chemin des Dames and the neighbourhood of Reims was carried through in fairly good order, though about Reims it was hastened by the transfer to that neighbourhood of the 2nd and 3rd American Divisions in succession. On October 13 the French entered Laon, and two days later found themselves confronted by the enemy in his new positions. Opposite Gouraud the Germans withdrew, when on October 8 the French attacked in force, into their Brunhilde position along the Aisne, from the west of Rethel, through Attigny, to Vouziers, just west of the northern edge of the Argonne.

The German retreat from the main British front between Cambrai and St. Quentin was, however, not carried through according to Ludendorff's plan. By incessant and skilful work on the part of the engineers, bridges were thrown across the Canal du Nord and the St. Quentin Canal, and the roads were made possible for traffic, while farther back the railways, both narrow and broad gauge, were repaired or relaid, so that as early as October 6, before the German rear-guards had been organised, the Fourth and Third Armies were able to begin the second Battle of Le Cateau. This battle culminated in a fine attack made on a front of seventeen miles by those armies at dawn on October 8.

It was a bold measure to attempt to assemble in darkness, on ground torn up by shell-fire and seamed with trenches and with the wreckage of wire entanglements, such a mass of troops on so wide a front, but the time had come to be bold. The immediate results of this attack were that the 9th Corps, 2nd American Corps and 18th Corps of the Fourth Army, all greatly assisted by tanks, made very important progress in the direction of Le Cateau, while the Third Army was able to complete the encirclement of Cambrai on the south. Debeney, continuing his role of extending the battle front of the Fourth Army southwards, simultaneously drove the Germans back east of St. Quentin.

The ultimate results were of much greater importance in their effect upon Ludendorff's plan. The enemy's intended orderly retreat became a rout, and the roads behind his front converging on the bridges over the River Selle were blocked with troops and transport, so that the time which was to have been employed in the systematic occupation of the Hermann position had to be devoted to restoring order amongst weary and dispirited troops and clearing away such of the impedimenta as could be saved from capture.

On October 9 the Canadians entered Cambrai from the north and the 57th Division from the south, and drove the last Germans out of the town, while the Fourth and Third Armies, led by cavalry patrols, took up the pursuit of the enemy retiring towards the Selle, and drove him across the field of the first Battle of Le Cateau, where Smith-Dorrien had fought von Kluck during the retreat from Mons. By October 12 the enemy was found to be established in the Hermann position, but his retreat to it had cost him 12,000 prisoners and 250 guns.

On the American front there was no question of a German retreat, and except in the northern part of the Argonne Forest the Americans had to fight hard for every yard of ground they gained. The slow struggle through the southern end of the forest had brought the Americans on October 1 to approximately its centre, and for a week little or no progress was made. Then, fortunately, it became possible to apply the plan, which had been originally attempted and had failed, of forcing the Germans to evacuate the forest by advancing on both sides of it. On October 6 and 7 troops of the American 28th and 82nd Divisions, after a desperately hard struggle, took the village and *château* of Chatel and the hills around it which dominate the eastern edge of the Argonne.

On October 8—that is, the same day on which the Third and Fourth British Armies made their dawn attack in the second Battle of Le Cateau—Gouraud had, it will be remembered, begun his advance to the Aisne, and by the 9th his troops were in position along the greater part of the western edge of the forest. Fearful of being cut off, the Germans thereupon evacuated the Argonne, and on October 10 the 77th American Division was clear of the forest and in touch with the Germans on the outskirts of Grandpré. East of the Argonne there was no such rapid progress, and the Americans fought their way slowly on to the forward positions of the Kriemhilde system, with which they were everywhere in touch by October 14. Five days before this Pershing had handed over command of the First American Army to General Liggett, for the continued arrival of American troops had made it necessary to form a Second American Army of the troops occupying the Woeuvre front, east of the St. Mihiel salient and opposite Metz.

Ludendorff appears to have been fairly well satisfied with the progress of his retreat by October 16. His left and centre were by then back in their new positions, which were strong, and his losses during the retreat, if heavy, had not been overwhelming. His right had not yet completed the retreat from Flanders behind the Scheldt, but he had good reason to believe that it would be able to do so. Accordingly on October 17 he spoke much more boldly to the German cabinet than he had done on October 1. Prince Max of Baden was proposing to pave the way for peace negotiations by offering to abandon unrestricted U-boat warfare and to guarantee that the German troops would not destroy French and Belgian towns during their retreat. The rumblings of revolution were growing louder, and it was vitally necessary to make concessions to the popular party, which had lost all confidence in the Great General Staff, and were becoming more and more determined to enforce peace.

It had become abundantly evident that the German people had only been induced to endure the rigours of the blockade and to hold on by the lavish promises of victory which had been given to them. It was therefore impossible, while the military situation on all fronts was going rapidly from bad to worse and decisions had to be taken quickly, to educate them to an attitude of endurance with the object of minimising the effects of defeat. The pretence that Germany had been fighting a defensive war, which had periodically been put forward by the *Kaiser* and his advisers whenever their campaign of conquest was checked, could not deceive anyone, and least of all the German people.

The popular sentiment in regard to war was summed up in the phrase, "World power or downfall," the assumption being that there was no doubt as to which of these alternatives would be Germany's fate. With rare skill the German Government and its military advisers had hitherto managed to obliterate the effect of their failure to obtain their chief aims by dazzling victories in secondary theatres of war. They had not succeeded in conquering France in 1914 according to plan, but this had been forgotten in the joy of gazing at the brilliant prospect opened up by the accession of Bulgaria, the overrunning of Serbia, and the opening of the road to the East.

The conquest of Roumania had obliterated the memories of Verdun; the collapse of Russia and the victory of Caporetto had been ample compensation for the long, costly and unfruitful struggle on the Western Front during 1917. Now, however, there was no carrot to dangle in front of the donkey's nose. Even in an autocratic country it is not possible to deceive all the people all the time, and the German people knew in October, 1918, that the victory which had been promised to them could never be obtained.

The revulsion of feeling and the collapse of confidence were such that no enthusiasm could be aroused for a war of endurance in defence of the Fatherland. Yet this was what Ludendorff proposed. He wished the negotiations to be continued with President Wilson, but refused to agree to the acceptance of any terms which would make Germany militarily defenceless. He protested energetically against the renunciation of the U-boat campaign, and claimed that the German Army should be allowed to take any and every measure which would delay the enemies' advance. But while he was actually pressing his views upon the German cabinet another blow had fallen upon him, and his new front had been broken.

The enemy's position along the River Selle, which was the connecting link between the Scheldt and his lines south of the Oise, was, as I have said, naturally formidable. His left flank opposite Debeney's army rested on a series of very defensible wooded heights which divided the valleys of the Selle and the Oise. On the front of the Fourth British Army the Germans held the eastern bank of the Selle, and had occupied the line of the railway which connects Le Cateau and Solesmes. This railway line runs through a series of embankments and cuttings, which provided the German infantry with excellent cover and their machine gunners with positions from which they could sweep the valley, while the rolling heights behind gave their artillery splendid opportunities for dominating the approaches to the river.

In front of the railway line a single, and as compared with the entanglements of the Hindenburg line not very formidable, belt of barbed wire had been erected, but the Selle, ordinarily an insignificant stream, had been dammed by the enemy and was in flood, and in itself constituted a serious obstacle to infantry, which would have to force its way across in face of machine-gun fire. The sites for a strong trench system had been marked out by digging down to a depth of about one foot, but the German infantry and engineers, weary and dispirited by their defeats, had not the energy to complete these trenches in the time at their disposal. None the less, the attack on such a position was a serious undertaking, particularly as the enemy, knowing that it covered the direct road to Maubeuge, had occupied it in great strength and had numerous machine-guns and a powerful artillery.

The Battle of the Selle began in the early hours of October 17 with an attack by Debeney's First French Army and the 9th, 2nd American and 13th Corps of the Fourth British Army against the German left, from Le Cateau southwards. The enemy fought well, the 27th and 30th American Divisions having a particularly hard task in their attack upon the railway line south of Le Cateau, where it ran along a commanding hill. It was only after two days of strenuous effort that the Germans south of Le Cateau were forced back behind the Sambre and Oise Canal. It was quite evident from this fighting that the enemy was making a desperate effort to hold up our advance. Appeals were issued to the German troops to remember the devastation, which they had seen in Belgium and northern France, and to save their country from a like fate.

But though they fought valiantly, they had lost confidence both in themselves and in their leaders, and they had none of the grit and staying power which distinguished the British soldier when he was in like straits. However, it still remained to tackle the German main position along the Selle west of Le Cateau, and this was done in a night attack by seven divisions of the Third Army and one of the First Army. A mist in the valley increased the cover afforded by night, and enabled the infantry and engineers to lay foot bridges across the Selle under the very noses of the enemy's machine gunners, and tanks to be brought down unseen into the valley.

At 2 a.m. on October 20 the British infantry advanced to the assault, and helped by the ubiquitous tanks, which succeeded somehow in getting across the river, they stormed the heights on the east bank after fierce fighting, for the Germans again fought hard.

The weather had broken, the ground was saturated, there was little shelter for the troops, the roads churned up by shell-fire and by the stream of traffic became rivers of mud, and both roads and railways were constantly being cut by mines, which the enemy had buried beneath them and fitted with delay action fuses, so that they would explode at irregular intervals after our troops had passed beyond, but the enthusiasm of the British troops was not to be denied. On October 23 the Fourth, Third and First Armies made a general advance on a front of fifteen miles between the Sambre and Oise Canal and the Scheldt. On the right the Germans were driven back into the Mormal Forest, in the centre our troops got within a mile of Le Quesnoy, and on the left approached Valenciennes. Thus, in the Battle of the Selle, British, French and American troops had made a breach, about thirty-five miles wide and nearly six miles deep, in Ludendorff's rallying line. The twenty-four British and two American divisions engaged had defeated thirty-one German divisions and had captured 20,000 prisoners and 475 guns.

I have mentioned that on October 14 the Americans were in touch with the forward positions of the Kriemhilde system. On that day there began an eight-day battle on the front from the Meuse to Grandpré, in which by incessant hard fighting the Americans broke into the formidable German defences at a number of points. On October 16 Grandpré was taken, while Gouraud on the American left stormed the heights about Vouziers and crossed the Aisne. On the 16th, 17th and 18th a succession of fierce attacks, in which four divisions took part, enabled the Americans to pierce the Kriemhilde line near its centre. The Germans fought desperately to hold the line and employed some of their best troops, including the 3rd Guard Division, the infantry of which was almost annihilated.

The most important result of this battle was to exhaust the German defensive power on the Meuse front just as Haig's attacks had exhausted it on the Cambrai-St. Quentin front, a secondary result being to straighten out the American line, so that by the end of the month it was well placed for another general forward movement.

I have already explained that Ludendorff's plan of deliberate withdrawal to the Meuse depended on holding off the British on the Selle and the Americans on the Kriemhilde line. He was endeavouring to assure his government that there was no cause for despair when the news of the Selle battle and of the American attacks on the Kriemhilde line reached them. It convinced them that there was no line upon which the German Army could be relied upon to stand, and it shattered what little faith they had left in their military adviser. On October 26 Ludendorff tendered his resignation, which was accepted, and the next day he left Great Headquarters. The capitulation of Turkey, following upon that of Bulgaria, and the decisive defeat of the Austrians on the Piave coupled with the never-ending tale of disaster on the Western Front, and the growing unrest in Germany left no glimmer of hope in the minds of the *Kaiser* and his ministers. While they were preparing to send in plenipotentiaries to Foch, he, in order to make assurance doubly sure, was setting the stage for the final advance.

CHAPTER 6

The Last Push

At the end of October Germany's Armies on the Western Front had suffered a series of crushing defeats, her navy was seething with mutiny, her working class population were on the verge of starvation, the German people were at last aware of the extent to which they had been deceived by their rulers, and all of her Allies had collapsed. The military power of the United States was but half developed, the output of the Allied munition factories had not reached its zenith. After a long and bitter struggle, we had won a definite superiority in the air, we had aeroplanes ready of a type capable of bombing every town in Germany, and the U-boat menace had been scotched, if not definitely mastered. There could be only one end to the war; the question was when that end would come.

The situation of France in 1870 after the Battle of Sedan had been, except as regards food stocks and the determination of the people to resist, more hopeless than was that of Germany on October 30, 1918. Almost the entire French Army as it had existed at the outbreak of the war had disappeared, and France, too, had realised that she had been deceived by those she had placed in authority over her. She overthrew the Government; under the inspiration of Gambetta's leadership, she created new armies and went on fighting for six months, during which she caused her apparently irresistible foe many moments of anxiety. Germany had no need to create new armies. Those she had in the field were still capable of prolonged resistance provided they were inspired with patriotic devotion, and determined not to yield until the last extremity.

Her enemies were still far from her frontiers, there were many strong natural barriers between the Allied Armies and the interior of Germany, and the German Armies, if permitted to fall back to these, would obtain a shorter and stronger battle front on which they might hold out throughout the winter. There was no precedent for a great and powerful nation, which was fighting for its existence, surrendering while it still had the means to resist. Therefore, it was necessary to continue to press the enemy until his means of resistance were destroyed or until his will to fight was finally broken. Foch therefore planned another great combined drive against him.

When Germany in 1914 first invaded Belgium and France by far the greater number of the German troops deployed on the Western Front had crossed the line extending from the Dutch frontier north of Liege to Metz, a distance of 115 miles. As the war went on and Germany developed her man power, her forces on the Western Front had been strengthened, and in the early months of 1918 they received a very great reinforcement consequent on the collapse of Russia. In August, 1914, some fifty-four German infantry divisions had passed between the Dutch frontier and Metz, and by the middle of 1918 the front of deployment of 115 miles had developed into a battle front extending from the North Sea near Nieuport to Pont-à-Mousson on the Moselle south of Metz, a great arc with a circumference of about 350 miles.

The maximum strength of the German Armies on and behind the circumference of this arc amounted in May, 1918, to about 190 divisions. These divisions were smaller than those of August, 1914, but their appurtenances, guns, mortars, machine-guns, aeroplanes and war material of all kinds had in the four years multiplied exceedingly. Even when Ludendorff had completed his retreat after the great Battle of September 26-October 3, his front from the Dutch frontier to the neighbourhood of Metz was not less than 250 miles in length, and the number of divisions which he had on that front and in reserve was not fewer than 160.

Therefore, in order to make good their retreat the Germans had to get back across the 115 miles about three times as many men and many times as much material as Moltke had sent westwards across that line in August, 1914. In fact, they had to get their armies through the neck of a bottle. It was like trying to force an oak plant, which has grown in four years from an acorn in a bottle of water, back into the bottle without destroying the plant; a difficult problem if the neck of the bottle were clear, but it was not. Behind the German centre lay the forests and mountains of the Belgian and Luxembourg Ardennes, a region traversed by few roads and fewer railways, and washed by the Meuse, which had a limited number of bridges. The main exits lay north and south of the Ardennes, in the north from Liége to Namur, in the south from Mézières to Longuyon.

The course of the Meuse from Mézières to Namur runs generally northwards, but at Namur, where the Sambre joins it, it makes a sharp bend eastwards. The consequence of this was that the German troops on the Scheldt on either side of Ghent would, when in their retreat they reached the longitude of Namur, still have fifty miles to march to the river, and would only find east of Namur four points of passage. If the British succeeded in crossing the Meuse between Namur and Dinant before the German forces in Belgium had got over the river, there was a probability that they would be driven against the Dutch frontier and forced to surrender; if the German centre had not made good its retreat before Gouraud and the Americans captured Mézières and Sedan it was in danger of being cut off.

There was, therefore, no longer any question of the leisurely retreat to the Meuse which Ludendorff had planned. It was essential to withdraw to the river as quickly as possible, but to do this without incurring irremediable disaster it was still as necessary as it had been since the end of September to delay to the utmost the British advance on Namur and the American progress towards Sedan.

This was the position of which Foch proposed to take advantage by continuing the general plan of his great battle. Gouraud and the Americans were to strike for Mézières and Sedan and block the southern exits, while the British Armies made for Maubeuge and Mons and threatened Namur before the Germans in western Belgium could get away. The advance on Namur would force the Germans to come out of the greater part of Belgium in a hurry or be cut off, and would save that sorely tried land from the destruction which was inevitable if it became the scene of pitched battles, while the advance on Mézières and Sedan would have the same effect on the German centre.

The French Armies in the centre were, therefore, to continue their role of harassing and delaying the German retreat, and the Belgian Armies were to keep the Germans busy on the Scheldt. The French troops on King Albert's right, however, with the help of two American divisions sent up to reinforce them, were to assist the British advance by forcing the line of the Scheldt about Audenarde.

On November 1 the last drive began, as had Armageddon, with a Franco-American attack, and again there lay in front of the American left a stretch of mountain forest, the Forest of Bourgogne, a northern extension of the Argonne. Again, the intention was to force the Germans out of the forest by a combined advance of the Americans to the east of it, and of Gouraud's army to the west. This time the plan was completely successful. On the right of the American battle front the 3rd American Corps attacked in the Meuse valley, while the 5th American Corps broke clean through such parts of the Kriemhilde line as it had not previously captured, and made an advance of about five miles in the one day.

Simultaneously Gouraud extended his hold on the heights on the eastern bank of the Aisne opposite Vouziers. The Germans were in no mind for a repetition of the Argonne struggle. Before the battle started their morale had begun to give way under the steady pressure of the American advance, and now it gave way altogether, while the American divisions which had done most of the hard fighting in October had either been rested and their ranks refilled, or had been relieved by fresh divisions, with the result that the First American Army was as full of vigour and energy as it had been on September 26, despite the continuously wet and cold weather on the bleak hills of the Meuse.

On November 2 the 1st American Corps on the left of the First Army drove forward six miles, captured Buzancy, and lined the eastern edge of the Bourgogne Forest, Gouraud at the same time reaching its western edge throughout its length. The Germans immediately evacuated the forest and began a general retreat before the First American Army and Gouraud's right. During the night of November 3, the infantry of the 2nd American Division, giving the weary Germans no time to reorganise a defence, made a remarkable pursuit and advanced in the darkness straight through the German lines for a distance of five miles. This great progress enabled the Americans to bring forward long-range guns and to shell the railway stations of Longuyon and Montmédy, through which the Crown Prince was trying to get away as much as possible of his war material.

The clearing of the Bourgogne Forest had enabled Gouraud to join hands with the Americans on November 3 to the north of the forest, and he thus obtained a straight front of some nine miles beyond the Aisne east of Attigny. He was now able to threaten the retreat of the German troops holding the formidable Brunhilde line farther west between Attigny and Rethel, by pushing forward his right wing in conjunction with the American advance. On November 4, he drove the enemy back from the southern portion of the canal which connects the Aisne near Attigny with the Meuse near Sedan. This manoeuvre compelled the Germans to fall back from the Brunhilde line in order to avoid being cut off from Mézières, and the French entered

Rethel on November 6.

Meanwhile, by November 5 the American front had sprung forward another six miles, and on the evening of the 6th, despite the endeavours of the German machine-gunners to delay the pursuit, a division of the 1st American Corps reached the Meuse opposite the southern outskirts of Sedan, twenty-one miles from its starting point of November 1. Gouraud, with a longer distance to go and with the resistance of the German troops, who had fallen back from the Brunhilde line, to overcome, did not reach his objective, Mézières, until the evening of the 10th. While the 1st and 5th American Corps were advancing northwards towards Sedan the right of the 3rd Corps began to strike out eastwards, and it crossed the Meuse and occupied Dun on November 4.

Thence on the following days, the 3rd, 2nd Colonial and 17th French Corps on the right of the First American Army gradually wore down the resistance of the Germans in the wooded Meuse hills, and on the morning of November 11, when the Armistice came into effect, the Franco-American front was within six miles of Montmédy, where the German Crown Prince had lived during the Battle of Verdun, when he was not in his dug-out on the Montfaucon Hill.

Though Montmédy was not entered by the Allies until the Germans had withdrawn in accordance with the Armistice terms, they found on arrival that defeat had not changed the German nature, for the little town was pillaged by the enemy's troops before they left. These operations on the east bank of the Meuse towards Montmédy were extended southwards by the Second American Army, which began the long threatened movement toward the Briey iron fields. The reasons for this development I must leave for the present to follow events farther north.

While the French and Americans on the southern battle front were completing the task set them by Foch, the British Armies were again in motion. The Germans at the end of October, after their defeat on the Selle, occupied the line of the Scheldt from Ghent to a point about two miles south of Valenciennes, whence their front ran southwards to the River Sambre, which it reached a little above Landrecies. The distance between the Scheldt and the Sambre on this line was not more than eighteen miles, and the southern five of these eighteen miles were taken up by the Mormal Forest.

Sir Douglas Haig's first care was, therefore, to get more room for his advance between the Sambre and the Scheldt, and particularly to

LANDRECIES ON THE SAMBRE, 1918

force the enemy to fall back from the tangle of reclaimed land, cut up by innumerable dykes, which stretches north of Valenciennes as far as the Condé Canal. Accordingly, on November 1, while the Americans and French were attacking on the Meuse-Argonne front, the 17th Corps of the Third British Army, and 22nd and Canadian Corps of the First Army, attacked south of Valenciennes, and after two days' heavy fighting had by the evening of November 2 turned the line of the Scheldt from the south, and the Canadian corps had entered Valenciennes.

This at once gave Haig the elbow room he required, and as there was no time to spare, if the enemy was to be prevented from making good his retreat to the Meuse, the Fourth, Third and First Armies attacked on November 4 on a thirty-mile front, from the Sambre Canal eight miles south of the Mormal Forest to the north of Valenciennes. The British right had the difficult tasks of crossing the Sambre Canal, which is as wide as the Scheldt Canal stormed on September 29, and contains more water, and of forcing a way through the Mormal Forest.

This forest was not so serious an obstacle as it had been in August, 1914, when after the Battle of Mons it caused the separation of the British Army into two parts, one retreating on each side of it, for the Germans had obtained a great quantity of timber from it for their trenches, huts and dug-outs, and they had also improved the roads through it. Nevertheless, it afforded a resolute enemy splendid opportunities for defence, and both it and the canal prevented the Fourth Army from making free use of its tanks.

The British Army was now fighting on the very ground on which it had first assembled in France, before it advanced to Mons, and was about to take complete revenge for its early misfortunes. A dense artillery barrage rolled forward, and behind it, with the help of tanks wherever they could be used, the infantry on the whole thirty miles broke into the German positions. On the right the 1st and 32nd Divisions of the 9th Corps fought their way across the canal near Catillon, and by nightfall were more than three miles to the east of it. Farther north the Germans were driven far back into the Mormal Forest, and troops of the 25th Division of the 13th Corps, crossing the Sambre on rafts, captured Landrecies at the south-east corner of the forest.

Landrecies was defended by a battalion of the German 1st Guard Reserve Division; it was in Landrecies that British Guards first met the Germans, when, on August 25, 1914, they repulsed a night attack in the streets of the town. North of the Mormal Forest the 37th Division and the New Zealanders, after repulsing a heavy German counter-attack, drove the enemy back beyond the Valenciennes-Avesnes railway, which runs through the centre of the forest from west to east, and the New Zealanders, surrounding the old fortified town of Le Quesnoy, compelled its garrison to surrender. By the evening the left of the Third Army, and the right of the First Army, were on a front five miles beyond Valenciennes. On the British right Debeney's First French Army had also forced a crossing over the Sambre Canal to the north of Guise and kept pace with the advance of our Fourth Army.

In this battle the resistance of the enemy was definitely broken and he never rallied again. The three British Armies captured 19,000 prisoners and 450 guns, and Debeney gathered in 5,000 more prisoners. South of Ghent the two French corps on King Albert's right, which each now had an American division with them, drove back the Germans along the Scheldt, and the 91st American Division captured Audenarde.

From this time until the end the pursuit was delayed mainly by the very complete destruction of the roads and railways by the Germans as they fell back, and by the consequent difficulty of getting up supplies to the troops. The enemy's difficulties in retreat were, however, much greater. Far into Belgium the roads were blocked with masses of transport and the railways with thousands of trucks, for the removal of which the Germans had not sufficient engines. Our aeroplanes swooping down from the sky attacked the German convoys and railway lines with machine-gun fire and with bombs, causing great destruction and frequent panics. A single battalion of the 25th Division on November 5 took possession of thirty guns, which the German artillerymen had abandoned when attacked from the air.

By November 5 our troops were well beyond the Mormal Forest. On the 7th the Guards entered Bavai, on the 8th the Fourth Army occupied Avesnes. On the 9th the Guards and 62nd Division occupied the fortress of Maubeuge, the French taking Hirson on the same day. On the 8th the Germans began to fly from the Scheldt, and the British Fifth and Second Armies, with the French and Americans on their left, who had been preparing to deliver a great attack on the river line on November 11, finding that the enemy were slipping away, followed hard after him and made rapid progress. Peruwelz, Tournai and Renaix were occupied in succession, while by a last dramatic stroke of fortune the 3rd Canadian Division entered Mons a few hours before the Armistice was signed.

There were many curious coincidences between our first and last contact with the Germans in arms. Officers of our cavalry who had fought at Mons in August, 1914, found themselves on November 11, 1918, on the scene of their original encounter with the German troopers; while most curious of all the 2nd Battalion of the Royal Irish Regiment, which had fought in the 3rd Division in the loop of the canal north-east of Mons on August 23, 1914, was with the 63rd Division entering that loop when hostilities ceased.

The opinion is widely held that the Armistice of November 11 was premature. It is argued that we had the German Armies at our mercy, and that the foundations of peace would have been more sure if we had ended the war by forcing the surrender in the field of a great part of those armies, or, failing that, had driven our beaten enemy back across the Rhine and followed him into the heart of Germany. The reception of the German troops by the German people, their march into the German towns through triumphal arches and beflagged streets with their helmets crowned with laurels, and the insistent statements in Germany that the German Armies had not been defeated, that the Armistice had been accepted to save bloodshed, and to put an end to the sufferings of the women and children aroused amazement and disgust in the victors.

There was very real anxiety lest after all we had failed to convince Germany that war did not pay; it was felt that we ought to have brought the realisation of what war means home to the German people in their own country, and that, had we done so, the long-drawn-out negotiations in Paris would have been concluded more speedily and more satisfactorily. It is worthwhile, therefore, examining the situation as it was at the time of the Armistice, and considering the case as it presented itself to the men who had to decide whether hostilities should cease or not.

There is no question but that the German Armies were completely and decisively beaten in the field. The German plenipotentiaries admitted it when they met Marshal Foch, and von Brockdorff-Rantzau admitted it at Versailles, when he said after the Allied peace terms had been presented to him:

> We are under no illusions as to the extent of our defeat and the degree of our want of power, ... We know that the power of the German Army is broken.

Even if these admissions had not been made, the condition of the

German lines of retreat to the Rhine is conclusive evidence of the condition of their armies. Every road was littered with broken-down motor trucks, guns, machine-guns and trench mortars. Great stacks of supplies and of military stores of all kinds were abandoned. Every railway line was blocked with loaded trucks which the Germans had been unable to remove. The sixty miles of railway in the valley of the Meuse between Dinant and Mézières was filled from end to end with a continuous line of German freight trains carrying guns, ammunition, engineering equipment, and other paraphernalia. On the Belgian canals alone over eight hundred fully charged military barges were found.

It is beyond dispute that on November 11 the lines of communication immediately behind the German Armies had been thrown into complete disorder by the streams of traffic which were converging on the Meuse bridges, disorder greatly intensified by the attacks of the Allied airmen. The German Armies, unable to resist on the fighting front, could no longer retreat in good order, partly because of the congestion on the roads and railways behind them, which not only hampered the movements of the troops, but prevented the systematic supply to them of food and ammunition, partly owing to the fact that there were not horses left to draw the transport of the fighting troops. The following description of the condition of the German Army at the time when it began its march back to the Rhine in accordance with the terms of the Armistice has been recently published in Berlin.

> Many of the units of the army were unable to move for lack of transport horses. Even those which were able to march had but little of their former mobility because the loss of horses had been so great. The majority of the troops were unaccustomed to long marches, the horses were in very poor condition, and the daily losses even during the retreat to the Antwerp-Meuse position had been very great. There was a deficiency of boots, winter clothing, hoof-pads, and frost nails, and winter weather might set in at any time. Almost all the casualty clearing stations, the ambulances and the hospitals were overcrowded owing to the continuous stream of wounded and sick, which poured in in consequence of the fighting which continued right up to the Armistice. (*Die Rachfuhrung des Westheeres*, Berlin, 1919.)

Not less remarkable is a report from the headquarters of one of the divisions of the 17th German Army of the Crown Prince Rupprecht's group. The number of the division is obliterated on the report, which is dated November 8, 1918, and was found in a Belgian farmhouse. I have therefore been unable to identify the division, but it appears to have been one of those which was opposed to our First Army. The report runs:

> The division can only be considered as unfit for battle. Owing to the extremely heavy casualties, to sickness and to numerous desertions, the average strength of regiments is under 600. (A German regiment consisted of three battalions, and its full strength was about 3,000 men and 64 officers.) Still more important as regards efficiency in battle is the shortage of officers, of which no regiment of the division has more than twelve, and one regiment has only nine. Almost all the machine-guns in the division have been lost or are out of repair, and half the guns of the artillery are deficient.
>
> Owing to lack of horses, less than half the transport of the division can be moved, and if the retreat continues many guns and vehicles will have to be abandoned. Owing to lack of petrol, much of the motor transport of the division cannot be moved. The division has not received rations for two days, and the condition of the horses which remain is becoming very bad, because owing to constant movement there is no time to collect supplies from the country, and forage for them is not arriving.

If ever armies were in a state of hopeless rout, the German Armies were in the second week of November, 1918. The morale of the troops was gone, the organisation of the services on which they depended for their needs had collapsed. This being so, why did we allow the German Armies to escape from a hopeless position? Why did we not at once follow up the military advantage which we had gained at such cost?

In order to get an answer to these questions I visited the fronts of the Allied Armies shortly after the conclusion of the Armistice. I there found, after travelling down the line from north to south, that amongst the fighting troops of the Belgian, British, French and American Armies the opinion was unanimous that they had got the Germans on the run and could have kept them on the run indefinitely, or until they laid down their arms. On the American front in particular, where there were large numbers of troops ready and eager to go forward who had not yet taken part in a great battle, there was a very strong feeling that they had been robbed of the fruits of victory.

When, however, I inquired the opinion of those behind the fighting fronts who were responsible for feeding the troops and keeping them supplied with all that was necessary to enable them to march forward, I heard a different story. Everywhere I was told that the Allied Armies, which were on or were marching towards the Meuse, had on November 11 reached, or very nearly reached, the farthest limit at which for the time being they could be kept regularly supplied. The reasons for this were twofold. In the first place the Allied lines of communication grew steadily longer as the Germans were driven back, and even before our victorious advance began the state of the railways and the amount of rolling stock in France had caused anxiety. For four and a half years the railway systems of north-eastern France had been strained to the limit of their capacity, and the effects of that strain were beginning to be serious in 1918.

Both we and the Americans had made great efforts to improve and extend the railway systems in our respective zones. During 1918 the British military railway administration in France built or reconstructed 2,340 miles of broad gauge and 1,348 miles of narrow-gauge railways, while to supplement the French rolling stock we sent to France 1,200 locomotives and 52,600 cars. The shipment across the Channel of such cumbrous and heavy objects as locomotives and trucks was a slow and difficult business, and the needs of the armies were always growing faster than were the resources of the railways. During the last four months of the war the weekly average load carried by the British military railways in France amounted to over half a million tons.

If these were our difficulties, those of the American Army were greater, owing to the rapid growth of the army during the latter half of the year 1918, the shortage of shipping capable of crossing the Atlantic, and the necessity of giving first place to the transportation of troops and of war material. Up to the end the railways under American control in France suffered from a deficiency in rolling stock, and had great difficulty in meeting the demands of the large forces engaged in the Meuse-Argonne battle at the end of an ever lengthening line of communications.

The French Armies, which in the middle of September had been extended along the outside of the great bow made by the German lines between St. Quentin and Verdun, had the longest distances to advance in following up the German retreat, and before the advance began the French Government had cut down the railway transportation in the interior of the country to the bare minimum necessary for the preservation of the industrial and social life of France, and even then was unable to meet the full demands of the French Armies and to supplement the railway material which Great Britain and America had been able to produce. The Belgian Armies had hardly any resources of their own and no means whatever of developing their means of transportation. The result of all this was that the mere lengthening of the Allied lines of communications by the German retreat, apart altogether from any other action by the enemy, threw a very great strain upon the Allied railway administrations.

The Germans were, however, very active and skilful in damaging the roads and railways before they retreated, and this damage was extended by the destructive power of the artillery of both sides. Every railway bridge, large or small, was blown up, the railway embankments were cut, long stretches of track were destroyed, the stations were burned down, and the telegraph lines were almost obliterated and the instruments removed. The Germans had left behind them mines buried under the railway lines, and these exploded often after the first damage had been repaired and the trains were running, with the result that there was constant interruption to the traffic. One of our army commanders told me that, owing to the constant explosion of mines behind his front, during the last stages of the advance of his army his railhead was retreating faster than his troops were advancing.

The consequence of this was that on November 11, despite the most strenuous and devoted work by all concerned in the repair and working of the railways, the farthest points at which supplies could be delivered by rail were from thirty-five to fifty miles in a direct line behind the front, and often double this distance by road. This gap had to be bridged by the motor transport, which, of course, had to use the roads. But the destruction of the roads by the Germans was as thorough as their destruction of the railways. Not only were the bridges destroyed, but mines were sprung at every cross-road.

I remember counting eleven mine craters on three miles of the main road between Le Quesnoy and Mons. This damage could only be very roughly repaired, while the wet weather and the heavy traffic of the German retreat and of our advance increased the work of destruction. The heavy motor lorries, loaded with supplies and ammunition, had to plough their way slowly through these broken roads from the railheads to the troops, and return to the railheads to fill up. At the time of the Armistice—the motor lorries were working in double and treble shifts, and the strain upon them caused by the bad roads and the incessant work was such that in the Fourth Army on November 11 more than half of the lorries at the service of the army had broken down. The troops were receiving no more than bare necessities, and at one time had with them nothing more than the day's food carried by the men.

The advance of the British Army towards Germany did not begin until November 17, six days after all fighting had ceased, and actually only sixteen of the fifty-nine British infantry divisions in France and Belgium at the time of the Armistice that is, less than one-third of our whole army moved forward. Though there was no interference by the enemy, and the advance was made by slow stages, it proved impossible to keep even this comparatively small part of our army supplied with their full rations, and at the beginning of December it was necessary to call a halt because the supply trains were running more than forty-eight hours behind scheduled time. A very similar story could be told of the situation on the Belgian, French, and American fronts.

Nor was the feeding of the fighting troops by any means the only problem of supply which the Allied Armies had to solve. The Germans in their retreat had left behind them in the liberated provinces of France and Belgium a large civilian population on the verge of starvation. In the French provinces on the British front alone there were nearly 800,000 persons to be fed, and during a period of six weeks, until the French Government could undertake the distribution of supplies, we distributed more than 5,000,000 rations amongst the civilian population, a task which threw an immense additional burden upon the transportation services.

The French Armies on their own front had very much larger numbers to deal with, and, as it taxed all their resources to repair the main roads and railways so that the troops on the front might be fed, many French villages and small towns off the main lines of communication remained isolated for long periods, and were only kept from starvation by having food brought to them by aeroplanes. Added to all this, the Germans as they retreated released large numbers of prisoners of war without making any provision for their feeding. The people of Belgium of their necessities made great sacrifices in order to do what was possible for these unfortunate men, whose sufferings were often intense, but their means were not equal to their generosity, and yet another burden was added to the work of supply.

This being the situation on the front at the time when the Armistice was signed and during the days which followed its signature, it is obvious that a great and rapid advance to and across the Meuse by the Belgian, British, French and American Armies, such as might have brought about the complete destruction of the German Armies and ended the war with a colossal Sedan, was out of the question. It is true that on November 11 two British cavalry divisions had passed through the front and were ready to pursue the enemy. Sir Douglas Haig has expressed the opinion that this cavalry would have been able to turn the retreat of the Germans on the British front into a complete rout, but it is very improbable that any action by such a comparatively small force of mounted troops would have been able to affect seriously the situation on the whole long front, and their influence, though it would certainly have been considerable, must necessarily have been local.

The plain fact is that on, or very soon after, November 11 it would, had hostilities been continued, have been necessary to call a halt of the Allied Armies between the Dutch frontier and the Meuse until the roads and railways behind them had been repaired and the services of supply were again able to work normally. That is to say, it would have been necessary to give the enemy a breathing space, which would have allowed him to restore some sort of order in his ranks and make good his retreat to the Meuse, where he would have been able to establish himself on a very much shorter front and in very strong positions. This would have entailed fighting at least one more great battle and have cost us very many lives.

There was, however, a part of the front on which the Allied Armies had made little progress and behind which their communications were in good order; that was the front between the Meuse, northeast of Verdun, and the Swiss frontier. As I have explained, Pershing's victory of the St. Mihiel salient had given Foch an opportunity for invading Lorraine, and the French marshal had all his plans ready for the extension of his long line of battle by an advance into Lorraine when hostilities ceased.

In fact, the manoeuvres preliminary to this advance had begun on November 7, when the three French corps immediately east of the Meuse attacked in the direction of Montmédy, a movement followed by the advance of the second American Army through the Woeuvre, as the country east of the St. Mihiel salient is called, towards the famous ironfields of Briey. The left of the Second American Army had driven the Germans back some three miles in the Woeuvre by the morning of November 11. The general plan for this new attack was that the left of the Second American Army should be protected by the advance of the right of the First American Army and of the three French corps on Longwy—the French fort on the Luxembourg frontier, about fifteen miles north of Briey, which had been captured in 1914 by the German Crown Prince in the first invasion of France—the Second American Army was to attack towards and across the Briey ironfields, which lie north of Metz, while another Franco-American attack was to be made east of the Moselle and to the south of Metz.

These two attacks, which were to have been in full swing by November 14, were intended to isolate the great German fortress. Now there is very little doubt but that this battle on the Lorraine front would have ended in another great Allied victory, for the Germans would have been greatly outnumbered and their troops on this part of the line were not of the best quality; but it is equally certain that it would have exposed a great part of Lorraine to the ravages of war, and very probably also to the same widespread destruction which the Germans had carried out during their retreat farther north.

The general situation at the time of the Armistice, then, was that the Allied Armies between the Dutch frontier and the Meuse were for the time being incapable of carrying on a sustained advance, though two British cavalry divisions were ready to begin a local pursuit on a portion of the British front. The Germans in front of them had been utterly defeated and were almost helpless, but we were not, and could not for some little time, be in a position to complete their destruction as a military force. It was, therefore, reasonably certain that if the Armistice had been refused the Allied Armies would have had to fight hard and would have suffered serious losses, while there was the risk of exposing the greater part of Belgium, including the cities of Brussels and Antwerp, and the great Charleroi industrial district—which were still in the hands of the Germans—to destruction.

Everything was ready for another battle on the Lorraine front, but this, too, would certainly have cost us many lives and have caused much damage to valuable property, which is today intact and in the hands of the French. The problem which the Allied and Associated Governments and generals had to decide was whether they would continue to fight on these terms or would impose such conditions of armistice upon the enemy as would render him militarily impotent. They decided on the latter course, and I think there are very few who would have taken upon themselves the responsibility of deciding otherwise.

The criticism of the decision to stop fighting on November 11 has been due to the feeling that the German people do not recognise that their armies were beaten in the field, and the fear that this state of mind may sooner or later cause them to fight again. My own conviction is that the reception of the German troops in Germany and the statements made in the German press and by the German people that the Armistice was not the consequence of defeat were not unnatural, and can be explained. In November, 1918, the German people could only get news of what was happening on the front through the newspapers, and the newspapers got their information through the military Press Bureau.

The officials of that bureau, either because they were so inured to lying that they could not tell the truth, or in the hope of staving off revolution by continuing to deceive the people, announced, from the first days when things began to go wrong for them right up to the end, that the German Armies were fighting splendidly, that the front was everywhere intact, and that the troops were falling back, slowly and steadily, according to plan to better and stronger positions. No inkling was given of the true state of affairs on the front, and the German people ascribed the surrender either to the revolution, if they were not in favour of it, or more generally to the desire of the new Government to get the blockade raised as quickly as possible.

When the German troops came back to their homes and began to talk, the truth gradually became known, and the German people were able to see for themselves the state of the army which had once been their god. I do not think that there is today (1919), any intelligent German who does not know that the German Armies were utterly beaten, though there may be many who would not admit as much to a foreigner.

It has begun to dawn upon most Germans that it is more disgraceful to admit that they accepted defeat, ignominiously surrendered their navy, gave up the greater part of their artillery and aeroplanes, handed over large quantities of rolling stock and military stores, and permitted the armies of their enemies to occupy the Rhine unopposed, that they did all this when they still had the power to fight on, than to acknowledge that their armies were defeated in the field. I do not believe that we shall in the future hear much more of the unbeaten German Armies, except perhaps from a few extremists like Bernhardi, nor do I believe that if we had not stopped fighting on November 11, it would have been possible to make Germany any less capable of resistance than she is today, (1919).

I set out in this book to describe the general course of the last great campaign on the Western Front. I am not, therefore, concerned with the story of the downfall of Bulgaria, Austria and Turkey, except in so far as these have contributed to the defeat of our chief enemy. The trials of the spring of 1918 had taught us that common sense which is the essence of strategy; we had learned that the Western Front was for us the vital front, and we had concentrated there every man who could be spared from other theatres of war; but Sir Charles Monro's expansion of the Indian Army had enabled us to replace the British troops withdrawn from Palestine with Indian troops who could not be employed in France.

Thus, Allenby was still powerful, while any weakening of the British and French forces in Macedonia had been compensated by the addition of a Jugo-Slav division to the Serbian Army and the growth of the Greek forces. The Germans had withdrawn all their troops in Italy to France, so that the Italians were not only able to dispense with part of the assistance which we and the French had given them after Caporetto, but were able to send a contingent to France, and even so were superior to the Austrian Armies on their front. Therefore, common sense indicated that as soon as Foch's policy of exhausting the German reserves in the West had taken effect, and Germany was no longer in a position to help her friends, every possible effort should be made on every front.

By that time, it had become clear that the direct road to Germany was the shortest road, that the barrier in the West was penetrable, and therefore, while the attack upon our enemies upon all fronts became general, there was no doubt as to where the main attack was to be made or any attempt to seek the defeat of Germany by taking the way round. Had there been no good reason to expect that the Allied Armies in France would be able to pierce the Hindenburg line, then, when the arrival of American troops had placed the safety of the Western Front beyond question, it might have been right to seek victory by the way round. Fortunately, this was not necessary, for it would have greatly prolonged the war.

So it happened that, while Foch was completing his preparations for Armageddon, Franchet d'Espérey was driving back the Bulgars, Allenby was overwhelming the Turks, and about a month later, on October 24, the Italians began the third Battle of the Piave. By the time that Austria collapsed Ludendorff's attempt to rally had been defeated, and the fate of the German Armies in the West was sealed. The

Italian victory, therefore, came too late to affect the main issue, nor did Allenby's campaign, though of vital importance in its influence on the future of the East, hasten by an hour the defeat of Germany. The defeat of Bulgaria, on the other hand, did, as I have shown from the statements made by Hindenburg and his advisers at the time, unquestionably weigh with the political and military leaders of Germany and helped to convince them of the hopelessness of their position.

The controversy between the advocates of an Eastern and of a Western policy, which so long agitated us, is a symptom of defective organisation. Conflict between the political demands for dispersal of force and the military demands for concentration are nothing new in war. It has always been a very difficult problem to adjust them, and in the case of a scattered Empire such as ours the problem is peculiarly complex. War, as the Germans were never tired of telling us, is an act of policy, and it is the business of the statesman to define policy in war as in peace. The soldier is as much his servant as the civilian administrator in Whitehall. It is the statesman's duty to determine the objects of the war, to say what interests are vital to the security of the nation and what may be neglected with impunity, to increase our power by bringing in Allies to our side, and to diminish that of the enemy by detaching from him potential or actual adherents to his cause.

War, however, is not an abstract problem. It is a struggle against an opponent whose intentions and resources can only be surmised from incomplete evidence. Miscalculations and mistakes entail loss of life and, maybe, disaster. Therefore, before the statesman decides on his policy it must be translated for him by experts into a definite plan which shows him what his policy entails in men and in time, and gives him the best possible estimate of how the enemy will endeavour to counter the plan. It is very easy to take a map and place one million men in the Balkans, or a quarter of a million in the Gallipoli Peninsula, and picture the results of their action when they have arrived. It is quite another matter to calculate accurately how long it will take to get the men to those places, to estimate what will be needed to maintain them when they are there, and to forecast what the enemy may do while they are moving to their positions.

Mr. Lloyd George's proposal, made early in 1915, to transfer the British Army to the Balkans would have been admirable had it been practicable. He maintained, with good reason, that such a manoeuvre would assure the safety of Serbia, bring in Italy, Greece, Bulgaria and Roumania on our side, enable us to complete the encirclement of the Central Powers, cut them off from Turkey and the East, would open up communication with Russia, and allow us to attack Austria in overwhelming force. It opened up a dazzling prospect when compared with Kitchener's prophecy of a war lasting three years and with the slow and costly process of wearing down the Germans in the West. The fallacy in the plan was that we had not the military power ready to provide for security in the West and in the East while it was in preparation.

It would have taken us many months to move an army to the Balkans and to equip it. While it was on the move it would have been incapable of action, and in the interval both the Western Front and Egypt would have been exposed to attack. Even if Germany was unable to get the Turks to organise an effective attack upon Egypt and did not again mass troops against France, there was no guarantee that she would not anticipate us in the Balkans, as from her central position she might readily do, and with the help of Austria, Bulgaria and Turkey destroy our expedition while it was concentrating. The translation of Mr. Lloyd George's plan into practical proposals involved a careful survey of ways and means and elaborate calculation of time and space.

These were the business of the soldier. But we had made the grave mistake of taking too narrow a view of our commitments when we first entered into the war. No one save Kitchener, who was only brought into the War Office after war had been declared, had foreseen that we would be engaged in a world war and a long war, and it took even Kitchener time to grasp that our part in such a war could only be directed from a great general headquarters in London. We allowed the General Staff at the War Office to be broken up, and it was long before it was built up again. The result of this was that the Government was deprived of expert assistance at the time when it was most needed, and individual Ministers devoted their energies, abilities and influence to advocating particular plans of campaign which appealed to them, in place of supporting one carefully thought out and agreed policy.

The Dardanelles Commission has made public the melancholy story of the inception of that enterprise. As a plan of campaign it promised, if successful, results as brilliant as Mr. Lloyd George's Balkan enterprise, while it had the advantage over its rival that it enabled us to make use of our sea power for offence and that it did provide from the outset a definite measure of protection for Egypt, for it was clear that the Turks would not venture to attack the Suez Canal while Constantinople was menaced.

The plan was faulty because Mr. Churchill had formed an exaggerated estimate of the power of naval guns against land defences, because the machinery for getting the expert naval opinion before the Government on this question was defective, and because we were drawn into a military enterprise for which we had not the means ready, when it was found that the navy had been given an impossible task. Owing to this same absence of organised expert advice, the Mesopotamian expedition was allowed to drift gradually into commitments which were beyond its powers.

So, our energies were exhausted in controversies which need not have arisen if the roles and responsibilities of the statesman, the soldier and the sailor had been clearly defined, and if the Government had been equipped with the means of surveying the whole ground from the outset, and of learning what various alternative policies entailed in men, guns, ships, material and time. In our special circumstances "sideshows" were inevitable. We had to protect India, and keep the Suez Canal open; we could not allow the Germans a free hand in Africa to organise native forces, at their leisure. We could not therefore concentrate all our forces in the Western theatre and leave the outlying parts of the Empire to look after themselves.

The fact was, however, that so large a part of our total power was required in order to make the Western Front safe that we were never able, until our enemies were on the verge of exhaustion, to conduct offensive campaigns elsewhere to a decisive issue. Because that truth was not realised in time, we frittered away our resources and prolonged the war. In the end circumstances compelled us to renounce our strategical heresies, and victory followed.

Not only was the defeat of the German Armies due to Foch's campaign in the West, but that campaign made victory possible in all theatres of war by discouraging Germany's Allies, who, like the German people, had been kept in the war by promises of victory, and by depriving them of her aid at the moment when they were most in need of it. The sudden change of the tide of fortune from the ebb to the full flood of victory, the vast extent of the operations, and the swift succession of blows struck made this campaign a stupendous climax to a stupendous war. In 118 days, the great German Army which set out confidently to capture Paris on July 15, 1918, had been utterly and completely broken.

It had been driven back to the French frontier, and made incapable of further resistance. During the period of rather less than four months which had elapsed since the beginning of the second Battle of the Marne the British Army had captured 188,700 prisoners and 2,840 guns; the French Army, 139,000 prisoners and 1,880 guns; the American Army, 44,000 prisoners and 1,421 guns; the Belgian Army, 14,500 prisoners and 474 guns a total of 385,500 prisoners and 6,615 guns. Many thousands of machine-guns and trench mortars and thousands of tons of war material of all kinds must be added to this tale of booty, while the enemy's losses in killed and wounded are estimated to have amounted to 1,500,000.

This wonderful result, which even as late as the end of September no one would have ventured to foretell, was due to many causes, of which, in the military sphere, three are predominant: the genius of Foch, the unexpectedly rapid development of America's fighting power, and the marvellous recovery of the British Army from its reverses of the spring. To Foch's genius I have already paid my tribute. In his *Principles of War*, which embodies his teaching at the French War College before the war, he says:

> Great results in war are due to the commander. History is therefore right in making generals responsible for victories, in which case they are glorified, and for defeats, in which case they are disgraced. Without a commander no battle, no victory is possible. . . . The will to conquer, such is victory's first condition, and therefore every soldier's first duty, but it also amounts to a supreme resolve, which the commander must, if need be, impart to the soldier's soul.

Foch's will to conquer wavered neither in the dark days of 1914 nor throughout the long period of trench warfare, when many in high places were talking of a deadlock and planning for a patched-up peace, nor in those still more critical days of March, 1918, when he was first called to the helm to steer the ship from the rocks, and the storm of the German offensive was at its height, nor when the Germans surprised him in May and a second time menaced the capital of France.

But the stoutest will in the world can at best refuse to admit defeat; it cannot compel victory unless it is accompanied by knowledge and skill. Foch had the knowledge and skill which come of long study and careful thought, and these he added to his iron will. Great results in war are due to the commander, and, therefore, our first tribute must be paid to Marshal Foch.

Even Foch could not have foreseen how nobly his will to conquer and his genius in planning would be supported. Early in April there had been one American division fit to take its place in the line; by November 11 twenty-four American divisions had fought in battle and had won, and there were many more ready to fight. I doubt if, even after the second Battle of the Marne, there was a single Allied general who believed that it would be possible for a great American Army to force its way triumphantly through the German lines. Many of the American divisions who fought in those last battles which brought us victory went into action with little or no experience of trenches, and with none at all of the hell on earth which constitutes a modern battle. The multiplicity of weapons and the complications of tactics which four years of war had produced, and the fact that an entirely new element had entered into war with the development of aircraft, all made the effective handling of troops in battle a far more difficult problem than it had ever been.

Neither the American generals nor the American staffs had had experience in fitting together the numerous parts of the military machine or in handling large bodies of troops. For all these reasons a great attack by American troops against intact German defences on the most difficult part of the front was a bold experiment. It was one thing to obliterate the St. Mihiel salient in thirty hours, to stop the German rush at the Marne, or even to drive the Germans from the Marne to the Vesle in co-operation with Allied troops. It was quite another matter to fight continuously on a front of some twenty miles for close on fifty days, through line after line of German trenches, in a battle which entailed the employment of nearly three-quarters of a million American troops. It was done because America placed the pick of her splendid manhood in the field, and that manhood went ahead at the job in front of it without counting the cost. By doing its job it gave us victory in 1918.

Of the achievements of the British Army in this last campaign, under its great leader whose calm judgment, coolness in adversity, unselfish patience, when unsupported at home, and bold decisions, when the time came to be bold, were vital factors in our triumph, a Briton can hardly write temperately. The "Old Contemptibles" of 1914 have become almost heroes of legend, and their wonderful recovery from the retreat from Mons, their advance to the Marne and the Aisne are rightly reckoned as amongst the proudest records of the British Army. I took part in the retreat from Mons and in the subsequent advance of our little army, and I saw both what our army had to endure in the spring of 1918 and what it accomplished in the last months of the war, and I am convinced that the achievement of the National Army of Great Britain transcends even that of her old Regular Army.

That National Army for six weeks, from March 21 until the end of April, withstood the full brunt of the greatest military effort of which Germany was capable. It was driven back at one point to a depth of forty miles, it lost 70,000 prisoners and 1,000 guns and suffered 300,000 casualties; 55 of its divisions were attacked by 102 German divisions, and still presented to the enemy a front he could not break. Then, starting on August 8, it fought uninterruptedly and victoriously for three months, driving the enemy back 120 miles, taking more than twice as many prisoners and more than three times as many guns as it had lost, and completely routing the German Armies by which it was opposed. This is a record with which any army coming fresh into the field might be content. That it was accomplished after four and a half years of bitter struggle is an achievement to which no words can do justice.

The soldiers of France were not less splendid. They had to endure first while Great Britain was making of herself a great military power, and then, when Great Britain's efforts were insufficient to turn the balance, while America was placing her armies in the field. The Germans had again and again boasted that France was bled white, that she was weary of the war and would not fight. From 1916 onwards the next winter was to see the collapse of France. From every trial, with her country ravaged, and many of her richest provinces in the hands of the most brutal tyrant of whom history tells, she rose again to a new effort, until at last she drove her oppressor back to her frontiers and her poilus marched triumphantly through Alsace-Lorraine to the Rhine.

The soldiers of little Belgium, who for more than four years had protected the last little strip of their country west of the Yser after the German tide of invasion had been stemmed on that river, had, under the leadership of King Albert, whose spirit was as indomitable as that of Foch, issued from behind their water-lines, had fought with a fire and dash wholly wonderful in an army which had long been condemned to inaction and had none of the means of replenishing its ranks at the disposal of the other Allies, and had conquered. It is idle to argue as to who won the war. Germany could not have been beaten in the field, as she was beaten, without the intimate co-operation of all the Allied Armies on the Western Front directed by a great leader, nor without the co-ordination for a common purpose of all the resources of the Allies, naval, military, industrial and economic.

If victory is to be attributed to any one cause, then that cause is not to be found in the wisdom of any one statesman, the valour of any one army, the prowess of any one navy, or in the skill of any one general. Our triumph was due to the justice of our cause and to the faith to which, even in the darkest days, the free peoples of the world held firmly—the faith that right is might.

ALSO FROM LEONAUR

AVAILABLE IN SOFTCOVER OR HARDCOVER WITH DUST JACKET

THE 9TH—THE KING'S (LIVERPOOL REGIMENT) IN THE GREAT WAR 1914 - 1918 by Enos H. G. Roberts—Mersey to mud—war and Liverpool men.

THE GAMBARDIER by Mark Severn—The experiences of a battery of Heavy artillery on the Western Front during the First World War.

FROM MESSINES TO THIRD YPRES by Thomas Floyd—A personal account of the First World War on the Western front by a 2/5th Lancashire Fusilier.

THE IRISH GUARDS IN THE GREAT WAR - VOLUME 1 by Rudyard Kipling—Edited and Compiled from Their Diaries and Papers—The First Battalion.

THE IRISH GUARDS IN THE GREAT WAR - VOLUME 1 by Rudyard Kipling—Edited and Compiled from Their Diaries and Papers—The Second Battalion.

ARMOURED CARS IN EDEN by K. Roosevelt—An American President's son serving in Rolls Royce armoured cars with the British in Mesopatamia & with the American Artillery in France during the First World War.

CHASSEUR OF 1914 by Marcel Dupont—Experiences of the twilight of the French Light Cavalry by a young officer during the early battles of the great war in Europe.

TROOP HORSE & TRENCH by R.A. Lloyd—The experiences of a British Lifeguardsman of the household cavalry fighting on the western front during the First World War 1914-18.

THE EAST AFRICAN MOUNTED RIFLES by C.J. Wilson—Experiences of the campaign in the East African bush during the First World War.

THE LONG PATROL by George Berrie—A Novel of Light Horsemen from Gallipoli to the Palestine campaign of the First World War.

THE FIGHTING CAMELIERS by Frank Reid—The exploits of the Imperial Camel Corps in the desert and Palestine campaigns of the First World War.

STEEL CHARIOTS IN THE DESERT by S. C. Rolls—The first world war experiences of a Rolls Royce armoured car driver with the Duke of Westminster in Libya and in Arabia with T.E. Lawrence.

WITH THE IMPERIAL CAMEL CORPS IN THE GREAT WAR by Geoffrey Inchbald—The story of a serving officer with the British 2nd battalion against the Senussi and during the Palestine campaign.

AVAILABLE ONLINE AT **www.leonaur.com**
AND FROM ALL GOOD BOOK STORES

www.ingramcontent.com/pod-product-compliance
Lightning Source LLC
Chambersburg PA
CBHW031618160426
43196CB00006B/188